Perception-based Marketing of Parishes

using the example of Catholic Academics and Students

Thomas Peters

Perception-based Marketing of Parishes

using the example of Catholic Academics and Students

A seminal inventory of church marketing activities.

BoD, Norderstedt/Germany, 2019

Bibliographic information of the German National Library:

The German National Library lists this publication in the German National Bibliography; detailed bibliographical data can be found on the Internet at http://dnb.dnb.de

Translation from the German language edition "Wahrnehmungsbasiertes Marketing von Pfarrgemeinden am Beispiel katholischer Akademiker und Studenten" by Tom Peters

Copyright © Springer Fachmedien Wiesbaden GmbH, a part of Springer Nature 2019. All Rights Reserved.

Forewords by Bischop Dr. Josef Clemens, Vatican City, and Prof. Mgr. Peter Štarchoň, Ph.D., Bratislava

Production and Publishing: BoD – Books on Demand, Norderstedt, Germany

ISBN: 978-3-7481-6025-0

Forewords

Bishop Dr. Josef Clemens, Vatican City,
Ex- Secretary of the Pontificial Council for the Laity

Globalization has significantly broadened and profoundly transformed our view of the world. The digitalization of media content has enabled previously foreign cultures, values and behavioral patterns to enter directly into our living rooms and into our children's rooms. As a result, young people, in particular, are confronted with the challenge of dealing with new impressions and influences often without sufficient background knowledge and without a clearly developed value system. Even the experience of elderly people and the Christian faith, which has been instrumental in shaping the western world and the enlightened Europe for over two millennia, can only provide limited guidance in our increasingly pluralistic, technocratic and secularized society. People look around and discover a steadily growing supply of alternative life coaching and orientation guides, more and more of these have no relation to religion or Christianity.

It is against this background that Thomas Peters explores the multitude of perspectives and dimensions based on which, and in accordance with which, respectively, Catholic parishes endeavor to present and popularize their liturgical (Leiturgia), charitable-social (Diakonia) and missionary-proclaming (Martyria) principal features in the most appealing manner. Here, church initiatives and programs increasingly find themselves in competition with secular providers of spiritual guidance, life coaches and ritual managers. Under these circumstances, it is all the more important to ensure that all activities and offers, the implementing and cooperating organizations, the acting persons and any existing and potential multipliers are linked together intensively, and that the goals, resources and communication efforts of all participants are coordinated in an optimal way.

In the course of my work as secretary of the Pontifical Council for the Laity, I was able to experience and support many "marketing campaigns" on the parish level and especially in the Catholic associations and communities. Looking back, I feel a deep respect for the personal dedication and a great joy for the valiant apostolic commitment of many Christian brothers and sisters in the various lay organizations.

In terms of direct church involvement at the local level, Catholic associations and the academic associations among them play a special role because of their extensive spiritual and material resources. In keeping with the spirit of the apostolic exhortation *Christifideles Laici*, these organizations of believers contribute towards building and strengthening the sense of community among members and provide in qualified training and education in all matters relating to faith. In addition, they motivate their members to resolutely express their faith, which primarily involves caring for and providing services to others.[1]

In his dissertation, Thomas Peters emphasizes the close relationship between Catholic Academics and their parish communities, as well as their student organizations. Using the Cartel Confederation of the Catholic German Student Associations (Cartellverband der katholischen deutschen Studentenverbindungen, CV), the largest confessional academic association in Europe, as an example, he demonstrates the useful potential of personnel, organizational, financial and communicative support provided by these lay organizations for matters such as the preservation – or reactivation – of parish life and work. In this regard, specific action recommendations for parishes and church (or church-related) institutions are to encourage contact to be established with this particular group of persons.

Especially at a time when local parishes are being forced to reorganize and, in many places, merge together in larger pastoral units, the helping, community-building and identity-forming strength of Catholic lay organizations becomes an increasingly important factor. May this book both inform and motivate its readers to actively shape and support a life led by Christian conviction in their personal environment.

Vatican City, December 2018

+ Bishop Dr. Josef Clemens

---

[1]   Cf. POPE JOHN PAUL II, Post-Synodal Apostolic Exhortation Christifideles Laici on the Vocation and the Mission of the Lay Faithful in the Church and in the World, December 30, 1988, in: *Verlautbarungen des Apostolischen Stuhls* Nr. 87.

Prof. Mgr. Peter Štarchoň, PhD, Bratislava,
Comenius University, Faculty of Management

I was honored to accept Thomas Peters' request for a short introduction to his brand-new book on parish marketing, given my deep appreciation and respect for his enthusiasm, his willingness, and everything that he has already accomplished through study and research – culminating in this publication. Moreover, Peters' own skills, expertise, abilities, and qualities are obvious, especially in terms of their direct applicability to practical values.

This book is truly innovative, inspirational, and of the moment; the powerful practical consequences of the resolution of its topic are remarkable. The author seeks to solve the problem of declining membership in religious (Catholic) organizations and find suitable strategies oriented towards encouraging involvement and voluntary engagement from particular target groups. In this context, marketing and communications have an important role to play, and can be used as a potent managerial and human-centric tool. The main results are presented in a review and synthesis of the current state of knowledge, analysis of the primary research results, and identification of potentially successful marketing and communication strategies oriented towards particular target groups. A fascinating discussion emerges from the secondary and primary research results, which can in turn be considered a stimulus for further research and implementation of particular marketing strategies as well.

Peters shows us how church communications should ideally be designed in order to successfully approach specific groups in the population with an affinity to the Catholic Church and with higher levels of education, and to recruit these people for the needs and purposes of the Church. In addition, he presents the elements of a marketing communication mix that are relevant to Catholic parishes, with a view to their student and graduate members on the one hand, and perception of the parish activities and programs specifically by these groups and identifying practical recommendations on the other. With respect to the appeal of the topic in terms of the Roman Catholic Church in Germany, particular recommendations and findings could be applied not only in other churches, but also similar (not only religious) organizations and non-profits.

It is my hope that this book will inspire its readers and be welcomed as a relevant source of knowledge.

Yours faithfully,
Peter Štarchoň

Table of Contents

List of Figures

Introduction

With about 23.6 million members, the Catholic Church is the largest religious community of faith in Germany and has been enjoying as such high esteem in the German population for its numerous charitable and social activities and institutions as well as for its offers of festive rituals at the occasions of important transitions between different stages of life.[2] However, this once powerful and not least politically influential people's church has been steadily losing members already since the 1970s; in the five year-period between 2011 and 2017 alone, this was more than 2,000,000 people at an average net loss in excess of 400,000 members annually, traceable to both instances of death and church leavings.[3]

The key causes of this decline in church membership have been an increasingly ageing German population and a loss of weight of not just the Catholic Church in society at large due to advancing secularization and pluralization of religious and church life: the differentiation in German society into increasingly disparate social milieus has been symptomatic of a growing alienation from traditional established structures and lifestyles while individualism and flexible, often non-committal orientations and affiliations that are in permanent flux have been on the increase.[4] All the while, this shift has been taking place against the backdrop of a prosperous state that has brought its population – on the basis of Christian values – life in peace and freedom devout of violence, oppression or poverty for over 70 years by now.

The decline in membership also has been complemented in the Catholic Church by a shrinking number of priests, deacons, religious and voluntary staff members. The result has been a profound change in religious and church life and not least in the structures and the performance ability of the Catholic Church as a socio-cultural non-profit organization that currently consists of more than 10,000 parishes and of

---

[2]   cf. HERMELINK, Jan (Ed.), LATZEL, Thorsten: Kirche empirisch: Ein Werkbuch zur vierten EKD-Erhebung über Kirchenmitgliedschaft und zu anderen empirischen Studien. Gütersloh: Gütersloher Verlag-Haus, 2008, pp. 101-103.

[3]   Author's own calculation based on data for 2012 to 2016 from: SEKRETARIAT DER DEUTSCHEN BISCHOFSKONFERENZ (Ed.): *Katholische Kirche in Deutschland: Zahlen und Fakten 2010/2011.* Bonn: DBM, 2010 – annual publications until 2017.

[4]   HILLEBRECHT, Steffen W.: Die Praxis des kirchlichen Marketings: Die Vermittlung religiöser Werte in der modernen Gesellschaft. Hamburg: E.B.-Verlag, 2000, pp. 13-22.

thousands of charitable and social facilities with more than a million staff members on a full-time or voluntary basis.[5]

In this context, the Catholic Church is faced with the challenge to professionalize its religious and social offers, its public, media and interpersonal presentation as well as its communication with members and marketing communication, and to adapt to the changed social and economic framework conditions.

Not out of missionary zest, but rather due to the emergency of the free fall in membership numbers, German dioceses have long began to analyze their structures and systems in order to use available resources more effectively and efficiently than before, to adapt their facilities to the challenges of an increasingly market-shaped religious environment[6], and to explore new potentials for the Church to fulfil its fundamental functions for example through milieu-specific activities and offers[7].

For that, the focus often is primarily on conservative maintenance and refurbishment measures with the aim of a "qualitative growth". Quantitative missionary goals in the sense of a new evangelization and recruitment of members in the form of measurable numbers of clients, visitors or members, up to newly founded Christian communities by now mainly have been implemented in Protestant environments.[8] On a complementary basis, the Catholic Church has been proceeding in accordance with various best practices and has been verifying for example also the marketing and communication concepts of successfully growing (or grown) parishes in the USA for suitable components and their feasibility for the German environment[9].

With a view to the decline in membership, the progressive shortage of priests and the erosion in support by voluntary helpers, it is becoming increasingly more urgent in

---

5   cf. SEKRETARIAT DER DEUTSCHEN BISCHOFSKONFERENZ (2017), ibidem, as well as DEUTSCHER CARITASVERBAND: *Caritas in Deutschland*. [retrieved on 2018-04-30], available at: https://www.caritas.de/diecaritas/wofuerwirstehen/millionenfache-hilfe.

6   Respective examples can be found in Chapter 3.3.4 of this thesis.

7   cf. GIESEN, Rut von: Ökonomie der Kirche? Zum Verhältnis von theologischer und betriebswirtschaftlicher Rationalität in praktisch-theoretischer Perspektive. Stuttgart: Kohlhammer, 2009, pp. 41-48.

8   Compare for example McGAVRAN, Donald Anderson: *Effective Evangelism - A Theological Mandate*. Phillipsburg: Presbyterian and Reformed Publishing Company, 1988 | SCHWARZ, Christian A.: *Praxis des Gemeindeaufbaus. Gemeindetraining für wache Christen*. Neukirchen-Vluyn: Schriftenmissionsverlag, 1987.

9   cf. REINHOLD, Kai, SELLMANN, Matthias (Ed.): Katholische Kirche und Gemeindeleben in den USA und in Deutschland: Überraschende Ergebnisse einer ländervergleichenden Umfrage. Münster: Aschendorff, 2011.

particular for parishes and their attached communities that operate at the local or regional level to identify and contact in a fitting manner in order to secure their fundamental functions and principal tasks those groups of persons that are able and willing to make available to the Church and for its purposes and the needs of church life on a sustainable basis their individual and professional skills and competences, their leisure time and not least their material and financial resources.

In this context, both the processes of promoting the message of the Church and its activities and offers as well as of designing, providing and delivering the church-specific benefits and services rely on effective internal and external marketing communication. This communication is the more important the more the persons involved in providing and delivering the service are making themselves available on a voluntary and free-of-charge basis, that is, as volunteer helpers.[10]

This is where the present thesis aims to contribute, with a discussion based on an inventory check of the church marketing mix of the notion of marketing from the church perspective; in doing so, the vital and core significance of communication is highlighted and explored in marketing of non-profit organizations such as parishes and church facilities and establishments.

As marketing and in particular marketing communication that is based on externally reflected perception can substantially contribute to improving the situation of the Church and its parishes, this thesis aims to provide parishes with conceptual and practical insights for a targeted, perception-based marketing communication of their activities and offers; perception-based because this thesis focuses in particular on the perception and judgement of how church communication, activities and programs are communicated mainly by those groups of persons that given their high affinity to the Church and their density of contacts actually are able to effectively evaluate these.

A population group that typically meets the socio-economic prerequisites to provide support that is so urgently needed by the Church is that of Catholic academics. Among these, of particular interest are those students and academics who are

---

[10] cf. BIEBERSTEIN, Ingo: *Dienstleistungs-Marketing*. Ludwigshafen: Kiehl, 2006, p. 45 | LICHTSTEINER, Hans et al.: *Das Freiburger Management-Modell*. Bern: Haupt, 2015, p. 49 f., p. 143 f. | SCHÜRMANN, Mathias: *Marketing. In vier Schritten zum eigenen Marketingkonzept*. Zürich: vdf Hochschulverlag, 2011, p. 260.

organized in Catholic student associations and their local societies in which they receive or have received an additional Catholic socialization during studies.[11]

The present thesis thus explores the question how church communication ideally must be designed in order to successfully approach groups in the population with affinity to the Church and with higher levels of education, and to recruit these for the needs and purposes of the Church. The general aim in the effort is to analyse and correlate the marketing communication mix of Catholic parishes with a view to their student and graduate members on the one hand, as well as perception of the parish activities and programs specifically by these groups, and to derive from these specific practical recommendations.

The research question and hypotheses herein are empirically explored and discussed on the example of members of the largest German academic association, which is the Cartel Confederation of the Catholic German Student Associations (CV)[12], and comprised and summarized with a view to the aspect as to how far the comprehensive Catholicism and affinity to the Church of this particular population group can be practically used towards securing the resources of "time, talent and treasure" needed by the church.

The CV is among the oldest academic association and was constituted over the course of formation of the landscape of the Catholic associations so successfully that already at the outset of the 20th century, it had more than 30 member-organizations. Today, the CV is the largest confessional academic association in Europe and with about 30,000 individual members in 126 member-organizations and about 250 local circles can be deemed representative of the Catholic corporate environment in Germany.[13]

---

[11] Details on the concept of the surveyed sample can be found in Chapter 5.1.1 of this thesis.

[12] cf. CARTELLVERBAND: *Webportal "Cartellverband.de"* [retrieved on 2018-04-30], available from: https://www.cartellverband.de/.

[13] cf. CARTELLVERBAND: *Wer wir sind.* [retrieved on 2018-04-30] available from: https://www.cartellverband.de/cartellverband/wer-wir-sind/.

1 The Roman Catholic Church in Germany

The Roman Catholic Church is the largest Christian community of faith, values, culture and solidarity in Germany. According to a publication by the German Bishops' Conference,[14] the association of the currently 68 German bishops, in 2016/2017 there were approximately 23.6 million members of the Catholic Church in Germany, which is around 28.5 percent of the population, thereof 47 percent are male and 53 percent female Catholics respectively.

1.1 Structure of the Roman Catholic Church

The Catholic population in Germany is organized in about 10,280 pastoral units, which are the prevalently local parishes. The structure is signified by large regional differences for example due to the Protestant alignment of northern German regions, or given the largely not religious population of eastern Germany (former GDR). Due to the progressive decline in membership, a number of parishes currently are being combined into parish associations or parochial unions, and some merged under one roof of a single newly established parish.[15]

Every parish belongs to one of the seven archdioceses (archbishoprics) and/or to one of the 20 dioceses (bishoprics), which in turn are assigned each to an archdiocese. At the regional level, always several parishes are combined into a deanery. Contrary to the global "universal church" or the Germany-wide "people's church", the dioceses and archdioceses also are referred to as "local churches". These are church administration districts that are headed by bishops or diocesan bishops. The Pope, who himself in his capacity as the Bishop of Rome is a part of the College of Bishops, is the global head of the Catholic Church and enjoys supreme legal and governing authority. [16]

While the dioceses and archdioceses and their parish associations and parishes are in terms of legal forms under German law organized as "corporations under public law" (Körperschaften des öffentlichen Rechts), charitable and social activities of the

---

14 cf. SEKRETARIAT DER DEUTSCHEN BISCHOFSKONFERENZ (ed.): *Katholische Kirche in Deutschland – Zahlen und Fakten 2016/2017* Bonn. DBK, 2017, p. 6-7, pp. 38-41.

15 DEUTSCHE BISHOFSKONFERENZ: *Aufbau der katholischen Kirche.* [retrieved on 2018-04-30] Available from: https://www.dbk.de/katholische-kirche/aufbau/

16 The hierarchical constitution of the Roman Catholic Church is described in: ROMAN CURIA: *Codes Iuris Canonici / Code of Canon Law.* Part II, Cann. 330-572. Vatican: Libreria Editrice Vaticana, 1983. [retrieved on 2018-04-30] Available from: http://www.vatican.va/archive/ENG1104/_INDEX.HTM

Church are depending on economic context and funding needs frequently organized as non-profit associations (eingetragener Verein, abbreviated: e.V.) or limited liability companies for charitable purposes (gGmbH), which as such enjoy preferential tax treatment.[17]

For the sake of completeness, as further organizations of the Catholic Church in Germany also new spiritual communities, monastic orders and secular institutions shall be mentioned as well as the coordinating body of the German layman's organizations, which is the Central Committee of German Catholics (ZdK).[18]

As of primary significance for Catholics in their faith life is the local parish or pastoral unit, the present thesis focuses on marketing and/or communication of parishes because: "For those who identify with the Church as an institution (...), the subject of their identification typically is the local parish – even if due to the more differentiated lifestyles in society, the significance of new pastoral spaces with target-group specific offers has been on the increase." [19]

1.2   Principal Features and Mission Components of the Church

The Catholic Church is traditionally grounded in and justified on the basis of the three main components of its mission (basic church practice):

- Liturgy (Greek: *leiturgia*): church services and in particular the celebration of the Eucharist, the administration of sacraments and common prayer;

- Diaconia (Greek: *diakonia*): service to others in terms of the entirety of all the charitable and social services of the Church, its members and its institutions;

- Witness/proclamation (Greek: *martyria*): the sustained transmission and spread of the Christian gospel.[20]

---

[17]   On the legal forms of church establishments and organizations, compare among others: WALTER, Christian: *Religionsverfassungsrecht in vergleichender und internationaler Perspektive.* Tübingen: Mohr Siebeck, 2016.

[18]   References to "the Church" in the following parts mean the Roman Catholic Church in Germany and its 27 dioceses and archdioceses.

[19]   KLENK, Christian: Zustand und Zukunft katholischer Medien. Prämissen – Probleme – Prognosen. Berlin: LIT Verlag, 2013, p. 220.

[20]   The term "gospel" is understood by Christians as the Good News about the incarnation of God in Jesus Christ, God's activity with and through Jesus Christ and his death and resurrection. Cf. BISCHÖFE DEUTSCHLANDS et al. (eds.): *Die Bibel. Altes und Neues Testament. Einheitsübersetzung.* Freiburg: Verlag Herder, 1980, 1 Kor 15,1.

The three components of basic church practice are sustained ever since the Second Vatican Council by a fourth principal feature that signifies the Church as an association of believers in which they join each other and God, namely

- Community of believers (Greek: koinonia).

The four principal features/mission components of the Catholic Church can be illustrated by means of a triangle the corner points of which – *liturgy, diaconia* and *witness/proclamation* – signify the church *community* of Catholics:

Figure 1-1: Principal features and mission components of the Catholic church (own illustration)

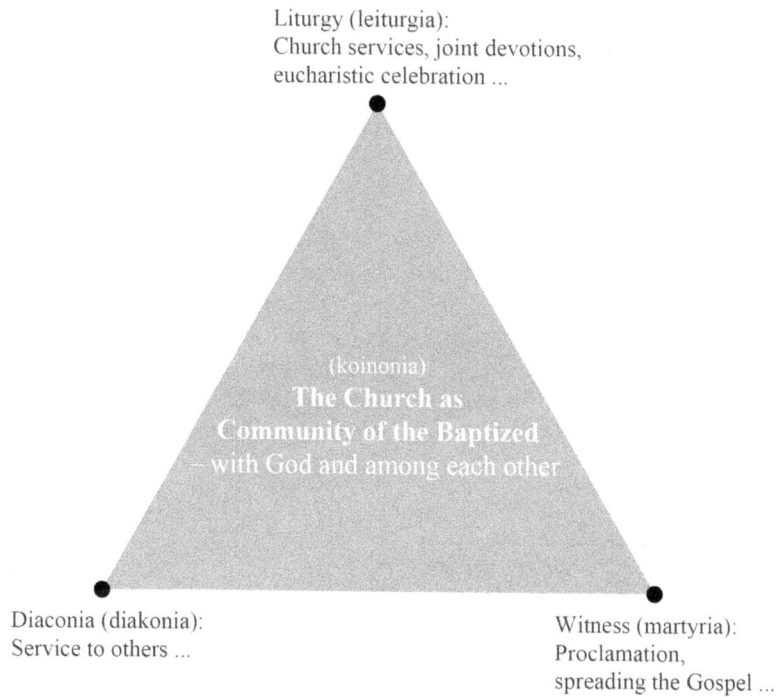

Liturgy (leiturgia):
Church services, joint devotions,
eucharistic celebration ...

(koinonia)
**The Church as
Community of the Baptized
– with God and among each other**

Diaconia (diakonia):
Service to others ...

Witness (martyria):
Proclamation,
spreading the Gospel ...

The outlined principal features and mission components give rise on the one hand to the large variety of church initiatives, facilities and services, and on the other to the particularity of church marketing that shall be explored and discussed in detail in Chapter 3 – Church Marketing.

1.3 Financing: The German Church Tax

As a territorially and episcopally organized corporation under public law, the Roman Catholic Church in Germany enjoys special dedicated status under church law,[21] offers labour relations similar to those for civil servants and has the right to levy taxes.[22] In this respect the Catholic Church in Germany differs significantly from churches in other countries.

Currently the Catholic Church levies against every baptized member nine percent (eight percent in the federal states of Bavaria and Baden-Württemberg) of their assessed payroll tax, income tax and capital gains tax as "church tax". By way of the church tax duty for members of recognized religious communities that has been in place since the German (interwar) Weimar Republic, the Catholic Church received in 2016 in excess of 6.1 billion euros complemented by about half a billion euros in additional state allowances and subsidies (Fig. 1-2).[23] Collection and administration of the church tax has been delegated by the Church to tax authorities of the federal states, which is are paid for by a compensation for administrative fees of about 3 percent that goes to the federal states.

Contrary to churches in other countries that are financed through member contributions, donations and foundation funds, collection actions, government funding and commercial and other activities, the Catholic Church in Germany is able to finance the majority of its pastoral and charitable/social activities, cultural efforts and building maintenance measures from the church tax. This though is added in Germany as well by state allowances and funding and the partly substantial income from church aid and relief organizations, some of which are active worldwide.[24]

---

[21] cf. DEUTSCHER BUNDESTAG: *Basic Constitutional Law of the Federal Republic of Germany.* Article 140140 in conjunction with Art. 137 (Weimarer Constitution), [retrieved on 2018-0430] Available from: https://www.bundestag.de/bundestag/aufgaben/rechtsgrundlagen/grundgesetz/gg_11/245152

[22] cf. MERTES, Martin: Controlling in der Kirche. Aufgaben, Instrumente und Organisation dargestellt am Beispiel des Bistums Münster, 2. ed., Gütersloh: Gütersloher Verlagshaus, 2000, p. 45 f.

[23] cf. VEREIN UMWIDMUNG VON KIRCHENSTEUERN: *Kirchensteueraufkommen beider Kirchen.* [retrieved on 2018-04-30] Available from: http://www.kirchensteuern.de/ | STATISTISCHES BUNDESAMT: *Statistical Yearbooks* until 2010 [retrieved on 2018-04-30] Available from: https://www.destatis.de/DE/Publikationen/StatistischesJahrbuch/StatistischesJahrbuchAktuell.html | DEUTSCHE BISCHOFSKONFERENZ: *Kirchensteuer.* [retrieved on 2018-04-30] Available from: https://www.dbk.de/themen/kirche-und-geld/kirchensteuer/ | SEKRETARIAT DER DEUTSCHEN BISCHOFSKONFERENZ (2017): ibidem, p. 59.

[24] SEKRETARIAT DER DEUTSCHEN BISCHOFSKONFERENZ (2017): ibidem, pp. 60-63.

Figure 1-2: Church Tax Revenues of the Catholic and the Protestant Church in Germany 1990–2015 (own graphic)

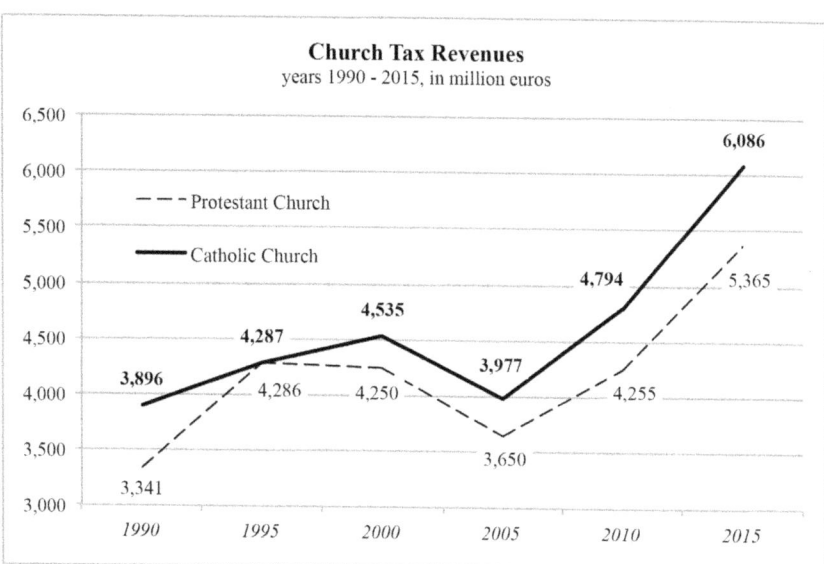

The church tax as well as other state payments to the Church are legally and from the church internal perspective in Germany not without controversy, as evidenced not least in the debate around the many members leaving the Church (cf. Chap. 1.4.3.6).

Unlike in the USA or France, for example, where churches, with the exception of state subsidies, largely have to sustain and fund themselves, the Catholic Church in Germany can rely on a fairly comprehensive financial backing that has seen a steady growth along with the growth in German incomes since 2005 (office assumption of Angela Merkel, who heads the Christian-conservative, central-right CDU party) and is legally based on tax law. This principal endowment with funds in order to sustain the Church's mission and the material goals of its organizations is taking place mostly irrespective of alignment of the Church offers to actual needs of its members, or to any changes thereof. Hence it comes as no surprise that not least with a view to the rising numbers of members leaving the Church, there are many and ever louder voices demanding to adapt and adjust the scope of operations of the Church and its offers more consistently and consequently to actual needs of all the members of the Church.[25]

A proof that a consequent orientation of churches on the needs of their audiences can be a great success has been supplied by the Willow Creek Community Church that was founded only relatively recently in Chicago, USA in 1972: the church has been aligning the entirety of its offers right from the beginning and in a targeted manner with the needs of an audience distant from the church and has been disregarding in the process the wishes of traditional churchgoers.[26] The result: today the Willow Creek Community Church counts with 20,000-strong visits to its church services among the three largest parishes in the US. For all its positive appeal, the pronounced marketing orientation of this American mega-parish is subject to a fairly contentious debate. Additionally on the basis of business economic considerations, Meyns (2013) concludes that the sc. "mega-churches" merely signify an organizational trend towards concentration, however not a religious growth trend that would be representative of society as a whole given that a half of such parishes shrink again to size after about 10 to 20 years.[27]

1.4   The Problem: Ongoing Decline in Membership

Eicken et al. (2010) bring membership trends in both the Christian people's churches in Germany (i.e., Protestant and Catholic) down to the variables of *leavings*, deaths *(funerals)*, *baptisms and joinings*, *immigration* plus other factors such as clearing up registries.[28] Figure 1-3 shows the relationship between entries of new members through baptisms, joinings and resumptions of membership, and departures through instances of death and leavings:

25   cf. TSCHEULIN, Dieter K. / DIETRICH, Martin: Zur Entwicklung und Bedeutung eines kirchlichen Marketings. (Zur Erfolgs- und Zielorientierung der Kirche) In: FAMOS, Cla Reto (ed.), KUNZ, Ralph: *Kirche und Marketing. Beiträge zu einer Verhältnisbestimmung.* Zürich: Theologischer Verlag, 2006, pp. 81-83 – as well as: NAGEL, Alexander-Kenneth: Marktförmige Religion – Ein Lernmodell für die deutschen Kirchen? In: SELLMANN, Matthias et al.: *CrossingOver – Inspirationen aus den USA.* Lebendige Seelsorge 3/2011. Würzburg: Echter, 2011, p. 155.

26   cf. WILLOW CREEK COMMUNITY CHURCH: *Willow Creek History.* [retrieved on 2018-04-30] Available from: http://www.willowcreek.org/en/about/history

27   MEYNS, Christoph: *Kirchenreform und betriebswirtschaftliches Denken. Modelle, Erfahrungen, Alternativen.* Gütersloh/München: Gütersloher Verlagshaus / Verlagsgruppe Random House, 2013, pp. 43-47.

28   EICKEN, Joachim, SCHMITZ-VELTIN, Ansgar: Die Entwicklung der Kirchenmitglieder in Deutschland. Statistische Anmerkungen zu Umfang und Ursachen des Mitgliederrückgangs in beiden christlichen Volkskirchen. In: *Wirtschaft und Statistik 6/2010.* Wiesbaden: Statistisches Bundesamt, 2010

Figure 1-3: Development of Membership in the Catholic Church 2010 – 2016[29]

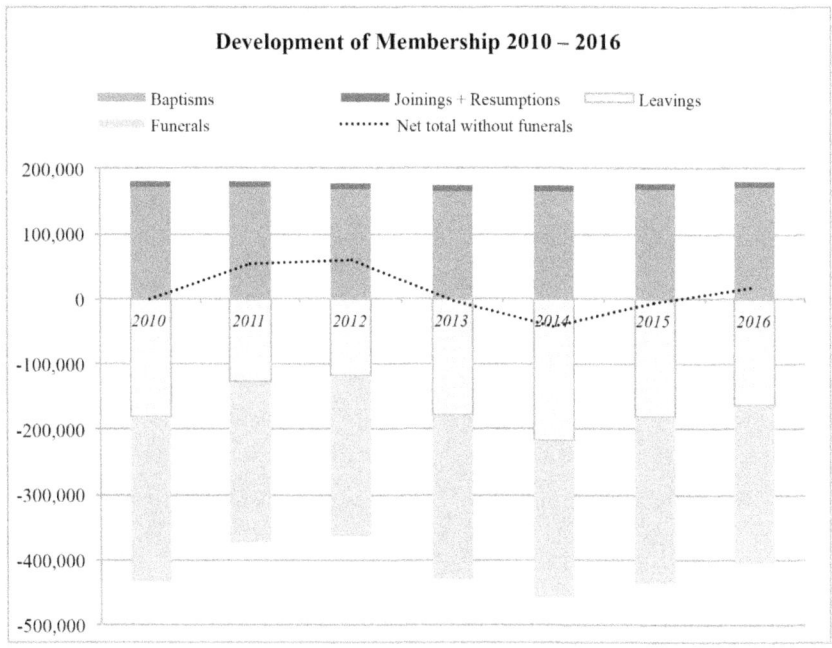

Both leaving the Church and baptism as well as joinings and resumptions of membership are preceded by deliberate decision-making processes. On disregading in this respect natural deaths, the decisions on leaving the Church were effectively compensated for over the past 15 years by decisions of entering the Church via baptisms and joinings/resumptions of membership.

1.4.1 Demographic Development

The high proportion of instances of death in departures of members from the Catholic Church can be explained using the sc. age pyramid of Germany. The age pyramid shows how the population structure in Germany has changed due to lower mortality, higher life expectancy and decline in birth rates: [30]

---

29   Source: SEKRETARIAT DER DEUTSCHEN BISCHOFSKONFERENZ, ibidem, own analysis of "facts and figures" 2010/2011 untill 2016/2017
30   PÖTZSCH, Olga, RÖSSGER, Felix: *Bevölkerung Deutschlands bis 2060. 13. Koordinierte Bevölkerungsabrechnung (28. April 2015).* Wiesbaden: Statistisches Bundesamt, 2015. p. 18.

Figure 1-4: Age development of the population in Germany (own graphic) [31]

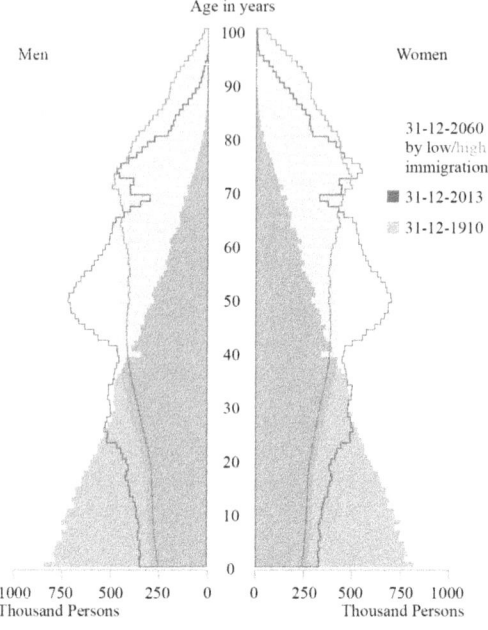

From the starting position of the classic pyramid-shaped form that was prevailing around 1910, recently the age pyramid has taken on the form of an onion or urn[32] the lower part of which continues thinning – which is strongly indicative of the deficiencies in births initiated with the sudden drop due to the advent of the birth control pill in the 1970s that has been continuing ever since. As a result, the German population consists in the meantime to almost a half of people past their 46th year of age (median age: 46.3), and one in five Germans already is 65 or more. In global comparison, only Japan has an older population.[33]

On the recurrent public debate around the causes of members leaving the Church, Eicken et al. (2010) conclude that "the demographic change has a substantial

31 Current population projections for Germany can be found online at [retrieved on 2018-04-30]: https://service.destatis.de/bevoelkerungspyramide/index.html#l=en

32 cf. BÄHR, Jürgen, JENTSCH, Christoph, KULS, Wolfgang: *Bevölkerungsgeographie*. Berlin, New York: de Gruiter, 1992.

33 UNITED NATIONS: *World Population Prospects 2017* [retrieved on 2018-04-30] Available from: https://esa.un.org/unpd/wpp/ – as well as: FEDERAL INSTITUTE FOR POPULATION RESEARCH: *Fakten: Bevölkerungsentwicklung*. [retrieved on 2018-04-30] Available from: https://www.bib.bund.de/DE/Fakten/Bevoelkerungsentwicklung/Bevoelkerungsentwicklung.html

influence on membership trends in both the churches and the decline in church membership thus cannot be solely equated with "leavings" and described with a monocausal explanation in the sense of "the church membership are scurrying away". Church members die without this being at least compensated by baptisms or joinings. Leavings thus only accelerate the demographically conditioned decline in membership".[34]

From the dying out of the older Church members prevalently with comprehensive Catholic socialization on the one hand and entries of increasingly ever more differentiated member groups with critical stances towards the Church on the other, long-term consequences ensue for the church offers and social infrastructures carried or sustained by the churches. This consequently implies the question how much the demographic change actually affects the trends in and structure of church membership and consequently the church offers that shall be explored in detail.[35]

1.4.2 Leaving the Church

Alongside the demographic change that is responsible for the majority of the decline in membership, the key cause mainly have been the growing numbers of members leaving the church, which both the major Christian churches in Germany have been struggling with already since the 1970s. A representative survey of the Sinus Sociovision Institute of Heidelberg confirmed in 2011 the steady shrinkage of both the major people's churches due to leavings. Over the period of the study, 3.2 percent of Protestant and 1.6 of Catholic Christians respectively decided to leave the church. The share of those who had been thinking about leaving but were still undecided was at 12.1 (Protestants) and 9.9 percent (Catholics).[36] In absolute terms this amounted in 2011 to a "depletion potential" of more than 5.5 million members of both the major churches, of which by the end of 2016 nearly a third actually left.[37]

---

[34] EICKEN, Joachim et al. (2010): ibidem, p. 587.

[35] ibidem, p. 576.

[36] FLAIG, Bodo: *Was wollen die Schäfchen?* In: ZEIT ONLINE. Christ & Welt, Ausgabe 52/2011. [retrieved on 2018-04-30] Available from: https://www.sinus-institut.de/veroeffentlichungen/downloads/download/was-wollen-die-schaefchen/download-file/174/download-a/download/download-c/Category/

[37] Own calculation, based on the last five annual editions of SEKRETARIAT DER DEUTSCHEN BISCHOFSKONFERENZ (2012-2017): *Zahlen und Fakten 2012/2013 – 2016/2017*, ibidem

Figure 1-5 explores the decline in membership in both the Christian people's churches and the rise in the numbers of members leaving the churches over a period of 15 years: [38]

Figure 1-5: Decline in Membership and Church Leavings 2001-2016 (own graphic)

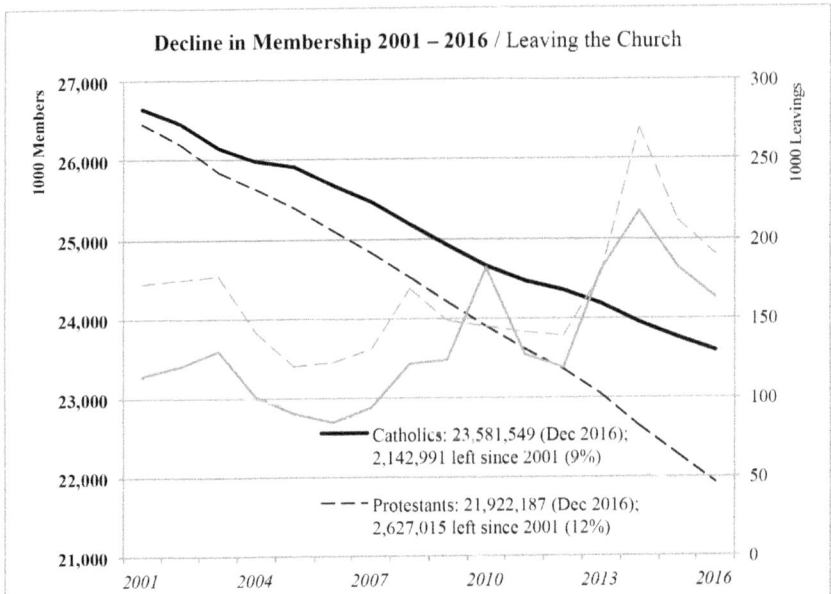

The growing numbers of leaving members strongly correlate with the church abuse scandals that were a trigger for a number of people particularly in early 2010 and in 2014.[39] Generally in considerations about leaving the church, there are frequently several, gradually cumulating motives that play a role. Some stimuli such a church scandal, personal disappointment or the church tax deducted from next gross salary may then precipitate the actual decision.[40]

---

[38] cf. MEINTZ, René: *Kirchenaustritt.de: Informationen zum Kirchenaustritt.* [retrieved on 2018-04-30] Available from: http://www.kirchenaustritt.de/statistik, with references to EKD.de, DBK.de, Destatis.de

[39] FOCUS ONLINE: *Missbrauchsskandal in der katholischen Kirche. Die wichtigsten Fakten seit 2010.* [retrieved on 2018-04-30] Available from: http://www.focus.de/politik/deutschland/rueckblick-zahlen-und-fakten-zum-missbrauchsskandal-in-der-katholischen-kirche_id_6511683.html

[40] INSTITUT FÜR DEMOSKOPIE ALLENSBACH: Kirchenaustritte. Eine Untersuchung zur Entwicklung und zu den Motiven der Kirchenaustritte (IfD-Umfrage 5065). Allensbach, 1992. p. 12.

1.4.3   Causes and Reasons for Leaving the Church

1.4.3.1   Main cause for Leaving: Alienation

According to a representative survey performed by the diocese of Rottenburg-Stuttgart in 2014,[41] the main cause for leaving the Church for over a third of the church members (35%) was identifiable with their *alienation* from the Church as an institution as well as from its parishes and organizations:

Figure 1-6: "Have you ever seriously considered leaving the church? - If so, why?" (open question)

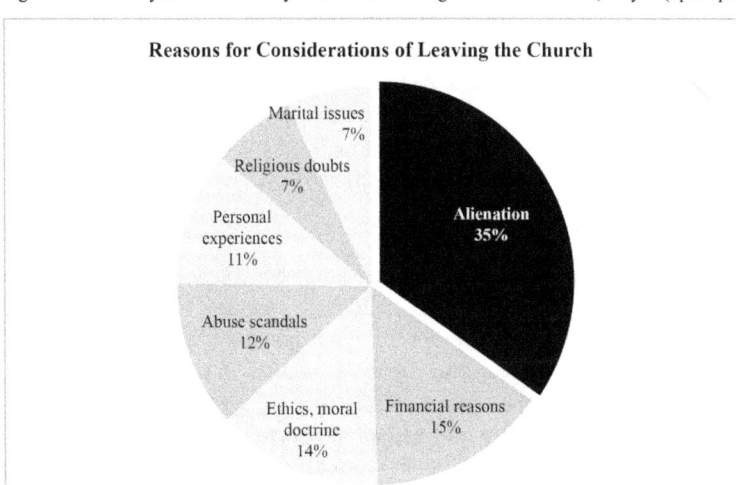

This alienation mostly is traceable to how the Church communicates with its members, "as its answers often do not relate at all to their questions and the respective worlds of thought and living frequently cannot be reconciled anymore".[42] The *church tax* (cf. Chapter 1.3) is indicated as a possible cause for leaving the Church by about 15 percent of Catholics. Another 14 percent gave as potential reasons the (obsolescent) teachings of the Catholic Church on *ethics and morals* and 12 percent of the respondents named *abuse scandals*.

The finding about *alienation* of church members has been confirmed also by a more recent study on leavings from the Church carried out by the diocese of Essen. Here

---

[41]   APP, Reiner, BROCH, Thomas, MESSINGSCHLAGER, Martin: *Zukunftshorizont Kirche: Was Katholiken von ihrer Kirche erwarten. Eine repräsentative Studie*. Ostfildern: Grünewald, 2014, p. 50.

[42]   ibidem, p. 51.

in an Internet survey over the period from March to May 2017, the more than 3,000 participants (of which 15 percent already had left the Church) indicated as reasons for leaving the Church in particular *alienation* and the *lack of attachment* to the Church as well as its "*attitudes being now out of step with time*".[43] These study results are a part of a research effort commissioned by the "Initiative zum Verbleib in der Kirche" (initiative to remain in the Church) whose results have been published in early 2018.[44]

The reasons and determinants of alienation of Christians from their church and/or parishes are multilayered and varied. Of particular significance here are the advancing secularization and progressive differentiation of society into a variety of increasingly different milieus, as well as the lack of religious socialization in families. These factors are explored in the following chapters, and finally also the financial reasons for leaving the church are examined in detail.

1.4.3.2 Changed Societal Framework Conditions

Hillebrecht (2000) examines the decline in church membership within the context of changed societal framework conditions that partly are mutually dependent and also affect each other.[45] As the principal reason for the decline in Catholic membership numbers, he mainly points out the *advancing differentiation in society*, as a result of which people no longer "see themselves as mutually interconnected limbs of the nation of God" but as individuals with freedom of choice in their respective social environment. He further lists as the consequences of the societal differentiation

- *Pluralism*: "Pluralism gives the individual the possibility of individual choice and so causes abandonment of the values and norms that are generally binding to all the people."[46] The end of the monopoly of the church, or of its privileged position in transmitting values and giving orientation ("endowment of sense/meaning"[47])

---

[43] cf. BISTUM ESSEN: *Kirchenaustritt hat viele verschiedene Gründe.* [retrieved on 2018-04-30] Available from: http://zukunftsbild.bistum-essen.de/die-bistums-projekte/die-bistumsprojekte/initiative-fuer-den-verbleib-in-der-kirche/kirchenstudie/ergebnisse-stimmungsbild-und-interviews/ – as well as: BISTUM ESSEN: *Das Zukunftsbild-Projekt.* [retrieved on 2018-04-30] Available from: http://zukunftsbild.bistum-essen.de/die-bistums-projekte/die-bistumsprojekte/initiative-fuer-den-verbleib-in-der-kirche/kirchenstudie/das-zukunftsbild-projekt/

[44] ETSCHEID-STAMS, Markus, LAUDAGE-KLEEBERG, Regina, RÜNKER, Thomas (ed.): *Kirchenaustritt – oder nicht? Wie Kirche sich verändern muss.* Freiburg: Herder, 2018.

[45] HILLEBRECHT, Steffen W.: Die Praxis des kirchlichen Marketings: Die Vermittlung religiöser Werte in der modernen Gesellschaft. Hamburg: E.B.-Verlag, 2000. pp. 13-22.

[46] ibidem, p. 14.

[47] The term "endowment of sense/meaning" fancied in church contexts (orig. German: Sinnstiftung) – according to Duden "the act of creating sense/meaning" (http://www.duden.de/rechtschreibung/Sinnstiftung, retrieved on 2018-04-30) implies the ability of a person or organization to "endow"

would now mean a different specific positioning of the church within a field of new competitors and their supposedly mutually substitutable offers.[48]

- *Individualism* as the antipode to pluralism that "shifts attachment to specific norms and values as well as the endowment of sense/meaning from fixed commandments to the level of freedom of decision of the individual".[49] In that sense some complementary notes from the 2013 Sinus Milieu Study: "The embedding of religion into the living world has largely been lost. (...) The Catholic faith and its ruleset nowadays directly contribute to finding the meaning of life only for some.[50] (...) In many respondents, faith is individualized – and not connected to the Catholic religion and Church. (...) The binding nature of the Catholic religion as a closed system of beliefs appears to have got lost in the wealth of religious and spiritual offers.[51] (...) Many assemble for themselves an individual patchwork of faith, drawing in the process from a number of, often far eastern sources."

- *Modernity* as adulation of the new under the influence of which the autonomous consumer doubts or rejects the preferability and existential necessity of existing, traditional meanings, offers or organizations as such, as well as

- *Secularization* in the sense of de-sacralization of everyday life, as a result of which things that by now have been taken for granted – including the church membership itself – have to be justified, and that goes along *inter alia* with lacking religious socialization of children (cf. Chapter 1.4.3.3).

In connection with secularization and modernity, Casanova (2009) claims the inability of Europeans to openly recognize Christianity as one of the constructive components of the cultural and political identity of Europe. Instead, Europeans would have stripped away their traditional Christian identities in a rapid and violent

---

another person with "sense/meaning" concerning specific situations, events or organizations, hence imbue matters with "meaning" and/or offer these to the other person to be internalized by the same. Here a critical examination is due whether "sense/meaning" can be endowed, given or transmitted at all. This is because "sense/meaning" is the result of a cognitive process that becomes apparent only *ex post*, i.e., is not attainable at all as of yet at the point of its supposed endowment. In this respect there is mainly the risk that what the "sense endowing instance" defines as meaningful and worthy of being endowed sense is not beneficial to the supposed "recipient of sense/meaning".

[48] cf. BUCHER, Rainer: Was geht und was nicht geht. Zur Optimierung kirchlicher Kommunikation durch Zielgruppenmodelle. In: sinnstiftermag 04, (2007) *Frreicht/Unerreicht – Welche Zielgruppen spricht Kirche heute noch an?* [retrieved on 2018-04-30] Available from: http://www.sinnstiftermag.de/ausgabe_04/titelstory.htm

[49] HILLEBRECHT, Steffen W.: Die Praxis des kirchlichen Marketings: Die Vermittlung religiöser Werte in der modernen Gesellschaft. Hamburg: E.B.-Verlag, 2000, p. 21.

[50] CALMBACH, Marc, EILERS, Ingrid, FLAIG, Berthold Bodo: *MDG-Milieuhandbuch 2013: Religiöse und kirchliche Orientierung in den Sinusmilieus.* Heidelberg/München: SINUS Markt- und Sozialforschung GmbH, 2013, p. 20.

[51] ibidem, p. 16.

secularization process that only by a matter of chance was coincidental with the historical process of the European unification and the German reunification. Despite this historically random coincidence, Europeans equated the European modern with secularization, so that as a result secularization would appear in keeping with the times and up-to-date.[52]

Fischer (2008) outlines the consequences of the differentiation of society into progressively different milieus as follows:[53] "The above needs of the petty bourgeois milieu are diametrically opposed to the ethos and the way of life of the milieus in the family tree of milieus identifiable with lines of professional work and practical intelligence, as the core values that are central to the family tree are self-responsibility and individual performance, which does not (...) exclude solidarity and prosocial behaviour, but does well exclude assignment to a patron-client relationship. Where churches intend to reach with their offers these milieus, then they must pick up their core values in the same way as they must respect their connection patterns and practical orientation." Further on, he agrees with the conclusions of Bremer et al. (2003)[54] by summing up that:[55] "The problem with the loss of connection (as does that of the problems with acquisition) is not, as frequently surmised, in the increase of secular, egoistic or hedonistic ways of life, but in the fact that the church has not sufficiently adapted yet to the shift in milieus and to modernized ways of life."

Hempelmann (2013) sees as problematic within the context of an increasingly differentiating society the following trends in milieus: while in the upper class and/or "upper segment", mentalities significantly move together and become mutually aligned, in the New Middle-Class Milieu, traditionally-oriented milieus and the Escapist Milieu there are substantial differentiation processes taking place. These produce not least pronounced "winners and losers" with regard to modernization,

---

[52]   cf. CASANOVA, José: *Europas Angst vor der Religion.* Berlin: University Press, 2009. p. 25, 29, 59.
[53]   FISCHER, Ralph: *Kirche und Zivilgesellschaft. Probleme und Potentiale.* Stuttgart: Kohlhammer, 2008. p. 49. Fischer refers in his work largely on the class theory-based milieu analysis according to Bourdieu and Vester, "as they a) do not disregard the aspect of rulership as well as the resulting relationships of subordinations and domination within society, and b) they do not attempt to explain the milieu affiliation of an individual voluntaristically but account for restrictive or enabling socioeconomic framework conditions". (ibidem, p.41).
[54]   BREMER, Helmut, TEIWES-KÜGLER, Christel: Die sozialen Milieus und ihre Beziehung zur Kirche. Von der 'Milieuverengung' zu neuen Arrangements. In: GEILING, Heiko (ed.): *Probleme sozialer Integration. agis-Forschungen zum gesellschaftlichen Strukturwandel.* Reihe ,Soziale Milieus im gesellschaftlichen Strukturwandel' Band 1. Münster-Hamburg-London: LIT, 2003. pp. 39-65.
[55]   FISCHER, Ralph (2008): ibidem, p. 49.

digitalization, blurring of the borders and individualization versus overload, the search for stability (regrounding), segregation and partial regression.[56] A key role in the process plays mastering new media and forms of communication. "This is opposed by growing déclassement processes, as exemplified by the slide of many in the New Middle-Class Milieu down to the underclass, but also permanent precarization of parts of the underclass. The classical middle class erodes and gets under differentiation pressures."[57]

Due to the differentiation of German society into increasingly different living worlds, the forces of cohesion are weakening both within society as a whole and also and in particular in those human communities in which there is a consensus about shared values and worldviews. Not least because of this, the Catholic Church as well is faced with the challenge to adjust the choice and quality of its activities, offers and people as well as in this regard in particular its interpersonal and media communication (cf. Chapter 3 – Church Marketing) to the changed societal framework conditions. In the process, not just milieu-specific religious and social needs of the many different stakeholder groups – including both members and non-members– need to be anticipated and satisfied in a targeted manner within the context of the Church's mission and the basic functions of the Church. There should be also more dedicated focus on renewal, deepening and passing on of religious and church relationships as they are grounded and perpetuated particularly in families and in primary education institutions.

1.4.3.3   Lack of Passing on of Religious Traditions Between Generations

The Bertelsmann Religionsmonitor 2013 performed a breakdown of the importance of religion in different age groups (Fig. 1-7).[58] For example in the group of 16- to 30-year olds, religion is less important (West: 42%/East: 21%) than for 31- to 60-year olds (48%/26%), who in turn deem religion less important than the above 60-year olds (70%/32%).

---

[56]   HEMPELMANN, Heinzpeter: *Gott im Milieu – Wie Sinusstudien der Kirche helfen können, Menschen zu erreichen.* 2. extended edition. Gießen: Brunnen, 2013. pp.67-73.

[57]   ibidem, p. 68.

[58]   POLLACK, Detlef, MÜLLER, Olaf: *Religionsmonitor. Religion und Zusammenhalt in Deutschland.* Gütersloh: Verlag Bertelsmann Stiftung, 2013, pp. 13-16.

Figure 1-7: Religious Socialization by Age Group

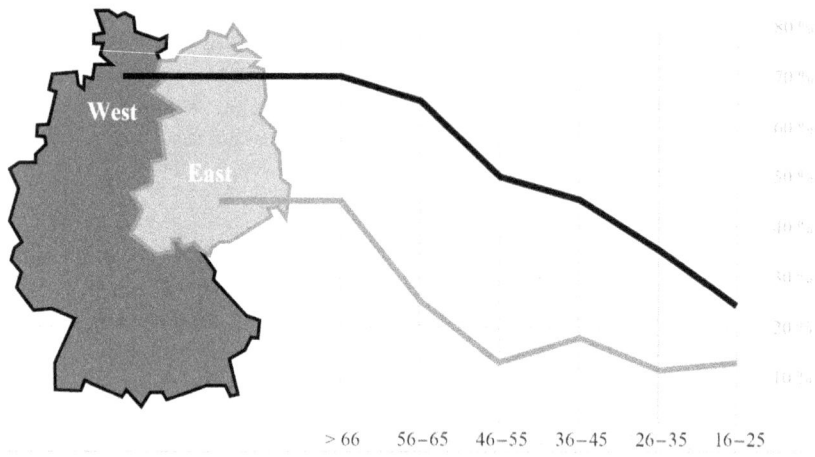

This could be traceable simply to a 'lifecycle effect' under which for today's youth, religion in their old age is going to be equally important as for the elderly of today. However, the authors rather presume here a sc. cohort effect, meaning a shift in religious orientation in the younger generations. This shift gets obvious on having a closer look at the breakdown in the passing on of religious traditions between generations – which principally includes a discontinuance in religious socialization of children at home where parenting takes place. Though in the former East Germany, the process was accelerated with the consequent suppression of religious activities by the (communist) GDR leadership, it is present and equally steady also in western Germany, "and it cannot be excluded that the west German figure approximates the east German figure even more over the coming years".

In 2010, 69 percent of the Catholic population on average deemed religious education of children important (versus 65 % in 1979).[59] This relatively stable level of recognition of religious education of children against previous periods however is contingent upon affiliation of the respondents with traditionally-oriented social environments: while 92 of the conservative and 84 percent of the tradition-conscious Catholics deem religious education of children important, the opinion is shared by

---

[59]   SCHULZ, Rüdiger, DE SOMBRE, Steffen, CALMBACH, Marc: *MDG-Trendmonitor. Religiöse Kommunikation 2010*, München: MDG Medien-Dienstleistung GmbH, 2010, p. 32.

only 53 percent of "modern performers" and merely by 34 percent of the "experimentalists", with both the categories accommodating significantly younger age groups.[60]

The Protestant Church deals in its regular examinations of church membership with leavings of its members since many years already, causally relating these *inter alia* to the decline in religious socialization within the family environment: "Who has left the church, mostly saw also the attitudes of their parents of being disinterested in the church and hardly was ever subject to deliberate religious education. Leaving the church appears the final point of a socialization process that began already in the generation before".[61] In addition to financial reasons for leaving, another principal cause has been in particular the loss of significance of the church, religion and faith to the individual. As runners-up in the list of reasons for leaving the church behind the statement "the church is not credible", there are indications such as that the church would be indifferent, religion would be unnecessary for life, faith would be irrelevant to the individual or it would not fit into modern society. Lower down in the list of potential reasons for leaving the church are negative experience and annoyances.[62]

The result of the substantially reduced or even ceasing religious socialization of young people is a loss of connection to the church and consequently the loss of its significance that adds to the probability of leaving the church. The progressive erosion of religious values also in evident from the changing shares of religious communities in the German population: [63]

---

[60] ibidem, p. 46.

[61] HERMELINK, Jan: Praktische Theologie der Kirchenmitgliedschaft: Interdisziplinäre Untersuchungen zur Gestaltung kirchlicher Beteiligung. Göttingen: Vandenhoeck & Ruprecht, 2000, p. 299.

[62] KUNZ, Ralph, SCHLAG, Thomas (eds.): *Handbuch für Kirchen- und Gemeindeentwicklung.* Neukirchen-Vluyn: Neukirchener Verlag, 2014, p.111.

[63] POLLACK, Detlef et al. (2013): ibidem, p. 32.

Figure 1-8: Development of Religious Denominations in Germany, 1950–2010

This means that in 2010, already nearly a third of the German population did not belong to any religious community anymore, with the Protestant Church in Germany even reporting over the 60-year period since 1950 a loss of about a half of its membership. This makes even the shrinkage of the Catholic portion from 36.7 to 30.2% relatively mild in comparison.[64]

1.4.3.4 Fewer Administered Sacraments

As before, still many couples decide to give their love a public imprint by entering into marriage. However, the number of weddings in which Catholic couples place their life together through the exchange of the sacrament of marriage under the providence of God has been in a significant downward spiral; the number shrunk from more than 100,000 weddings in the late 1980s initially rapidly to only 48,524 in 2010 and then continued in a steady decline to 43,610 in 2016.[65] This trend negatively affects the transmission of religious traditions in the family environment, as no Catholic socialization of their children can be expected from couples that only have had a civil marriage ceremony, and already in interconfessional marriages, religious socialization of children is significantly limited.[66]

---

[64] Chapter 3.4.1.5 deals in more detail with the topic of "religious socialization" in connection with the bundles of church marketing objectives.

[65] SEKRETARIAT DER DEUTSCHEN BISCHOFSKONFERENZ (2017): ibidem. p.45

[66] BIRKELBACH, Klaus: The decision to end church membership: Affiliation vs. church taxes. In: Zeitschrift für Soziologie 28 (2), 1999. pp.136-153.

Irrespective of the decline in the number of births, since nearly three decades three out of four newborns with at least one Catholic parent are Catholically baptized.[67] The baptized children go almost without exceptions all to first communion, and seven out of ten of these children renew their baptismal vows several years later in confirmation. These long-term steady proportions however do not change anything about the fact of the long-term decline in administered sacraments in absolute numbers.

The esteem church rituals such as church wedding, baptism of a child and other occasional services over further course of life are held in and whether they are used however are of surprisingly high significance to staying in the Church.[68] This finding has been confirmed by numerous studies including also the Sinus Milieu Study 2013; for many Catholics, it still is and remains difficult to simply give up their Catholic identity and to go the route of the "ultimate step", particularly where ecclesiastical services would still be needed on family occasions, in emergencies or at the end of life. The fear of "simply being thrown into ground somewhere" is a vital argument for staying in the Church particularly for those who would otherwise keenly prefer to leave due to their various grievances about the Church.[69]

1.4.3.5 Missing Sacerdotal Offspring

Along with the decline in Catholic socialization and the loss of significance of the Catholic Church in society, also ever fewer young people decide to take up a spiritual vocation or spiritual life. The number of diocesan and monastic priests specifically has gone down by about 30 percent from 19,707 in 1990 to 13,856 in 2016; in the same year, only 103 new candidates for priesthood were admitted for training.

Simultaneously however, the number of active deacons on a full- or part-time basis has grown from 1,469 in 1990 to 3,296 in 2016. Further also in 2016, as many as 4,537 parish workers and 3,200 pastoral workers (both male and female) were active on behalf of the Catholic Church – an unprecedented high number of people never seen before.[70] The increase in full-time staff members is traceable among other things also to the fact that as a result of ageing and the decline in membership, a number of core honorary functions cannot be populated anymore with volunteers. The tasks

---

67   SEKRETARIAT DER DEUTSCHEN BISCHOFSKONFERENZ (2017): ibidem. p. 44. | Idem:
     Katholische Kirche in Deutschland - Zahlen und Fakten 2010/2011, p. 12, 13.
68   cf. HERMFLINK, Jan (ed.), LATZEL, Thorsten: Kirche empirisch. Ein Werkbuch zur vierten EKD-
     Erhebung über Kirchenmitgliedschaft und zu anderen empirischen Studien. Gütersloh: Gütersloher
     Verlagshaus, 2008. pp. 101-103.
69   CALMBACH, Marc et al. (2013): ibidem. p. 27 and 31.
70   SEKRETARIAT DER DEUTSCHEN BISCHOFSKONFERENZ (2017): ibidem, p. 42.

such job entail are taken on by full-time staff members or external firms, which in turn for many parishes constitutes an additional financial burden and cost factor.

1.4.3.6 Financial Reasons for Leaving the Church

Birkelbach (1999) has supplied a proof in several consecutive surveys among grammar school students in the German federal state of North Rhine-Westphalia that the probability of leaving the Church for young people rises at the point in time they enter the labour market, i.e., start earning their own money, by a multiple of four to six.[71] Sociodemographic factors such as education, age or gender played hardly any role in this respect. Key was religious socialization in the family: there is a close relationship between own distance from the Church and that of one's parents as remembered, and the probability of later leaving the Church about doubles if there are parents of different confessions.

Concerning the coming generation, the Sinus Youth Study 2016 though concludes that the Christian youth do not show pronounced readiness to leave the Church even at a relatively low connectedness to religion:[72] "As one currently does not pay the church tax as of yet, leaving the Church can wait (...) Moreover, one often resents the inconvenience of getting information about the necessary bureaucratic procedures." However, it remains to be seen how the current attitudes of the youth on the church tax and belonging to the Church change later over the course of their life, because "the more one is exposed to the conditions of economic reality and cultural pluralization, and the more they are, especially at the beginning of her working career, forced into a mobile and autonomous way of life, the more they are likely to also opt for that one step [of leaving the Church]".[73]

About 15 percent of Catholics indicate according to the PRAGMA study from 2014 as a possible cause for leaving the Church the church tax.[74] A similar result was obtained by the Allensbach Institute for Demoscopy in a national survey already in 1992 as there were 13 percent of Catholics (versus 46 percent of Protestants) who had left the Church due to the church tax, though only 20 percent of the respondents actually knew the amount of their church tax payments.[75]

---

71   BIRKELBACH, Klaus: ibidem.
72   CALMBACH, Marc, BORGSTEDT, Silke, BORCHARD, Inga, THOMAS, Peter Martin: *Wie ticken Jugendliche 2016? – Lebenswelten von Jugendlichen im Alter von 14 bis 17 Jahren in Deutschland*. Wiesbaden: Springer Fachmedien, 2016, p. 349.
73   HERMELINK, Jan (2000): ibidem, p. 291.
74   APP, Reiner et al. (2014): ibidem, p. 50.
75   INSTITUT FÜR DEMOSKOPIE ALLENSBACH (1992): ibidem, pp. 20-24.

The portal "www.kirchenaustritt.de", which features prominently in the results of Internet search engines, offers information and statistics on leavings from the Catholic and Protestant Churches in Germany. Visitors of the webpage are asked using predefined answers about the key reason in their opinion for leaving the church.[76] In 2016, 46.9 percent of the total of 47,740 respondents indicated to leave the church because of the church tax; another 30.4% were dissatisfied with the church as an institution and/or its officials and office holders. 16.9 percent did not believe in God (anymore).

Nevertheless in the highly divisive survey, neither demographic data were collected nor was it recorded whether the respondents had left the church already, making the results of the survey of limited use in strictly scientific terms. Still, the high proportion of financial reasons to leave could imply these are going to grow in significance in the future.

On summing up the demographic trends and the different causes for leaving the Church, what remains in consequence of the decline in membership is the deteriorating ability of the Church to fulfil its basic functions, namely testimony and proclamation of faith, liturgy, the charitable and social services to others in need and building the community of the Church. For this reason, targeted involvement of laymen in the tasks and functions of the Church and professional coordination of volunteer functions in the Church are set to grow in importance in the future.[77]

---

[76] MEINTZ, René: *Kirchenaustritt.de.* ibidem.

[77] According to the results of a survey among 1,000 full-time church staff members and volunteers performed through e-mail, Twitter and Facebook in March 2017, 21.8 percent of the respondents saw as the largest problem in their parish the lack of members of the coming generation in volunteer functions: cf. LEITLEIN, Hannes: Die zehn größten Probleme der Gemeinden. In: *ZEIT ONLINE. Christ & Welt, Ausgabe 03/2017.* [retrieved on 2018-04-30] Available from: http://www.zeit.de/2017/03/kirche-gemeinde-probleme-ehrenamtliche-befragung

For examples of respective activities of German dioceses, see Chapter 3.3.4.

2 Church and Business Economics

This part does not aim at delving into or exploring the fundamental debate in pertinent church-related literature on the theological acceptability of a business economic view on Christian churches. For that there are comprehensive treatises of the debate *inter alia* in Fetzer (1997)[78], Thomé (1998), Hillebrecht (1999), Bruhn (2000), Mödinger (2001), Tscheulin/Dietrich (2003), Famos (2006), Giesen (2009) and elsewhere. Especially in more recent contributions to the debate, a business economic perspective on the Christian church not only is being legitimized but even deemed a necessity with a view to its sustainable development potential in the face of the progressive decline in membership and the resulting cost and competitive pressures.

Nevertheless, a comprehensive assessment of the church from the business economic point of view still remains a difficult undertaking as under the generic umbrella of the church, there are many different organizations with various legal forms and diverse objectives. Though their conditions of operation economically and leadership-wise are generally similar to other types of organizations, the business economic perspective completely disregards the spiritual and transcendental aspect of the "salvation goods of the church"[79] and the "church value mission":[80] "(...) An economistic constriction would have fatal consequences to church life. This is because the church does not have just a customer pool but membership, and it does not have just an offer, but a mission".[81]

In any examinations of the church from a business economic perspective, firstly the question arises about how to best to interpret the church and its parishes and facilities as an organization in business economic terms. Given the large variety of offers and structures of church organizations as well as their assumption of some tasks of the state on behalf of the same and network-like interconnections with state authorities, private enterprises and households, as the relatively best fitting concept to subsume the church and its parishes under appears that of non-profit organizations (NPOs).

---

[78] FETZER, Joachim: Mut zu Entscheidungen. BWL und Kirche: eine Einführung in ökonomisches Denken und Handeln. In: BRUMMER, Arndt, NETHÖFEL, Wolfgang (ed.): *Vom Klingelbeutel zum Profitcenter? Strategien und Modelle für das Unternehmen Kirche*. Das Sonntagsblatt, Hamburg: Hanseatisches Druck- und Verlagshaus, 1997, pp. 51-60.

[79] STOLZ, Jörg: Kirchen im Wettbewerb. Religiöse und säkulare Konkurrenz in der modernen Gesellschaft. In: FAMOS (2006), ibidem, p. 111.

[80] MÖDINGER, Wilfried: *Kirchenmarketing: Strategisches Marketing für kirchliche Angebote*. Stuttgart: Lucius und Lucius, 2001, p. 22.

[81] KUNZ, Ralph: Grenzen der Vermarktung – Marketing zwischen Ökonomisierung und Gemeindeaufbau. in: FAMOS (2006), ibidem, p. 30 – A more detailed treatise of the "mission" of the church and its activities and offers this gives rise to is provided in Chapter 3 – Church Marketing.

For example Kotler concluded in his NPO-specific elaborations on marketing already in 1978[82] that marketing as a management tool would not be exclusively suited for example for commercial companies only but instead be highly pertinent to the issues and challenges faced by non-profit organizations. This notion is to be explored further in the following parts firstly by summing up the particular features of non-profit organizations and then examining these for similarities with the establishments and organizations of the Catholic Church.

2.1 The Third Sector: Non-Profit Organizations In-Between the Opposing Forces of the Market, of the State and of Private Associations

In early 1990s, German political scientist Adalbert Evers recognized the rising socio-political significance of organizations of the sc. "third sector" (private associations of volunteers with a non-profit making purpose). In his examinations, he concluded that third sector organizations with the norms and values they operate under find themselves in a conflict area of a kind he termed the "Welfare Triangle" (cf. Fig. 2-1 on page 30). The corner points of this triangular conflict area are defined by where the respective motivations prevail of "profit" (market), "redistribution" (the state) and "self-responsibility" (family, community). Due to their central position in this conflict area, third-sector-organizations are "simultaneously influenced by state policies and legislation, the values and practices of private business, the culture of civil society and by the needs and contributions that come from informal family and community life." [83]

With the aim to re-evaluate the diverse relationships and services provided between private firms, the state, family-like communities and the spreading voluntary associations at hand, the John Hopkins Comparative Nonprofit Sector Project (CNP) was launched almost concurrently with Evers' publications in Baltimore/USA in 1991. Down to the present day the project aims to:[84]

- *Document the scope, structure, financing, and role of the civil society sector in solid empirical terms;*

- *Explain why this sector varies in size, composition, character, and role from place to place and identify the factors that seem to encourage or retard its development, including differences in history, legal arrangements, religious*

[82]   KOTLER, Philip: *Marketing für Nonprofit-Organisationen.* Stuttgart: Poeschel, 1978, p. 14.
[83]   EVERS, Adalbert, LAVILLE, Jean-Louis (ed.): *The Third Sector in Europe.* Cheltenham / Northampton: Edward Elgar, 2004, pp. 15-16.
[84]   JOHN HOPKINS UNIVERSITY, Maryland (USA): *Comparative Nonprofit Sector Project (CNP) of the Center for Civil Society Studies.* [retrieved on 2018-04-30] Available from: http://ccss.jhu.edu/ research-projects/comparative-nonprofit-sector-project/

> *backgrounds, cultures, socioeconomic structures, and patterns of government policy;*

- *Evaluate the impact these organizations have and the contributions they make, as well as the drawbacks they entail;*
- *Highlight this set of institutions by disseminating the results of the work;*
- *Build local capacity to carry on the work in the future.*

The CNP in the meantime has been implemented by the John Hopkins University – Center for Civil Society Studies in more than 45 countries worldwide. Based on the data obtained from the initial surveys in 13 countries, Salamon and Anheier (1992)[85] have devised the following five criteria based on which an establishment is classifiable as a non-profit organization (NPO). These are:

1. A certain degree of formalization, such as the presence of statutes, rules and regulations or organization plans (but not necessarily of a legal form);
2. Run by a private entity/person independent from the state and from profit-making enterprises, coupled alongside with its
3. Legally and organisationally autonomous administration;
4. The use of any profits possibly made solely to fulfil the organization's purpose (no profit distribution to entities/persons running the organization), as well as
5. Voluntary in all the aspects of membership, involvement and contributions.[86]

The five criteria that already have been declared as an international standard remain tried and tested in practice up to this day, however with national modifications and/or extensions in existence depending on political and economic systems of different states and the typical structures of the family-based and family-like communities.

To exemplify the fluent transitions between the areas of market, the state, family communities and NPOs as well as in particular to point to respective differentiation problems, Pestoff (1998) finally integrated the five criteria by Salamon/Anheier in a clear and descriptive manner with Evers' Welfare Triangle:[87]

---

[85] SALAMON, Lester M., ANHEIER, Helmut K.: *Defining the nonprofit sector. A cross-national analysis.* Manchester: Manchester University Press, 1992, p. 33 f.

[86] cf. LICHTSTEINER, Hans, GMÜR, Markus, GIROUD, Charles, SCHAUER, Reinbert: *Das Freiburger Management-Modell für Nonprofit-Organisationen.* 8. edition, Bern: Haupt, 2015, p.17.

[87] cf. PESTOFF, Victor, DEFOURNY, Jacques, HULGÅRD, Lars: *Social Enterprise and the Third Sector. Changing European landscapes in a comparative perspective.* New York: Routledge, 2014, p. 252.

Figure 2-1: The Third Sector and the Welfare Triangle

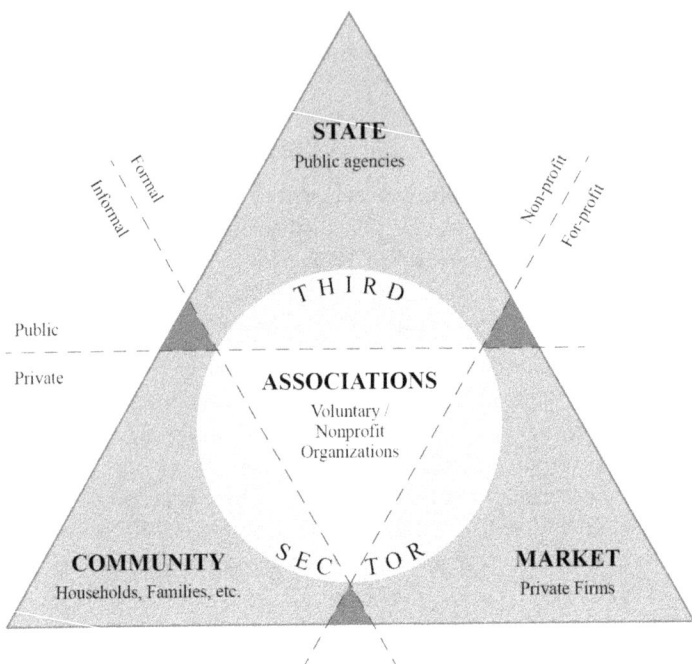

2.2 Analogies between Church/Parishes and NPOs

Using the five criteria by Salomon/Anheier (1992), churches and parishes now can
be examined for any first apparent similarities with non-profit organizations.

1. Degree of formalization: the Catholic Church has a formal set of
   organizational rules and regulations that has been written down as formal law
   with its own judicial instances in the "Codex Ius Canonici".[88]
2. Run by private persons/entities: All the facilities of the Catholic Church are
   owned by its dioceses, parishes and establishments that
3. Are administered as NPOs independently in legal and organizational terms
   from third parties.
4. Any profits made from its operations are used to fulfil the Church's mission
   and to meet its charitable and social aims; there is no profit distribution to
   shareholders.

---

[88]   cf. ROMAN CURIA: *Code of Canon Law*. ibidem.

5. Membership and involvement in the Catholic Church are voluntary. The membership fee however is obligatory in Germany (and only in Germany) and is assessed and levied as church tax on the income of members of the Church.

Where an organization meets all the five criteria, it is classifiable according to its scope operations within an international classification system ("ICNPO" – International Classification of NPOs) also devised by Salamon/Anheier into one of 12 Groups of NPOs. Under this internationally recognized standard, Group 10 (Religion) breaks down in its code 10.100 (Religious Congregations and Associations) into[89]

- *Congregations – churches, synagogues, temples, mosques, shrines, monasteries, seminaries and similar organizations promoting religious beliefs and administering religious services and rituals – and*
- *Associations of congregations – associations and auxiliaries of religious congregations and organizations supporting and promoting religious beliefs, services and rituals.*

This means a distinction between organizations that directly proffer messages of faith and religious rituals and practices (parishes), and social groupings and organizations that mainly provide services arising from the fundamental religious intention. Obviously it would be somewhat arbitrary to include churches and their parishes among non-profit organizations solely on the basis of their religious activities, as this would likely mean to ignore the various and important education, training and social/charitable service facilities run by the church as well as its national and international networks.

For example, the German Caritas Association alone, which is a charitable union of the Catholic Church and with about 8,000 legally independent carriers of its operations, around 590,000 staff members and approximately 500,000 voluntary helpers the largest private-law employer in Germany, could on closer look likely fit any of the ICNPO Classifications. The "Caritas", as it is known in Germany, organizes the social work of the Catholic Church and further is also present in the following lines of work:[90]

---

[89] SALAMON, Lester M., ANHEIER, Helmut K.: *The International Classification of Nonprofit Organizations: ICNPO-Revision 1, 1996.* Working Papers of the Johns Hopkins Comparative Nonprofit Sector Project, no. 19. Baltimore: The Johns Hopkins Institute for Policy Studies, 1996, p. 20.

[90] DEUTSCHER CARITASVERBAND e.V.: *Caritas in Deutschland. Millionenfache Hilfe.* [retrieved on 2018-04-30] Available from: https://www.caritas.de/diecaritas/wofuerwirstehen/millionenfache-hilfeGERMAN CARITAS ASSOCIATION: *Caritas in Germany – Tasks, organisation, and financing.* [retrieved on 2018-04-30] Available from: http://www.caritas-

- Health aid and assistance: hospitals, rehabilitation facilities, welfare centers, assistance to Aids patients, hospices etc.;
- Child and youth welfare: kindergartens and daycare centers for children, children's and youth homes, educational counselling ...;
- Family assistance: women's shelters, counselling centers, pregnancy counselling etc.;
- Welfare for the elderly, including residential and nursing homes, daycare centers, menu and emergency call services;
- Assistance to the disabled/psychiatry: residential/nursing centers, outpatient care;
- Other social aid: drug counselling, homeless assistance, railway mission, crisis line etc.

Further also the Catholic Church supports through its aid networks including their international variety diverse projects and organizations in a number of fields.[91] In doing so, there is at least one example of church engagement for every ICNPO Group (see Fig. 2-2 on the next page).

2.3   The Catholic Church as a Socio-Cultural NPO

Giesen (2009) concludes in her observations on church economics:92 "Despite some efforts to the contrary that emphasise the profit-making aspect of the church's operations, the idea of the church as a non-profit organization may be deemed largely undisputed." Lichtsteiner (2015) defines in this respect as non-profit organizations (NPOs) – including all their synonyms such as non-for-profit, non-business and non-government organizations – "those productive social systems that complementary to the state and to market-driven commercial enterprises fulfil specific needs or perform specific tasks of promotion, representation of interests and influencing (to material goals) on behalf of their members (self-help) or third parties"[93]. As churches have the primary task to pursue the cultural and societal interests and needs of their members,[94] he assigns them to "socio-cultural NPOs". Consequently the German Catholic Church, its facilities and organizations are subsumed in the following parts as such.

---

germany.org/cms/contents/caritas-germany.org/medien/dokumente/info-graphic-on-task/caritas-infografik-2016_en-version_170421.pdf?d=a&f=pdf

[91]   SEKRETARIAT DER DEUTSCHEN BISCHOFSKONFERENZ (2017), ibidem, p. 59 f.
[92]   GIESEN, Rut von: *Ökonomie der Kirche?* Ibidem, p.157.
[93]   LICHTSTEINER, Hans et al. (2015): ibidem, p.19.
[94]   Ibid., p. 20.

Figure 2-2: ICNPO classes and correlating examples from the Catholic Church

ICNPO	Area of Activity	Correlating examples from the Catholic Church
Group 1	Culture and Recreation	Religious publications, art and devotional objects, architecture and monuments
Group 2	Education and Research	Kindergartens, schools and universities95 under church leadership, Study of "Addiction Aid"
Group 3	Health	Hospitals, hospices and sanatoria of the Maltese Order; Caritas hospitals and sanatoria
Group 4	Social Services	Life coaching, social counselling services etc., children's homes, retirement homes, refugees
Group 5	Environment	Caritas environmental declarations/campaigns, Encyclical "Laudato Si" of Pope Francis
Group 6	Development and Housing	Renovabis, Misereor, Adveniat, Caritas and Parishal Neighbourly Help, CV-Afrikahilfe
Group 7	Law, Advocacy and Politics	Justitia et Pax, Encyclical "Dignitatis Humanae", consumer protection of KDFB
Group 8	Philanthropic Intermediaries and Voluntarism Promotion	Pax Christi, Papal Lottery, Caritas Refugee Relief, Caritas (approx. 500,000 volunteers)
Group 9	International	Caritas International (emergency aid and disaster management), Maltese International
Group 10	Religion	27 German (arch-) dioceses with more than 10,000 parishes, numerous Catholic associations
Group 11	Business and Professional Associations, Unions	Media (Tellux TV, Dom-Radio, Weltbild Publishers), Banks/Insurances, Realty. GKD union
Group 12	Not elsewhere classified	(...)

In legal terms, German dioceses and archdioceses with their parishes and parochial unions are organized under the German system of legal forms as public corporations (*Körperschaften des öffentlichen Rechts*), [96] while in particular the charitable and social activities of the Church depending on economic context and funding needs increasingly tend to be organized as non-profit associations (eingetragener Verein,

---

[95] In the winter semester 2015/2016, 356 professors worked at the theological institutes, universities and faculties of the Catholic church teaching 20,693 students. Cf: SEKRETARIAT DER DEUTSCHEN BISCHOFSKONFERENZ (2017), ibidem, p. 21.

[96] cf. DEUTSCHER BUNDESTAG: Basic Constitutional Law of the Federal Republic of Germany, Article 140. Ibidem.

abbreviated: e.v.) or limited liability companies for charitable purposes (gGmbH), which as such enjoy preferential tax treatment. Further also as legal forms, there are some foundations and cooperatives (in the fields of residential construction, banking).

In addition to attributes that are generally valid for NPOs such as being run by private entities, independent operations strictly focused on fulfilling the organization's purpose and voluntary membership/member contributions, Christian churches have four special features that fundamentally set them apart from other non-profit organizations and have far-reaching consequences for their competitiveness:[97]

(1) Their mission is grounded in religion. (2) They aim at covering all spheres of life of their members. (3) They offer a large variety of religious, church-related and economic goods. (4) They offer the promise of religious goods of the higher and highest order. In contrast to other NPOs and service enterprises, the church primarily is bound to fulfil its religious and missionary purpose and only then by the needs of its members.[98] This primary alignment of the church to its religious mission gives rise to strategies and services that are provided irrespective of their prospect of market success partly free of charge or at a price that is set politically. Church organizations easily tend to, as do many other NPOs, due to their relative independence from the market to pursue a strategy that, once set, is not reviewed further, and hence frequently are less about management than they are about administration.[99]

A model that undertakes to account for this specific issue is the Fribourg Management Model for Non-Profit Organizations that is explored in the following parts. This business economic model interprets NPOs primarily as communities of values and cultures the stakeholder groups of which share certain similarities in their opinions and ways of life and the activities and services of which that serve to fulfil the organization's purpose are carried as opposed to staff members many a time by members engaging as volunteers.

---

[97] STOLZ, Jörg: Kirchen im Wettbewerb. Religiöse und säkulare Konkurrenz in der modernen Gesellschaft. In: FAMOS (2006), ibidem, pp. 97-98. Stolz defines "religions" as "systems of symbols that refer to the transcendental".

[98] cf. KUNZ, Ralph: Grenzen der Vermarktung – Marketing zwischen Ökonomisierung und Gemeindeaufbau. In: FAMOS (2006), ibidem, p. 30.

[99] cf. GIESEN (2009): ibidem, p.152-153.

2.4   The Fribourg Management Model for NPOs

Lichtsteiner (2015) specifically defines an NPO as a social system with a concrete purpose that is grounded in its values and/or culture and that is met by organized provision of corresponding performance based on respective management of resources. He assigns to this basic conception within the Fribourg Management Model for Non-Profit Organizations the management areas of "system management", "marketing management" and "resource management".[100]

While system management represents the normative and strategic level of management in an NPO in which its mission, guiding principles/philosophy as well the ensuing strategies, structures and systems are defined, resource management refers to acquisition/provision, administration and development of necessary operational, personal and financial resources (cf. Fig. 2-3, next page).

Marketing management is according to the Fribourg Model of special and core significance as its scope is about designing the varied interactive and exchange relationships both internally such as towards members, staff and volunteers, and externally towards potential members and sponsors, marketing agents and cooperation partners, political bodies, society at large etc.:[101] "The task of marketing is to align performance and communication with meeting the organization's purpose and with generating benefits for members and clients and influencing third parties, with the marketing tasks arising in acquisition, internally and in delivering performance".

This principal role of marketing and of (marketing) communication internally and in delivering performance is dealt with in detail in Chapter 3 herein and applied in particular to service-related needs of the Catholic Church and of its parishes.

---

[100]   LICHTSTEINER, Hans et al. (2015), ibidem, p. 62 ff.

[101]   This implies profound similarities with service marketing that is defined as well by Bieberstein (2006) as a marketing concept for designing in a target-oriented manner the exchange processes with external and internal partners: "Internal marketing aims at designing the exchange relationships with in-house persons in order to create the personal and organizational prerequisites for an efficient external marketing. External marketing is the actual core focus area of the concept as it does not deal just with designing and marketing tangible and intangible results of performance but also with the process of delivering the performance". In other words: service marketing must deal in its marketing considerations not only with the result of the service process and with marketing individual performance but also with designing the service potential and how the performance is provided. – BIEBERSTEIN, Ingo: *Dienstleistungs-Marketing*. 4., revised and updated edition, Ludwigshafen: Kiehl, 2006, p. 45.

Figure 2-3: Structure Logic of the Fribourg Management Model for NPOs

Basic conception of a NPO   *Implementation in the Management Model*

NPO as a system
- Purpose and goal-oriented
- Producing performances
- Social
- Depending on environment

NPO-mission: Fulfillment of purpose
- Collective self-help for members
- Support, Furtherance of third parties
- Representation of interests, Lobbying
- Assigned (para-state) tasks

Fulfillment of purpose via performance
- Individual services for members
- Collective performances for a group

Provision of Performance by Means
- Procuring, managing, developing ressources
- Members, honoraries, employees, volunteers
- Finance (fees, donations etc.)
- Tangible means
- Cooperations

SYSTEM MANAGEMENT
comprising the entire NPO system:
- Defining management philosophy models
- Designing structures and processes
- Developing and managing instruments

MARKETING MANAGEMENT

Purpose of the NPO
- Creating benefit and effect towards special exchange partners
- Consistently implementing the incentive-contribution principle towards all reference groups

Fulfillment of purpose of the NPO
- Designing and providing of special performances
- Design and use of *communication* in the procurement, internal and output (sales) area

RESSOURCES MANAGEMENT
Procuring, designing, managing and using ressources and potentials to fulfill the purpose:
Ensuring motivation, efficiency and sService capability

2.5 NPO Marketing means NPO Communication

The outline of marketing tasks in the Fribourg Management Model for NPOs makes the comprehensive focus evident in NPO marketing on communication, as communication does not only play a role in NPOs in fulfilling the organization's purpose (cf. Fig. 2-4, next page [102]) – including positive self-presentation in order to

---

[102] WYMER, Walter et al.: Nonprofit marketing: Marketing management for charitable and non-governmental organizations. London: SAGE Publications, 2006, p. 14.

build personal and institutional relations, to acquire funding or recruit voluntary helpers and volunteers – but also in specifying and conveying its original organization's purpose and mission.

Figure 2-4: Non-profit Marketing Functions

Attracting funding	Submitting grant proposals to government agencies and foundations, conducting annual campaigns and capital campaigns, organizing planned giving, seeking corporate donations, holding special events, etc.
Attracting volunteers	Understanding where to reach potential volunteers, what message will appeal to them, how to deliver appeal, etc.
Building relationships	Developing and maintaining relationships with board members, corporations, volunteers, clients, donors, funding agencies, government, media, the public, etc.
Communicating	Advertising, publicizing, conducting public relations, reaching clients, maintaining government relations, carrying out advocacy and education

An NPO thus in any communicative and media presentations conveys "key aspects of its self-conception and its culture, its personality and its stances"[103] with the aim to be perceived by its stakeholders through this auto-communication coherently and positively as far as possible. The more NPOs in the effort convey stable content and standardized information, the more clear-cut their positioning and the more successful the cultivation of a sustainably positive image.

As though modern consumer societies are faced with information overflow, by far not all information that is disseminated finds its target. Quite on the contrary, there is a highly active, increasingly subconscious information filtering and selection ongoing in recipients that NPOs, hence also including the Church and its parishes, must take into account when designing their marketing strategies and in particular their communication efforts.

---

[103] LICHTSTEINER (2015), ibidem, p. 206.

3   Church Marketing

In their treatise "Zur (Un-)Vereinbarkeit von Marketing und Kirche" (On the (In)compatibility of Church and Marketing), Tscheulin/Dietrich (2003) conclude that "church marketing mainly is associated with communication policy measures", while "refraining from considering the implementation of measures ostensibly focused on the public". [104] This is no surprise given that the Church as a socio-cultural non-profit organization (NPO) and community of believers in God is dependent in conveying its messages and pursuing its tasks and objectives on both personal and media communication. In doing so in the Church and its parishes, aggressive market targeting postures or "guerrilla actions" mainly from consumer goods marketing that have been coming up with ever new and unprecedented forms of embarrassment at ever shorter intervals have been largely avoided.

In the following chapter, the insights from NPO marketing are applied to the German Catholic Church and its parishes. This is complemented by a detailed treatise of the notion of marketing in church contexts and an outline of the portfolio of church marketing tools with a particular focus on (marketing) communication of parishes.

3.1   The Origin of Church Marketing

"Church marketing" actually can be traced to as early as the very beginnings of Christianity, specifically as Jesus Christ after his resurrection sent out his apostles into the world with the utterances [105] "Go into all the world and preach the gospel to every creature!" (Mk 16:15) and "Go therefore and make disciples of all nations." (Mt 28:19). Translated into marketing vocabulary, this mission given by Jesus means to state, distribute and spread his message of faith and salvation (*product*) [106] in an already saturated, prevalently Jewish religious market (*place*) in personal contact with the target audience by personal example, word of mouth and later through writings (*promotion*) in order to bring about in this way a positive change (*price*) in the audience – for example in the form of conversion through internalized tenets of

---

[104] TSCHEULIN, Dieter K., DIETRICH, Martin: Zur (Un-)Vereinbarkeit von Marketing und Kirche – Eine anbieterorientierte Analyse des kirchlichen Marketings. Freiburg: Albert-Ludwigs-Universität, 2003, pp. 26-27.

[105] BISCHÖFE DEUTSCHLANDS et al.: *Die Bibel*. Ibidem. Mk 16:15 as well as Mt 28:19.

[106] The „4 P" – Product, Price, Place, Promotion – are deemed the classic instruments of the marketing mix, originally proposed by: MCCARTHY, Edmund Jerome: *Basic Marketing: A managerial approach*. University of California: R.D. Irwin, 1960.

faith, declaration of faith and joining the Christian community, of changed priorities in life and/or changed social behaviour, passing on and so perpetuating faith etc.

The origin of the idea that churches and parishes need to market themselves is attributed to Berger (1967), who stated – considering the consequences of secularization – that religious traditions could no longer be imposed on society in an authoritarian manner and that they need to be marketed:[107] "It [the religious tradition] must be "sold" to a clientele that is no longer constrained to "buy". The pluralistic situation is, above all, a *market situation*. (...) What happens here, quite simply, is that the religious groups are transformed from monopolies to competitive marketing agencies. Previously, the religious groups were organized as befits an institution exercising exclusive control over a population of retainers. Now, the religious groups must organize themselves in such a way as to woo a population of consumers, in competition with other groups having the same purpose."

40 years on, Bucher (2007), surprisingly, concludes in a similar vein[108]: "Religion since some time has been socializing in radically new ways. Religious practice is entrusted, as are many other things, to the freedom of the individual. (...) This is something entirely new in particular for Catholics given that up until and well into the 1960s they still used to be coached in a caring manner by their Church. Such efforts of course remain even today, nevertheless the decision about whether or not to follow them now is with the individual. For the Catholic Church, this means a revolutionary realignment: suddenly the Church is dependent in its actual existence on the reservation of consent of its own members and has undergone a transformation from a religious community of fate into one of many providers in the market of religions and the meaning of life." Kunz (2006) details this shift in church offers towards a 'buyer's market' as follows: [109] "Firstly, the Church as a provider of explanations to the meaning of life finds itself in a *competitive situation*. Secondly, it must economize its resources, as with the declining membership, its *means become more limited*." Though sustainable management of resources and customer-oriented marketing would be vital according to Kunz, a strongly economic focused management would have had fatal consequences for the life of the Church. This

---

[107] BERGER, Peter L.: *The Sacred Canopy: Elements of a Sociological Theory of Religion*. Garden City: Doubleday, 1967, pp. 137-138.

[108] BUCHER, Rainer (2007): *Was geht und was nicht geht*. Ibidem.

[109] KUNZ, Ralph: Grenzen der Vermarktung – Marketing zwischen Ökonomisierung und Gemeindeaufbau, in: FAMOS (2006): *Kirche und Marketing*. Ibidem, pp. 30 f.

because the Church would have not just a customer pool but its membership, and it would not just peddle an offer but have a mission. On the consequent alignment of religious undertakings with demand, Mödinger stresses out (2001):[110] "The measure of all things here is not the religious expert but the religious need from which expert knowledge can be derived and constituted ever anew."

In response to the societal changes outlined above and in Chapter 1 of this thesis, the topic of 'marketing' has been paid increasing attention and ascribed increasing significance by the Church. This is reflected also by pertinent marketing literature. For example over the period 1990 to 2000 alone, at least 25 concepts and 17 empirical studies were published on the larger subject of 'church marketing'.[111] Also since 2000, there has been a surge in interest in applying and/or transposing existing marketing concepts – including for marketing communication – to church contexts and needs.[112]

---

[110] MÖDINGER, Wilfried (2001): ibidem, p. 33.

[111] STEVENS, Robert et al.: *Concise the Encyclopedia of Church and Religious Organization Marketing*. New York: Haworth Press, 2005. – Many of these prevalently US publications use "church" and "parish" synonymously. The two terms in their German translation – both as "Kirche" – however may have entirely different meanings in German speaking areas, with the term (Kirche) being used either as a summary term for the church as a whole/universal church (cf. Chapter 1, page 6 herein), or in the meaning of a church building.

[112] cf.: [marketing communication] SELF, Donald R. et al. (eds.): *Marketing Communications for Local Nonprofit Organisations: Targets and Tools*. New York: Haworth, 2001 | RUPP, William T., SMITH, Alan D.: A Study of the Interrelationships between the internet and religious Organisations: An Application of Diffusion Theory. in: *Services Marketing Quarterly 24 (2)*, 2002. p. 29 | DAEHN, Michael: *Marketing the Church: How to Communicate Your Church's Purpose and Passion in a Modern Context*. St. Louis: Lulu, 2006 | VOKURKA, Robert J. et al.: Church Marketing Communication Methods. The Effect of Location and Impact on Growth. In: *Services Marketing Quarterly 24 (1)*, 2002. p. 17-32 | STIELSTRA, Greg et al. (eds): How to Market Your Church. In: *Faith-Based Marketing: The Guide to Reaching 140 Million Christian Consumers*, New Jersey: John Wiley & Sons, 2012 | FÜRST, Gebhardt (ed.): *Katholisches Medienhandbuch. Fakten – Praxis – Perspektiven*. Kevelaer: Butzon & Bercker, 2013 | [brand image] ABREU, Madalena: The brand positioning and image of a religious organisation: an empirical analysis. In: *International Journal of Nonprofit and Voluntary Sector Marketing 11 (2)*, 2006. p. 139-146 | GIESEN, Rut von (2009): ibidem, pp. 215 ff. | CASIDY, Riza: How great thy brand: the impact of church branding on perceived benefits. in: *Int. Journal of Nonprofit & Volun. Sector Marketing 18 (3)*, 2013. pp. 231-239 | USUNIER, Jean-Claude, STOLZ Jörg (eds.): *Religions as Brands. New Perspectives on the Marketization of Religion and Spirituality*. London: Routledge, 2014 | [service quality] SANTOS, Jessica, MATHEWS, Brian P.: Quality in religious services. In: *Int. Journal of Nonprofit & Volun. Sector Marketing 6 (3)*, 2001. p. 278–288 | TKACZYNSKI, Aaron: Take me to church: What ministries are of perceived value for attendees from a nonprofit marketing perspective? In: *Int. Journal of Nonprofit & Volun. Sector Marketing 22 (3)*, 2017, c1581 | [marketing strategy] PERL, Paul, OLSON, Daniel V.A.: Religious Market Share and Intensity of Church Involvement in Five Denominations. In: *Journal for the Scientific Study of Religion 39*, 2000. pp. 12–31 | RODRIGUE, Chistina S.: Marketing Church Services: Targeting Young Adults. In: *Services Marketing Quarterly 24 (1)*, 2002. p. 33 | DAVIS, Justin L. et al.: Stale in the pulpit? Leader tenure and the relationship between market growth strategy and church performance. In: *Int. Journal of Nonprofit & Volun. Sector Marketing 15 (4)*, 2010. pp. 352–368 | HIRSCHLE, Jochen: "Secularization of Consciousness" or Alternative Opportunities? The Impact of Economic Growth on Religious Belief

3.2 Definitions of Church Marketing

Due to the changing market environment and market stances among both providers and consumers, a radically different communication landscape and not least digitization of business processes, "marketing" has undergone many redefinitions since the early 20th century and has been systematically advanced among others by US economist Philip Kotler and his German colleague Heribert Meffert.[113] In current business economics, marketing is construed as a market-oriented management approach that is integrated into the entirety of business processes and "that combines both a function-specific dimension and a cross-functional dimension".[114] While the function-specific dimension refers to the typical tasks of marketing departments such as market research, brand management and brand strategy, customer acquisition and retention etc. (marketing functions), the cross-functional dimension of the notion of marketing stipulates consequent alignment of all the corporate areas, resources and activities with the market with the aim to satisfy the needs and expectations of customers and other stakeholders (marketing processes).

As the leading global scientific body in the field of marketing, the American Marketing Association (AMA) claims the official and generally applicable definition of the notion of 'marketing'. Its latest version of 2007 that was last confirmed as binding by the AMA board in 2013 reads as follows: [115] *"Marketing is the activity, set of institutions, and processes for creating, communicating, delivering, and exchanging offerings that have value for customers, clients, partners, and society at large."*

---

and Practice in 13 European Countries. In: *Journal for the Scientific Study of Religion 52 (2)*, 2013. pp. 410-424 | Dietlein, Georg: *Kirche im Aufbruch: Ein Change Management-Ansatz für die katholische Kirche*. Norderstedt: BoD, 2015 | [market orientation] FAMOS (2006): *Kirche und Marketing*. Ibidem. | WHITE, Darin W., SIMAS, Clovis F.: An empirical investigation of the link between market orientation and church performance. In: Int. Journal of Nonprofit & Volun. Sector Marketing 13 (2), 2008. pp. 153-165 | MULYANEGARA, Riza Casidy et al.: An empirical investigation on the role of market orientation in church participation. In: Int. Journal of Nonprofit & Voluntary Sector Marketing 15 (4), 2010. pp. 339-351.

[113]   For more information on „Entwicklung des Begriffsverständnisses des Marketing" (Development of the conceptual understanding of marketing) see: MEFFERT, Heribert, BURMANN, Christoph, KIRCHGEORG, Manfred: *Marketing. Grundlagen marktorientierter Unternehmensführung*. 12th revised and updated edition, Wiesbaden: Springer Gabler, 2015. pp. 11-13.

[114]   MEFFERT, Heribert et al. (2015): ibidem.

[115]   AMERICAN MARKETING ASSOCIATION: *Definition of Marketing*. [retrieved on 2017-12-07] Available from: https://www.ama.org/AboutAMA/Pages/Definition-of-Marketing.aspx (definition from 2007, approved July 2013 by the American Marketing Association Board of Directors)

3.2.1   Examples of Definitions of 'Church Marketing'

In church contexts, a systematic definition of the notion of marketing was first posited by Shawchuck/Kotler/Wrenn in 1992. The definition reflects both the missionary goals of the church – i.e., its mission to spread its message of salvation and to lead by example in spreading the Christian faith – and contains a first processual notion of marketing: [116]

"Marketing is the analysis, planning, implementing and control of carefully formulated programs, in order to determine voluntary exchange with specific target groups, in order to accomplish the missionary objectives of the organization. (...) More, marketing is a process destined to build the response capacity of a religious organization towards the numerous groups whose needs must be satisfied in order to achieve success in its efforts."

At its core also heavily drawing on Kotler, German theologist and advertising specialist Wilfried Mödinger (2001) tried to advance the notion of marketing towards a mutually beneficial balancing of interests that needs to be approached in economic terms between the provider and the consumer by defining that: [117]

"Marketing is the attitude, way of thinking or behaviour that is not driven entirely by the initiator's interests alone but also consciously considers the needs and expectations of the people who interact with each other as equal (market) partners. On the basis of this attitude, way of thinking or behaviour, marketing includes analysing, planning, implementing and checking on carefully devised programmes aimed to encourage and control voluntary exchange processes and/or exchange relationships relative to chosen and defined market partners (markets) so that a planned corporate objective can be met in terms of its substance and economically."

Famos (2006) interprets church marketing as an important and perhaps even crucial part of the tasks of church leadership, as it concerns all the aspects of activities of the church. In the process – similarly to Mödinger (2001) – an integrative model is to be presumed: [118] *"Marketing can function as a stimulus everywhere, not just in some selected fields of activities of the church. (...) In competitive contexts, marketing is to be implemented rather as a strategic alignment of all the activities and all the*

---

[116] SHAWCHUCK, Norman, KOTLER, Philip, WRENN, Bruce, RATH, Gustave: *Marketing for congregations: choosing to serve people more effectively.* Nashville: Abingdon Press, 1992, p. 22.

[117] MÖDINGER, Wilfried (2001), ibidem, p. 60.

[118] FAMOS (2006): *Kirche und Marketing.* Ibidem, pp. 27-28.

structures towards exchange with the relevant stakeholder groups in order to secure the existence and prosperity of the organisation." A strictly sectoral marketing approach would be not sufficient for the large national church organizations to be able, after many years of existence without competition, to adapt to a market-like situation, though awareness of the competitive situation – notably not just with respect to other religious communities but perhaps even more so vis a vis the offers of the entertainment industry – has grown significantly.

Finally, Reising (2006) in his highly regarded blend of strategic marketing and theological references to the bible "Church Marketing 101" emphasizes the comprehensive nature and image-defining effect of church marketing by referring in his definition in particular to corporate identity aspects such as corporate behaviour and corporate communication: [119] *"(...) marketing is much more than promoting things. Marketing requires thinking it through. It involves every entity and interaction that fosters the outside world's perception of your organization. When you do not pay your bills, you're marketing. When you do not cut the grass, you're marketing. When you talk over the heads of your 'prospects' or fail to serve them, you're marketing. You are shaping perception in the hearts and minds of your members and target community – that is the very definition of marketing."* Briefly: "Marketing is the management of perception."

Reising hence emphasises in his interpretation of marketing the individually different types of people and their perception of the church as an institution, a service or even as a person. Meffert (2008) elaborates on this in more detail: *"In that sense each individual's level contains important signifiers of the image perceived by different target groups. Church marketing may set to an extent the levers with which to control the perceived image, ultimately however marketing must convey the brand's core and build a relationship marketing, meaning relations with believers. In this aspect there are substantial deficiencies in the approach of both the major churches."* [120]

---

[119] REISING, Richard L.: *Church Marketing 101. Preparing Your Church for Greater Growth.* Michigan: Baker Books, 2006, pp. 23-24.

[120] MEFFERT, Heribert: Kirche im Zeitalter der Marken. In: sinnstiftermag 03 (2008). *Bekannt/Unbekannt – Was kann Kirche von moderner Markenführung lernen?* [retrieved on 2018-04-30] Available from: http://www.sinnstiftermag.de/ausgabe_03/interview.htm

3.2.2   Proposal for a Definition of 'Parish Marketing'

With a view to the interpretations and definitions of marketing and church marketing provided above[121], here the author's own definition shall be presented of the notion of marketing for church purposes that accounts for the special situation of local and regional pastoral care units – parishes, parish associations and parochial unions – in Germany and their facilities and establishments, which is why instead of "church marketing", the (more fitting) term "parish marketing" is used:

"Parish marketing are the activities, facilities and processes in order for a parish to fulfil its basic church functions with respect to leading by example in spreading the message of salvation and faith, its communal liturgical services and loving service to others, so meeting the needs and expectations of all the internal and external stakeholder groups of the church according to the gospel for the parish to grow and develop in terms of both quality and quantity."

3.3   Examples of Successful Church Marketing Approaches

In the following parts, some examples shall be provided of how religious and/or specifically Catholic denominations mainly in the USA have developed systems and processes for reinvigorating and diversifying the life of parishes in both quantitative and qualitative terms. Obviously the contexts of US parishes, and hence also the insights gained from their marketing and market research projects, are not fully applicable one on one to German parishes. Firstly as opposed to the German registration system, in the USA as "Catholics", only those people can be registered who voluntarily report to or have registered voluntarily with a parish; those who practice their faith without being connected to a parish are not accounted for in the statistics.[122] Secondly, US parishes are funded exclusively by donations and contributions of their members and sponsors; there is no church tax levied and collected with the aid of the state and no subsidies and/or considerations for taking on social and education tasks of the state, as is both the case in Germany. In particular the last aspect mentioned makes US parishes act inherently and in terms of their basic principles towards both potential and existing members more in a market-compliant

---

[121]   Further authors who explore marketing from different church-relevant perspectives can be found in: ANGHELUTA, Alin Valentin, STRAMBU-DIMA, Andreea, ZAHARIA, Razvan: Church Marketing. Concept and Utility, pp. 173-175. In: *Journal for the Study of Religions and Ideologies (JSRI), Vol. 8, No. 22*. Bucharest: Acad Econ Studies, 2009. pp. 171-197.

[122]   The first sentence of the US Bill of Rights prohibits the Congress from passing laws either to establish a religion or to prohibit free exercise of religion. A detailed comparison of the different environments for churches to operate in can be found in: NAGEL, Alexander-Kenneth: Marktförmige Religion – Ein Lernmodell für die deutschen Kirchen? In: SELLMANN, Matthias et al.: *CrossingOver*. ibidem.

manner, i.e., with a more consistent focus on their needs and a stronger emphasis on recruitment as compared to their German counterparts.[123]

Further also US Christians, who generally identify as more religious than German Christians, have, perhaps due to their still persistent self-reliant attitudes stemming back to the era of the founding fathers, a more casual attitude to societal changes including the secularization trends observable there as well. Problems are addressed and solved earlier and in a more consequent manner there, and solutions are devised, tested and optimized, including at times in own informal effort, instead of – as seen in various German dioceses – appointing business consultancies to deal with the problems at hand, or even having the problems elaborately analysed and studied by dedicated scientific institutes for years on end.

Among the most outstanding projects to date to explore the US church culture and the options for applying the experiences made and systems used there in the German landscape of pastoral care is the dialogue project "CrossingOver" launched by the Theological Faculty at the Ruhr University Bochum, Germany in 2004.[124] The project scope is an interactive learning process within the official framework of which a total of 60 German pastoral workers made over the period from 2005 to 2011 experience visits, each four to six weeks long, to the Chicago Archdiocese in the US. In the wake of the project based on the ideas hatched there, eight flagship test projects were drafted. The dialogue project that in the meantime was concluded continues scientifically via funding of basic research that draws inspirations from the practical learning processes concerning church life in the USA and aims to interconnect science with practical pastoral learning processes within the German context.[125]

Pott (2011) outlines four "learning impulses from overseas" [126] that constitute tried and tested aspects of successful US parish growth concepts and seem viable for inculturation in the German pastoral landscape:

---

[123] More detailed information on this *inter alia* in: POLLACK, Detlef, ROSTA, Gergely: Religiöse Vitalität und soziale Heimat – Ein Vergleich katholischer Gemeinden in Deutschland und den USA, pp. 64-66, as well as: REINHOLD, Kai: Patizipation und ihre Auswirkung auf die Gemeindemitglieder, pp. 178-180. In: REINHOLD, Kai, SELLMANN, Matthias (eds.): *Katholische Kirche und Gemeindeleben in den USA und in Deutschland. Überraschende Ergebnisse einer ländervergleichenden Umfrage.* Münster: Aschendorff, 2011.

[124] Detailed information can be found on the project website as well as in the 21 publications listed there: DAMBERG, Wilhelm: *CrossingOver. Kirche der USA erfahren, Kirche hier neu denken.* [retrieved on 2018-04-30] Available from: http://www.crossingover.de/index.php?id=30&L=0

[125] cf. ibid.: *Projektarchitektur.* Ibidem. [retrieved on 2018-04-30] Available from: http://www.crossingover.de/index.php?id=2&L=1%20order%20by%201000

[126] POTT, Martin: Pastoral als Gegenstand von Organisation und Planung – was lernen wir von den USA? pp. 162-163. In: SELLMANN, Matthias (2011): ibidem.

- The *welcoming culture* in which guests and members are greeted personally in a highly accommodating ambience and welcomed in the spirit of hospitability.

- The mission statement as a clearly worded declaration of commitment of the parish to its (local) mission, for example: Our mission is to be consistently engaging, transforming and serving those here, near and far.[127]

- *Stewardship* – an individual's shared responsibility signified by investing one's "time, talent and treasure" in the life of the parish.[128]

- Recognize, accept and proactively design *learning by change* as the principle of life-long learning, flux and change.

The following chapters 3.3.1 to 3.3.4 now provide some examples of comprehensive marketing approaches in the church context. Of course, it could be argued from the business economic viewpoint that the examples rather amount to change management concepts[129] as opposed to marketing concepts. As though church marketing is shaped mainly by communication (Chapter 2.5) and the retention of existing and, in particular, acquisition of new members is both a basic church function and a special marketing communication task (cf. Chapter 1.2 and 3.4 of this thesis), the concepts outlined may well be deemed viable for use in church marketing.

3.3.1   The US Church Growth Movement

For the concept of the US church growth movement, the missionary to India and evangelical theologian Donald Anderson McGavran (1897-1990) can be credited. He came in analysing Christian missionary work of his own and of others in India and in various African countries *inter alia* to a conclusion that individual proselytizing attempts in different segments of the population as mostly practiced as the time at missionary stations were largely unsuccessful[130]. Only by focusing missionary efforts on homogeneous small groups that were open to the Christian faith and in which multiple persons made their joint decision to join the Christian faith and then reported about their new faith to their friends, neighbours and relatives, success

---

[127]   cf. TRINITY VINEYARD CHURCH, Texas: *What we do / Our mission.* [retrieved on 2018-04-30] Available from: http://www.trinityvineyardchurch.com/about-us/our-purpose/what-we-do/

[128]   An explanation of the term "stewardship" is provided in Chapter 3.4.3 herein.

[129]   cf. DIETLEIN, Georg: *Kirche im Aufbruch: Ein Change-Management-Ansatz für die katholische Kirche.* Norderstedt: Books on Demand, 2015 | DOPPLER, Klaus, LAUTERBURG, Christoph: *Change Management. Den Unternehmenswandel gestalten.* 12th updated and extended edition, Frankfurt am Main: Campus Verlag, 2008.

[130]   BLÖMER, Michael: Die Kirchengemeinde als Unternehmen: Die Marketing- und Managementprinzipien der US-amerikanischen Gemeindewachstumsbewegung. Münster: LIT Verlag, 1998. pp.19-27.

finally came. According to the sociological "principle of homogeneity" described by McGavran (1955), it is easier for people to become Christians if they do not have to overcome any race, class or language barriers ahead of the conversion, and to remain Christians if they can keep their cultural identity and the sense of community with their family members.[131] According to McGavran, fully adjusting to the target group and its needs only is possible in homogeneous parishes. Visiting a parish is made easier to a non-Christian if the people there come from the same homogeneous unit and there is a familiarity with the way they treat each other, the language they use and their thinking patterns. In contrast in heterogeneous parishes, it would be difficult to adequately approach the large number of target groups. Ultimately the different people would have to necessarily adapt to the cultural form mostly of a single dominating group within the parish.[132]

In 1965, McGavran founded at the Fuller Theological Seminary in Pasadena, California, the *School of World Mission* [133] at which tens of thousands of pastors and missionaries of hundreds of different confessions were trained and that up to the present is deemed the center of the US church growth movement. The movement that identifies explicitly as interdenominational and interconfessional[134] grew in the following years *from its origins* of an international civil rights movement politically inclined to the left and/or an antiwar, largely student-affiliated movement ("Jesus marches") and its continuation in the Hippie movement to also reach a number of European countries.

Based on systematic research of a large number of growing US parishes, Wagner (1981) posited for the first time the seven indicators of growth of a parish. These are [135]:

(1) The pastor: A pastor who is a 'possibility' thinker, and whose dynamic leadership has been used to catalyze the entire church into action for growth.

(2) The people of the church: A well-mobilized laity with has discovered, has developed and is using all the spiritual gifts for growth

(3) Church size: A church big enough to provide the range of services that meet the needs and expectations of its members

---

[131] McGAVRAN, Donald Anderson: *The Bridges of God. A Study in the Strategy of Missions.* Eugene: World Dominion Press, 1995.

[132] cf. BLÖMER (1998): ibidem. p. 106-107.

[133] McGAVRAN, Donald Anderson: *Effective Evangelism - A Theological Mandate.* Phillipsburg: Presbyterian and Reformed Publishing Company, 1988, pp. 79-82.

[134] BLÖMER (1998): ibidem, p. 29.

[135] WAGNER, C. Peter: *Your Church Can Grow.* Eugene: Wipf & Stock Publishers, 1981, pp. 36/47f./147.

(4) Structure and functions: The proper balance of the dynamic relationship between celebration, congregation and cell.

(5) Homogeneous unit: A membership drawn primarily from one homogeneous unit.

(6) Methods: Evangelistic methods that have been proved to make disciples.

(7) Priorities: Priorities arranged in biblical order.

In his comprehensive treatise of the US church growth movement, Blömer (1998) concludes[136] that "the evangelization principles of the church growth movement are most similar to the principles of the sc. "customer-oriented marketing". (...) The management principles correspond to several principles of some modern management approaches that emphasize the importance of "soft", i.e., human and social factors to corporate productivity". In fact, there is an analogy of a kind between the seven indicators of growth according to Wagner and the also seven indicators within the 7S model devised about at the same time by the business consultants with McKinsey Peters and Waterman[137] (The pastor ~ Style, The people ~ Staff, Church Size ~ System, ...Functions ~ Skills, Homogeneous Unit ~ Structure, Methods ~ Strategy, Priorities ~ Shared Vales). On a critical note regarding the church growth movement in the USA, Blömer adds that [138] – notwithstanding all its apparent success – its proponents partly had tended towards a technocratic feasibility approach and that its focus would be mainly on quantitative growth. Further the growth movement would be insufficiently reflected in biblical and theological terms, the human dimension of a parish put on equal footing with its respective spiritual dimension, an examination of the church growth movement from the perspective of (social) sciences on the whole despite the numerous surveys and case studies would be impossible and it would be lacking systematic and systemic thinking.

3.3.2 The "Natural Church Development" in Germany

In Germany, Christian A. Schwarz is deemed the most prominent proponent of the church growth movement. Son of a Protestant priest and not as yet influenced at the time by the US church growth movement, Schwarz devised in 1984 along with his father Fritz Schwarz the German first "theology of developing parishes". After his studies of evangelic theology, Schwarz was intensely involved with the US church

---

[136] BLÖMER (1998): ibidem, p. 38, in reference to pertinent authors such as Philip Kotler, Tom Peters/Robert Waterman et al.

[137] PETERS, Tom, WATERMAN, Robert Jr.: *In Search of Excellence. Lessons from America's Best-Run Companies*. New York: HarperCollins, 1982.

[138] BLÖMER (1998): ibidem, pp. 220-227.

growth movement and also experienced it firsthand for several months in US Pasadena. Ever since, he has been undertaking in his papers and publications to apply many of the movement's principles to the German environment.[139]

Schwarz (2003)[140] uses to explain his conceptual approach for natural growth of parishes a quote from the bible: "Consider the lilies of the field, how they grow" (Mt 6:28). Schwarz here is not after vigorously studying and praising the beauty of these plants but principally after exploring the natural growth mechanisms of lilies with a particular view to those factors that affect the growth either negatively or positively. In his considerations on growth, the "minimum factor" occupies a prominent place[141] as lilies only prosper as good as the soil, availability of light and water, the surrounding plants etc. permit. Schwarz transplants this idea to the growth potential of a parish.

In order to advance his approach further, Schwarz initially conducted in the 1980s surveys among 400 German speaking parishes; in these efforts, he looked for "parish growth principles that are valid irrespective of culture, theological background and religious affiliation"[142]. As a result, Schwarz identified eight indicators of a growing parish to further explore which he carried out between 1994 and 1996 perhaps one of the most comprehensive international studies on the growth of parishes. Using standardized questionnaires, in a total of 1000 parishes of 20 different denominations from 32 countries always 30 unpaid volunteers (where possible) and the pastor or parish priest in charge were asked about the previously identified growth indicators. Unfortunately, the sheer amounts of data have not been scientifically documented and evaluated in a testable manner to this day.

By 2003, Schwarz performed a total of more than 25,000 empirical surveys of growing and not growing Christian parishes respectively, further strengthening the case for his eight principles of growth for natural ("biotic") growth of parishes. These are specifically:

(1) An empowering leadership style: "Leaders who use their authority specifically to guide other Christians towards authority and maturity may see how this automatically and naturally contributes to growth." Quality and growth of a parish in the process are best sustained by the readiness to accept help from outside.[143]

---

[139] SCHWARZ, Christian A.: *Praxis des Gemeindeaufbaus. Gemeindetraining für wache Christen.* Neukirchen-Vluyn: Schriftenmissionsverlag, 1987.

[140] SCHWARZ, Christian A.: *Natürliche Gemeindeentwicklung in der katholischen Kirche.* Vallendar: Patris Verlag, 2003. p. 9.

[141] Ibidem, pp. 50-60.

[142] Ibidem, p. 19.

[143] Ibidem, p. 23.

(2) Talent-oriented pool of workers: [144] "The task of parish leadership merely is to help the parish members to identify the skills and abilities they have been endowed with by God and to find a type of service they can provide that makes best use of the skills and abilities." Schwarz' studies further have found a high correlation between individual happiness in life of the survey participants and the extent to which Christians live and work in accordance with their spiritual talents and abilities, in which he assigns a particularly vital role to training workers in accordance with both the objectives pursued and their talents.

(3) Passionate spirituality: "Do Christians live their faith with devotion, vigour, with fire, with passion?" This growth principle is opposed by practicing faith and holding church services simply as performance of duties, and by defending orthodoxy.[145]

(4) Efficient structures: Instead of entrenched structures, rigid routines and long-standing traditions, living structures have to be created that facilitate multiplication and perpetuation of the work: [146] "Leaders are there not just to lead but to produce other leaders" ("the section head principle").

(5) Inspiring church services: A key differentiation criterion between growing and non-growing parishes is whether or not attendance at church services is a joyful and inspiring experience for the visitor, i.e., one can "enjoy it". A church service is neither about "pleasing the pastor or God"[147], including by urging others to visit church services, and being rewarded for this loyalty, nor about imbuing the church services with an introverted-like spiritualism. "Where church services are celebrated in an inspiring manner, observations are that they seemingly attract people as if by themselves." [148]

(6) All-encompassing small groups: The most important growth principle according to Schwarz is for parishes to deliberately promote the constitution of small groups in which apart from spiritual impulses also the trials and tribulations are shared of day-to-day life,[149] and "that these small groups reproduce by way of multiplication".

(7) Evangelisation that focuses on the needs: Only ten percent of Christians have the spiritual gift to effectively spread the message of faith, and it is important to identify

---

[144] Ibidem, p. 24.

[145] Ibidem, p. 27.

[146] Ibidem, p. 28 – quote: "The results of our research confirm for the first time that the disease symptom of traditionalism that is so widespread in Christendom correlates negatively with both growth and quality of a parish."

[147] Ibidem, p. 31.

[148] Ibidem; In marketing, this attraction effect is achieved via pull (vs. push) strategies; see MEFFERT, Heribert et al., ibidem, p. 593.

[149] Ibidem p. 33.

these persons and use their evangelistic skills and abilities accordingly in a targeted manner. Generally, it is the task of every Christian to bring people outside the church they have good personal relationships with into contact with the parish. A key prerequisite to that however is "that the parish fully adapts its evangelistic offers to the questions posed by and the needs of non-believers". [150]

(8) Loving relations: In contrast to technocratically acting parishes the events of which often have an artificial and fake/preposterous feel to them, "growing parishes have on average a measurably higher 'loving quotient' than stagnating or declining ones." The laughter in the parish – be it in private meetings, invitations, when sharing compliments etc. – significantly relates to the parish quality and its growth. [151]

Pursuant to the "minimum factor" mentioned above, for the growth of the parish it is now vital to address on a priority basis those variables that pose the strongest limits to its growth. In this way, the parish will see, as did the lily mentioned by Schwarz, a natural growth in its resources that will sustain its growth for as long as another minimum factor manifests to limit further growth, etc.. Schwarz continues to analyze the extent of presence and trends in these variables by means of a standardized survey of 30 active parishioners.

For further operative work on growth, Schwarz gives parishes the tool of "six biotic principles"[152] on implementing which a self-regulating organisation shall, in a manner similar to a living organism, develop with its own unique identity:

- *Principle 1 – Network effects*:[153] All the areas within a parish and all the quality variables of natural growth of a parish are interconnected in a network of interdependencies and affect each other. Due to this, for example regular consultancy meetings of the workers responsible for the individual areas and appropriate communication systems are a must.

- *Principle 2 – Multiplication*: "In the same way as the true fruit of an apple tree is not an apple but another apple tree, the true fruit of a (faith) group is not a new Christian but a (faith) group; the true fruit of a leader is not their successors but new leaders; the true fruit of an "evangelist" are not converts but new evangelists."

---

[150] Ibidem, p. 35.

[151] Ibidem, p. 36.

[152] Ibidem, pp. 61-82.

[153] Schwarz refers in this principle as well as in deriving his concept to various publications of biocyberneticist Frederic Vester, in particular "Neuland des Denkens" (1997) and "Unsere Welt – ein vernetztes System" (1996).

- *Principle 3 – Conversion of energy*: Instead of – for example – revolting in defiance against social trends and changes, or succumbing in resignation to seemingly inevitable fate, energy conversion is about using the power momentum of the current situation so that it can give rise to something positive.

- *Principle 4 – Multiple benefits*: Thoughts should be given to how parish work can generate not just momentous benefits in its day-to-day dealings but also how workers (in particular leaders) may also share their responsibilities and competencies with several other persons, thus passing on and spreading their skills and expertise.

- *Principle 5 – Symbiosis*: The strengths and needs of the parish as a whole and of its workers and members need to be mutually aligned in a symbiotic relationship so that win-win relations may ensue.

- *Principle 6 – Functionality*: "A good tree cannot produce bad fruit" (Mt 7:17) and "You will know them by their fruits" (Mt 7:16); All the activities are to be designed so that they are measurable in terms of success or failure, and in terms of their benefits and/or contribution to parish growth.

The well-known theologist and sociologist of religion Paul Michael Zulehner writes in his preface to Schwarz' (2003) publication *Natürliche Gemeindeentwicklung in der katholischen Kirche* (Natural Growth of Parishes in the Catholic Church):[154] "Catholic parishes have the choice of setting off to break new ground, or perish. Parish growth thus becomes one of the primary future challenges for our parishes."

3.3.3   CARA – Parish Life Surveys and Services (U.S.)

The origins of the Center for Applied Research in the Apostolate (CARA) founded in the USA in 1964 had to do with demands of contemporary leaders of US missionary societies for a national research institute in order to support research work in third world countries. While the evangelical part of the US church growth movement around Donald A. McGarvan was focusing from 1965 on the Fuller Theological Institute in Pasadena, its Catholic counterpart of a kind was founded near the Catholic University of America in north-east Washington D.C. as Center for Applied Research in the Apostolate (CARA), and then moved soon thereafter to the premises of Georgetown University.[155]

From early on, CARA began dealing with changes in socio-cultural, political, moral and religious values, including in other parts of the world. In collaboration with other

---

[154] Ibidem, p. 2.
[155] cf. CARA – Center for Applied Research in the Apostolate: *The CARA Story*. [retrieved on 2018-04-30] Available from: http://cara.georgetown.edu/about-us/cara-story/

research institutions in Europe, the "European Values Study" (EVS) was launched in 1978[156] that was later developed in cooperation with Gallup[157] into "World Values Survey" (WVS) from 1981 onwards. Today, WVS conducts surveys of the values and attitudes as well as of individual perception of 'happiness' in over 100 countries worldwide and compiles the "Inglehart-Welzel cultural map", according to which countries can be split into specific cultural regions.[158]

CARA counts among the leading research institutions in the USA and carries out studies in social sciences on behalf of all types of organizations and establishments of the Catholic Church. Among others, for example White/Corcoran (2013) as well designed their exemplary "rebuilt" project[159] on the fundamental analyses of the "CARA Parish Life Survey". Based on its research work to date and analyses of parish life for a total of over 800 Catholic parishes, CARA posited the "seven elements of parish life" to which the CARA Parish Life Surveys refer to:[160]

(1) Community: The sense of community within a parish includes the sense of belonging at the parish and how it welcomes people in a friendly, inclusive, non-judgmental way (internally focused).

(2) Worship means the expression of the sacramental and prayer life of parishioners at Sunday liturgies and other sacred celebrations, including the fostering of individual spiritual growth (personal prayer, private devotions).

(3) Leadership – of the pastor, pastoral staff, parish council, and key organizations – involves forming a vision, planning the future, evaluating the efforts, as well as optimizing the organizational structures.

(4) Formation includes all aspects of parish life involving explaining, informing, and forming parishioners of all ages in Scripture, Church teaching, and tradition (religious education of children and adolescents, youth work, religious education for adults etc.).

---

[156] cf. Website of the EUROPEAN VALUES STUDY. [retrieved on 2018-04-30] Available from: http://www.europeanvaluesstudy.eu/
[157] cf. Website of GALLUP. [retrieved on 2018-04-30] Available from: http://www.gallup.com/home.aspx
[158] cf. WORLD VALUES SURVEY (WVS): *Inglehart-Welzel Culture Map 2017.* [retrieved on 2018-04-30]   Available   from: http://www.worldvaluessurvey.org/images/Culture_Map_2017_conclusive.png
[159] WHITE, Michael, CORCORAN, Tom: Rebuilt: Awakening the Faithful, Reaching the Lost, and Making Church Matter. Indiana: Ave Maria Press, 2013. p. 5.
[160] cf. CARA - CENTER FOR APPLIED RESEARCH IN THE APOSTOLATE: *Seven Elements of Parish Life.* [retrieved on 2018-04-30] Available from: http://cara.georgetown.edu/wp-content/uploads/2015/01/Seven-Elements-of-Parish-Life.pdf

(5) Stewardship involves challenging parishioners to share their time, talent, and treasure with the parish (cf. Chapter 3.4.3 of this thesis).

(6) Social Justice includes all parish work directed at advancing social concerns in the wider world, nation, and local community (externally focused).

(7) Evangelization includes all efforts to witness to the Gospel. It focuses especially upon reaching out to inactive Catholics and the unchurched (externally focused).

CARA surveys the level of presence of and trends in each of these elements of parish life – in contrast to the surveys under "Natural Growth of Parishes" that strongly focus on parish staff (cf. Chapter 3.3.2 of this thesis) – by means of sc. "In-Pew Surveys". Under these on specific weekends, questionnaires are distributed after a brief introductory sermon to all adult visitors to church services and collected again after only 12 minutes, or they can be subsequently thrown in a box at the entrance door. The survey method that in the meantime has proven itself with best results in the US offers according to CARA several advantages,[161] including direct inclusion in the survey in addition to full-time employees and volunteers also and in particular of parish members faithful to the church. Also several persons thus are reached from the same household, and also captured are those persons that reside in other parishes. The questionnaires, with different selection of questions for each parish, are compiled each from a pool of 600 tested and proven questions and variations thereof on the seven elements of parish life.

The collected data are processed by CARA into parish-specific and comparative evaluation reports the summaries of which are meant to be subsequently published in parish media with better reach such as the parochial magazine, parish news and websites as well as offered in presentation events.[162] "How the parish further utilizes the report's findings often depends upon the initial reasons for conducting the survey. In many cases, the report findings are a launching point for the development of a parish strategic plan. In other cases, a specific ministry or issue addressed in the survey may be the subject of further parish study and planning."

3.3.4   Parish Development on the Example of German (Arch-) Dioceses

The comprehensive marketing approaches with cross-functional scope outlined above pursue by virtue of their history and evolution mainly the goal of spreading

---

[161]   cf. CARA: *Why in-pew surveys work best.* [retrieved on 2018-04-30] Available from: http://cara.georgetown.edu/wp-content/uploads/2015/01/Why-In-Pew-Surveys-Work-Best.pdf

[162]   cf. CARA: *What to do after the CARA report is delivered.* [retrieved on 2018-04-30] Available from: http://cara.georgetown.edu/wp-content/uploads/2015/01/What-To-Do-After.pdf

the message of faith and of pertinent, initially qualitative but later also consistently quantitative growth of the churches and parishes.

With a view to falling membership numbers, most of German dioceses have been actively addressing the progressive societal changes already, and have launched and initiated as part of the process a number of development measures the scope of which includes both the parish staff and members as well as the interested public. To use in this regard the term "marketing" at this stage already would be apparently premature as the final output to be (prospectively) presented and offered in the internal and external "religious market" is currently still being tested and/or under development. However, given the fact that under these change management projects, all the partial areas of church life are to be examined on a cross-functional basis for their benefits to members and the "church of tomorrow" and redesigned accordingly, these shall be briefly outlined here using several examples: [163]

- The archdiocese of Cologne, Germany has been treading since 2014 a "pastoral path of tomorrow"[164] that incorporates conceptual elements from both the US church growth movement and the Natural Growth of Parishes according to Schwarz (cf. Chapter 3.3.2): participation in decision making through shared responsibilities (archdiocese of Cologne) – "efficient structures, the section head principle" (Natural Growth of Parishes, Schwarz); leadership and participation – "an empowering leadership style"; charisma orientation – "talent-oriented pool of workers"; spiritual focus – "passionate spirituality". In a consequent approach, the archdiocese makes sure by using dedicated administration instances that the parish priests in charge can (and must) focus on their actual pastoral and priestly tasks instead of being preoccupied with administrative matters of the parish.

- Under the title "Church on the Spot – Designing the Church in Many Spots", the diocese of Rottenburg-Stuttgart goes a growth path under which local parish life is to be aligned to the needs of the future. In a three-stage pastoral development plan, the south German diocese is to devise by 2019 and decide on strategic, systemic and structural solutions.[165] In doing so, firstly

---

[163] A comprehensive outline of innovative projects of the different Catholic organizations is provided at the website of KAMP (Katholische Arbeitsstelle für missionarische Pastoral): *Pastorale Innovationen*. [retrieved on 2018-04-30] Available from: http://www.pastorale-innovationen.de/

[164] ERZBISTUM KÖLN: *Pastoraler Zukunftsweg.* [retrieved on 2018-04-30] Available from: http://www.erzbistum-koeln.de/erzbistum/pastoraler_zukunftsweg/ as well as: *Neue Wege für Pastoral und Verwaltung.* [retrieved on 2018-04-30] Available from: http://www.erzbistum-koeln.de/kirche_vor_ort/neue-wege/

[165] cf. DIÖZESE ROTTENBURG-STUTTGART: *Entwicklungsschritte im Geist Gottes planen und gehen.* [retrieved on 2018-04-30] Available from: https://www.kirche-am-ort.de/entwicklungsplan-und-abschlussbericht.html

the spiritual attitudes in parishes are to be examined and new missionary, diaconal, communicative and sacramental perspectives developed. This is followed by devising strategies that accommodate the priorities and cooperation forms of future pastoral and social offers as well as their concrete implementation planning.

- In the diocese of Hildesheim, local parishes refer to the attributes of the "Hildesheim model" under which the church is to develop ecumenically, in spiritual and religious terms, with an awareness of mission and purpose, with a focus on talents of its members and in particular on local needs and contexts.[166]

- Under its own "pastoral plan", the diocese of Münster is to develop into a living and missionary church for its area.[167] For that sake, firstly the God-given talents, gifts and motivations ("charismas") of all the members and helpers are to be discovered, appreciated and used for pastoral purposes. All along, members of all age groups and different stages of faith, of all types of attachment to the church and from all social environments are encouraged and aided to proffer, spread, renew and advance their message of faith.

- The diocese of Essen devised in 2013 in the wake of the experience of a failed structural reform in 2008-2009 a multilateral dialogue process "An Image of the Future – You Change the Church" that is unique of its kind in Germany. Over the course of the process, the remaining 43 parishes in the diocese were invited to come up from the perspective of "The Church in the Year 2030" with reference documents for how they intend to adapt their respective offers and structures to the ever changing general social and church contexts.[168] The strategic considerations that are due to be finalized in 2017 use many insights from the Sinus Milieu research that with a view to its broad acceptance in the German Catholic Church is explained in detail not least in Chapter 4.2 – Milieu-specific Orientation of Church Action.

The above examples of the individual dioceses illustrate that there are different perceptions in the Catholic Church of the issues facing its members and consequences thereof that have given rise to equally different concepts and measures

---

[166] cf. BISTUM HILDESHEIM: *Lokale Kirchenentwicklung.* [retrieved on 2018-04-30] Available from: https://www.lokale-kirchenentwicklung.de/

[167] cf. BISTUM MÜNSTER: *Pastoralplan.* [retr. on 2018-04-30] Available from: pastoralplan-bistum-muenster.de/fileadmin/user_upload/pastoralplan/downloads/2013/web_pastoralplan_20130218.pdf

[168] cf. BISTUM ESSEN: *Zukunftsbild im Bistum Essen.* [retrieved on 2018-04-30] Available from: http://zukunftsbild.bistum-essen.de/

adjusted for regional contexts. This implies a question as to how far the vehicle of a general strategy with clearly defined and transparent objectives and with measurable milestones in quantitative and qualitative terms can be actually useful for the Catholic community of faith.

Sobetzko et al. (2017) decscribe the ongoing procedures in the German dioceses as follows: [169] "The ecclesiastically historic present age within the German dioceses is a present age of papers, models, programmes and plans. There is hardly a diocese that does not have a new programmatic structure and in its own way deals with the trinity of pastoral goal-setting, personnel planning and financial resources. The whole scenario resembles a major construction site. And some is standing at the fence like a little boy, staring through the net and hoping, in view of the deep excavation pits, the high tower cranes and the straying yellow helmets, that there is someone who has the plan for the whole thing."

3.4 Objectives of Church Marketing and Marketing Communication

Pfister (2000) stresses out in his observations on church and marketing[170] that church marketing does not aim "to adjust or change the message the church is committed to and that is outside of its decision-making powers: it [church marketing] is rather at the service of this message, or even more, it wants to be of help for the message to be communicated more clearly and accurately for better comprehension". Accordingly, the objective of church marketing is to convey at the service of the message of the gospel precisely this message universally through personal example as well as through interpersonal and media communication. By extension, this clearly makes a perspective on church marketing as communication to spread the message of faith insufficient. In reality, parishes pursue by spreading this message also a variety of other goals, from announcing, or boosting acceptance for, their concrete parish offers, through recruiting volunteers or selling goods up to financing charity projects.

In marketing literature, marketing objectives are split into economic marketing objectives that primarily pursue quantitative aims such as sales, turnover, market share, contribution margin, profit and yield, and psychological/psychographic marketing objectives such as name recognition/awareness, image and attitude,

[169] SOBETZKO, Florian, SELLMANN, Matthias: *Gründer*innen Handbuch für pastorale Start-ups und Innovationsprojekte*. Würzburg: Echter, 2017, p. XVI.
[170] PFISTER, Xaver: Marketing im Dienst der Kirchen. In: BRUHN, Manfred, GRÖZINGER, Albrecht: *Kirche und Marktorientierung – Impulse aus der Ökumenischen Basler Kirchenstudie*. Freiburg (CH): Universitätsverlag, 2000. p. 142.

customer satisfaction, buying preferences and customer retention[171] that rather pursue a qualitative promotional effect. Pepels (2015) gives as key psychographic target variables knowledge and understanding (cognition) of promoted offers, a liking (affection) for a particular offer or provider as well as creating and/or amplifying the desired effects on actions (conation).[172] Marketing communication and advertising accordingly is primarily meant (in an informative manner) to make an offer known in new markets, and/or make it better known in existing markets. Additionally in an environment of objective interchangeability of many products and services, the emotional components of the advertising message are meant to affect how the offer and/or provider are viewed in a positive direction. Both the communication measures pursue the aim to condition the prospective buyer to a specific offer, thus boosting acceptance and sales chances of the offer.

Psychographic advertising objectives are not equal to economic advertising objectives but precede them instead, as reaching an economic advertising objective such as sales or turnover obviously is contingent on the effects and successful implementation of measures under psychographic objectives, such as an improved image. "The key aspect however, marketing communication (...) only is able to actively control the dimension of psychographic advertising objectives (promotional effect)"[173] while the target persons at the same time are subject to a variety of other, non-advertising related influences. Pepels gives as an example in this respect "word of mouth", which at the latest since the advent of word-of-mouth marketing (WOMM) as a separate marketing discipline has controllable dimensions.

Non-profit organizations do not pursue primarily economic objectives but fulfil their purpose (mission) defined by the values or culture they represent primarily through communication and activities/services fit for the purpose. Due to this complexity, it is recommended in considering church marketing objectives not to restrict one's perspective to economic control variables only but rather to extend it to also include psychographic marketing objectives that may well include or have economic objectives attached to them. In reference to this complexity of objectives, some authors use in this respect terms such as "aggregated systems of objectives" or marketing guiding principles[174]. For clarity's sake even in operationalizing complex

---

[171] BRUHN, Manfred: *Marketing. Grundlagen für Studium und Praxis.* 12th revised edition. Wiesbaden: Springer Gabler, 2014. p. 26.

[172] PEPELS, Werner: *Marketing-Kommunikation. Einführung in die Kommunikationspolitik.* 3rd revised and amended edition. Berlin: Duncker & Humblot, 2015. p. 37.

[173] Ibidem, p. 38.

[174] Becker recognizes the following aggregated systems of objectives: market share and distribution objectives, positioning objectives, image and name recognition objectives, buyer reach and buying intensity as well as customer satisfaction and customer retention. cf.: BECKER, Jochen: *Marketing-*

bundled marketing objectives, the marketing objectives must be defined in a clear hierarchic order and precisely enough to allow both planning and success verification. Above all however, the marketing objectives must be realistic with a view to the particular competitive situation as well as the resources and chances of a parish or establishment.[175]

Fischer (2008) speaks with a view to the aims of Christian parish work of a "divine mission" that is not changeable and is imposed on every single parish. This mission however "always needs to be translated into action and completed differently according to its specific context in the three dimensions of church activities – 'spreading the message of faith', 'figurative action' and 'local community'."[176]

Figure 3-1: The Mission of God to His Church according to Fischer (2008)

The Mission of God to His church
You shall love the Lord your God with all your heart and with all your soul and with all your mind. This is the great and first commandment. And a second is like it: You shall love your neighbour as yourself. – Mt 22:37-39
Truly, I say to you, as you did it to one of the least of these my brothers,6 you did it to me. – Mt 25:40
Go therefore and make disciples of all nations, baptizing them in the name of the Father and of the Son and of the Holy Spirit, teaching them to observe all that I have commanded you. – Mt 28:19

Due to different contexts and options of individual parishes to define and pursue bundles of objectives that would cover all the dimensions of their activities, only some generic marketing objectives and marketing guidelines can be provided herein for parishes:

- Retention and recruitment of new parish members (and with that church members)

- Social change

- Generation of sustainable support: Stewardship

- Sales promotion of products and services

- Positioning objectives

Konzeption: Grundlagen des ziel-strategischen und operativen Marketing-Managements. 7th, revised and extended edition. München: Vahlen, 2001, pp. 65-82.

[175] KOTLER, Philip (1978): ibidem, p. 62.
[176] FISCHER, Ralph (2008): ibidem, p. 189 f.

3.4.1 Retention and Recruitment of Parish Members

One of the original goals of the Catholic Church is to bring people faith in the Triune God and to aid them in loving God from all their heart.[177] As religious faith cannot be inherited by birth and much less imposed on an individual in the post-modern age but relies on positive internalization and voluntary adoption, the core church function of spreading and conveying the message of faith targets an "inner reversal" of the individuals approached, also commonly referred to as "conversion". The initial aim in spreading the message of faith hence is passing on faith via enthusiasm that triggers conversion, or through an inner change of an individual's consciousness and their resulting ambition to become a better human being within the meaning of the Catholic message of faith. The inner reversal ideally goes along with a change of the convert's or believer's social behaviour.

Consequently under the marketing guiding principle of "Retention and Recruitment of Parish Members", all those measures can be subsumed that aim to obtain as a result the community of believers (koinonia/communio) and stabilize it in qualitative terms through growth in competences, and in quantitative terms through new members. The measures are construed as a bundle of objectives and can be broken down according to the degree of novelty of a member into retention/recruitment of parish members through infant baptism, adult baptism, integration of new residents and administration of sacraments:

3.4.1.1 Retention and Recruitment Through Infant Baptism

Infants and toddlers without religious capacity may join the church at the wish of their parents and godparents by the act of infant baptism. The marketing focus here on the one hand is on the baptized child's parents, godparents and family who will be responsible over the coming years for the child's Catholic upbringing and socialization, and on the other also on young couples and married couples for which infant baptism is a likely potentiality in the coming years.

3.4.1.2 Retention and Recruitment Through Adult Baptism

In 2016, 171,531 people joined the German Catholic Church through baptism, with most of them in their first year of life.[178] Of these, slightly less than 7,200 children were older than seven and 3,200 persons older than 14 years of age. Children with religious capacity, adolescents and adults who previously were part of another religious community, or were not in any religious community at all, may join the Church at their own wish through adult baptism. Here the focus in potential

---

[177] cf. Chapter 3.6.1.2 – The Faith as Ecclesiastical "Core Product"
[178] SEKRETARIAT DER DEUTSCHEN BISCHOFSKONFERENZ (2017): ibidem, pp. 44-46.

marketing activities is after the baptized person mainly on the group of their closer friends and relatives.[179]

3.4.1.3 Retention and Recruitment Through Administration of Sacraments

Alongside the festive act of baptism as an initiation ritual, the Church also performs other "rites of passage" for specific stages of life or on specific occasions at which special sacraments are administered. These "occasional services" include the first communion (176,297 children in 2016), confirmation (149,796 adolescents in 2016; corresponds to 7 out of 10 children who received the first communion), the marriage/wedding ceremony (43,610 in 2016), pertinent jubilees, and the anointing of the sick and the funeral ceremony (243,323 in 2016). The church marketing activities in this respect target the group of closer friends and relatives of the persons concerned.

3.4.1.4 Retention and Recruitment Through Integration of New Residents

Catholics and their families who have recently moved in to the parish area are to be approached proactively and, most importantly, personally by the parish representatives or its head, or pastoral workers. By virtue of the German church registration system, parishes typically receive information on newly arrived Catholics. This moment poses a unique opportunity to personally welcome the new fellow residents as neighbours, to invite them to church services and to inform them about the various offers and activities of the parish. In doing so, it is important not to handle this as a one-off action, but to integrate the newcomers gradually into the life of the parish.[180]

3.4.1.5 Ensuring Catholic Socialization of Children

Within the context of the progressive shift in religious orientation of Germans[181], religious socialization within the family is ascribed primary significance as it represents the first and foremost socialization instance per se: according to Religionsmonitor by the Bertelsmann Stiftung (2013), core values such as "independence", "assertiveness", "compliance with rules" and "fair treatment of all people" are transmitted mainly in the family, with runners-up being the school and

---

[179] As part of activities of the US church growth movement (cf. Chapter 3.3.1), 14,000 parish members were asked about who or what brought them to Christian faith and to the church. The key stimulus came for 75 to 90 percent of the respondents from a friend or relative. This result has been confirmed also for the German speaking areas: cf. ARN, Win, ARN, Charles: *Master's Plan for Making Disciples*. Pasadena: Church Growth Press, 1984, p. 43. | SCHWARZ, Christian A. (1987): *Praxis des Gemeindeaufbaus.* Ibidem.

[180]   c   f. in this context also the "offers for coping with contingencies" and the "culture of welcome" in: ETSCHEID-STAMS, Markus et al.: *Kirchenaustritt – oder nicht?* Ibidem, p. 292, 295.

[181] cf. chapter 1.4.3.3: Lack of Passing on of Religious Traditions from Generation to Generation.

the social network of friends, which are only then followed by the religious community.[182]

In any case though, the parents cannot be left alone with their religious education task by the parish, as implied by a research report on religious socialization in Christian families published in 2017. In the report, Künkler et al. (2017) supply a proof that religious education specifically in Catholic families plays in comparison with other Christian families a smaller role (see Fig. 3-2, next page). [183]

The authors have further found out that members of the Protestant and Catholic Churches rather prefer an "instructive" as opposed to an "indicative" form of education, and that the instructive religious education is particularly well-pronounced especially in the Catholic Church. This of course invites interpretations. The problem of declining transmission of religious traditions in the family accordingly may causally relate *inter alia* to the following aspects:

- The intrafamily religious education is far too vague in terms of being "indicative" and consequently not concrete, or "instructive" – in the meaning of catechetical – enough;

- The Church officials do not claim the parental commitment to education given on the occasion of the (Catholic) infant baptism early and consequently enough, as a result of which

- The Church officials do not sufficiently meet its responsibility for education as regards proactive support to the family in which the religious education takes place.

Only when religious education in the family as the primary socialization instance can be deemed effectively ensured, the supporting and consolidating role may come in of the Church offers of upbringing, education, and leisure activities.

---

[182] POLLACK, Detlef (2013): ibidem, pp. 24-27.
[183] KÜNKLER, Tobias, FAIX, Tobias, SANDMANN, Tim: Aufwachsen in einer christlichen Familie. Eine empirische Studie zur christlich-familiären Erziehung. Forschungsbericht. Kassel: empirica, 2017, p. 84 as well as pp. 93-95.

Figure 3-2: Role of the Christian Faith in the Parenting by Denomination
          n=1751 (cases not belonging to any community are not shown),
          scale from 1 "no role at all" to 5 "very large role"

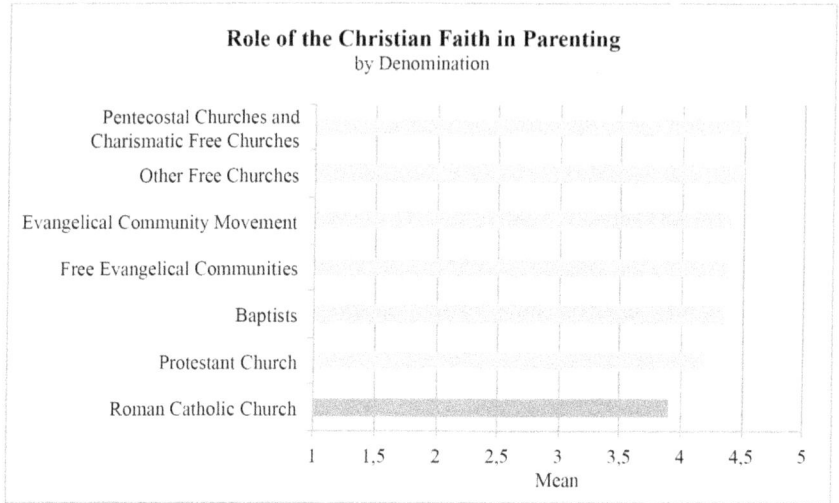

3.4.2 The Marketing Guiding Principle of Social Change

Alongside the bundle of marketing objectives for the recruitment of new and retention of existing and/or new generation members, another bundle of objectives for the Catholic Church is initialisation of social changes and of a pertinent change in consciousness that is consistent with its message of faith. Kotler (1978) recognizes four types of 'social change' that are principally focused on in the implementation of ideational goals of non-profit organizations including church establishments and organizations: [184]

- Bringing about a 'cognitive change' for example through public information and/or awareness campaigns the content of which must be interesting, clear in its message and correspond to the perceived values of the target group.

- Animating a preferably large number of persons to perform a (one-off) specific activity, i.e., a 'change in direct relation to an activity' that however must be preceded by understanding and acceptance of the desired change.

---

[184] KOTLER, Philip (1978): ibidem, pp. 285-294.

- Bringing about a behaviour change in the positive direction to one's own benefit, the sustainability of which however depends on entrenched behaviour routines and alternative modifications of behaviour.

- Changing the tenets of faith or perceived values in sc. 'value changes' that can only be reached providing that the value change does not interfere with a person's self-image and positive attitude towards life with resulting dissonance and is not subsequently filtered out in an act of "rationalization".

Here as examples, mainly the various fundraising campaigns can be mentioned of church relief agencies in which through concrete argumentative presentation of deficiencies and/or of those in need (cognitive change), one-off (e.g. donations) or permanent (e.g. sponsorships) voluntary commitments are to be secured. Finally, social changes with regard to individuals and in society at large also can be achieved by declaring an extraordinary church year such as a „Holy Year of Mercy".

As a side note here, the marketing discipline of "Social Marketing" can be explicitly pointed out[185] the aim of which is to achieve through systematic persuasion work a preferably large-scale change in consciousness with behavioural changes in the population mostly concerning socio-political or economic subjects.

3.4.3 Stewardship, Providing Systematic Support

Closely related to the marketing guiding principle of "social change" is that of "stewardship". The latter is about generating consistent support by individual and particularly competent, or preferably a large number of members of the parish who have a sense of shared responsibility for the well-being of the parish and engage on behalf of the parish, so making their individual contribution.

This stewardship, which has been a core component of pastoral concepts in Christian churches in the USA since the 1980s,[186] deals with targeted appeal to, or invitation of, the parish members to consistently support the life of the parish with their "time, talent, and treasure" – including time and talent that goes into all forms of voluntary

---

[185] KOTLER, Philip, ROBERTO, Eduardo: *Social Marketing.* Düsseldorf: Econ-Verlag, 1991, pp. 37-76.

[186] "Stewardship", from "steward" in the sense of a caretaker/administrator, refers to the attitude of Christian responsibility that corresponds to that of a good custodian capable of managing the assets and resources that have been entrusted to them by God in a prudent manner, and sharing the assets justly with others, in particular those in need of help. In more detail on the theological concept of "stewardship" from sources close to the Catholic Church, see:
ROMAN CURIA / International Theological Commission: *Communion and Stewardship. Human Persons Created in the Image of God (2004).* [retrieved on 2018-04-30] Available from: http://www.vatican.va/roman_curia/congregations/cfaith/cti_documents/rc_con_cfaith_doc_200407 23_communion-stewardship_en.html – as well as: INTERNATIONAL CATHOLIC STEWARDSHIP COUNCIL (ICSC): *Website of the ICSC.* [retrieved on 2018-04-30] Available from: http://catholicstewardship.com/

work, and "treasure" in terms of funds and other items of value to finance the activities, buildings and establishments of the parish. Consequently, stewardship means an attitude under which in gratitude for the God-given vital commodities, a part of the commodities is brought in accordance with individual possibilities into the community for the benefit of all.

While under "treasure", mainly all kinds of monetary and in-kind donations, including financial and investment aid, are subsumed, "time" means making one's own free time available to handle all types of tasks and auxiliary tasks, and "talent" the voluntary engagement of persons with special professional or individual skills, abilities and relationship networks that could be beneficial to the parish.

A particularly valuable, living stewardship and consistent support of the church applies always where people who are committed to the church discover their predestination to become a deacon, priest or to lead a consecrated life for example in a monastic community.

3.4.4 Sales Promotion of Products and Services

Parishes and church establishments have a comprehensive portfolio of goods and services[187] they offer to the parish members but also to third persons not connected to the church. Contrary to religious goods of the higher and highest order[188] such as the life of faith, forgiveness of sins or resurrection, for marketing concrete church products and services in general, four market area strategies are available as options:[189]

- *Market penetration*: Existing products and services are offered in existing markets (such as to parish members, or within an association of parishes) in a more active and visible manner.

- *Market expansion*: Existing products and services are offered on new markets (subject to an analysis of competitive situation).

- *Product expansion*: New products and services (true innovations, differentiated versions or upgrades, product-related services) are offered on existing markets.

---

[187] cf. chapter 3.6.1 – The ecclesiastical "product".
[188] cf. FAMOS et al. (2006): *Kirche und Marketing*. Ibidem, pp. 98-104.
[189] PEPELS, Werner: Kommunikationsmanagement. Marketing-Kommunikation vom Briefing bis zur Realisation. Stuttgart: Schäfer-Poeschel, 1994, pp.56-64.

- *Diversification*: New products and services are offered on new markets (for this purpose, there are concepts by different authors concerning target group or milieu-specific offers, or milieu-sensitive pastoral care [190]).

Both in developing and in launching new products and services via marketing communication, detailed knowledge of the target groups to specifically approach on the existing and/or new markets is an absolute must. What market area strategy is ultimately the most viable for a particular parish offer must be assessed and decided by the parish concerned depending on its local, regional, or diocese-specific competitive context and actual market chances.

Finally concerning sales marketing, a quote from Nagel (2011) who concludes with a view to applicability of successful US strategies in the German 'church market' that German churches should stay true to their core competences "instead of constantly dabbling as a result of the general restructuring panic always in new fields of business".[191] Low-threshold "bait offers" that actually are not representative in any way of the church portfolio are to be avoided according to Nagel. Instead, the task would be to convey that quality work of value has its price, which might come either in the form of comprehensive engagement on behalf of the parish, or in charges for a particular good or service. "Instead of commodification – the goods-like packaging and conditioning of religious goods – the aim should be to effectively communicate the nature of the church as a public good", which connects directly to the next bundle of marketing objectives:

3.4.5 Positioning Objectives

Finally, there are diverse, mostly psychographic positioning objectives that may be pursued by a parish regarding its popularity and recognition, image and preferability of its offers and activities. Such objectives may include for example:

- Presence in its particular urban setting as a strong and multifaceted community (of faith)

- To be a preferred point of contact/place of pastoral care, search for meaning, spirituality

- To be a serious contact person for religious goods of the higher and highest order

---

[190] cf. FAMOS (2006): *Kirche und Marketing.* – "Konkretionen", p. 135 ff. | HEMPELMANN, Heinzpeter: *Gott im Milieu.* Ibidem. | SELLMANN, Matthias, WOLANSKI, Caroline (eds.): *Milieusensible Pastoral. Praxiserfahrungen aus kirchlichen Organisationen.* Würzburg: Echter, 2013.

[191] NAGEL, Alexander-Kenneth (2011): Marktförmige Religion – Ein Lernmodell für die deutschen Kirchen? p. 159. In: SELLMANN, Matthias et al. (2011): *CrossingOver.* Ibidem.

- To be a partner/guide for successful religious upbringing and education of children and adolescents

- To be an oasis of calm in the winds of change, a safe haven, a lifeline in case of need

- To be an appreciative network for individual aid and contributions

- The church and the parish as an attractive employer (employer branding)

Following the outline of the fundamental aspects of marketing of the Catholic Church and of its parishes and establishments, now the ecclesiastical target groups shall be explored including their different social characteristics.

3.5 Ecclesiastical Target Groups

3.5.1 Preliminary Considerations

A quote by the Apostle Paul that is frequently being used in scientific contributions on church marketing outlines his target group-specific approach in spreading the Christian faith during his many travels in which he covered considerable distances for his time from Jerusalem to present-day Slovenia: [192] "To the Jews I became like a Jew, to win the Jews. To those under the law I became like one under the law (though I myself am not under the law), so as to win those under the law. / To those not having the law I became like one not having the law (though I am not free from God's law but am under Christ's law), so as to win those not having the law. / To the weak I became weak, to win the weak. I have become all things to all men so that by all possible means I might save some." According to Reising (2006),[193] Paul here breaks down the ethnic group of the Jewish population strategically into those Jews who were faithful to the Jewish law with its religious practice, the less religious Jews ("the lawless") as well as the sick and the poor ("the weak"). Paul adjusts his arguments individually to every one of these target groups so as to win them over for the Christian faith. Even more: Paul lives and even works for a while with the different people, tribes and occupational groups,[194] in order to learn their daily routines and their ways of life and so to ideally place his message – this is a target group-specific approach bar none. Now, how could this idea be transplanted to the current needs and concerns of the Church?

---

[192] cf. BISCHÖFE DEUTSCHLANDS et al.: *Die Bibel*. Ibidem,1 Cor. 9:20-22.

[193] REISING, Richard L. (2006): *Church Marketing 101*. Ibidem, pp. 79-81.

[194] cf. BISCHÖFE DEUTSCHLANDS et al.: *Die Bibel*. Ibidem, Acts 18:3-4.

The Church target groups are a relatively broad variety as the Church's mission to spread the message of gospel and faith generally applies to all people. This means that principally every person with their different needs or disadvantages, or seeking ones, count among the public masses the activities and offers of the Catholic Church are open to:

Figure 3-3: Target Groups of the Catholic Church (own graphic)

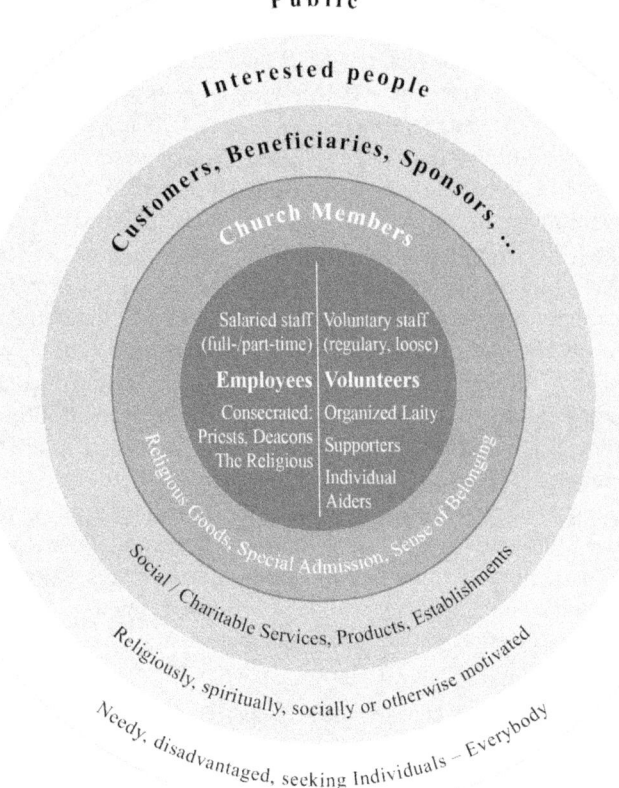

Within this broad mass, there is the circle of interested persons who gravitate towards the Church out of religious, spiritual, social or other motivations. Among these, as a first more narrow target group, those persons can be comprised who participate in the social and charitable establishments and organizations of the Catholic Church as customers, beneficiaries or even sponsors. Any members of these first three spheres do not necessarily have to be members of the Catholic Church, who constitute the fourth group of persons located within the target groups of the Catholic Church.

The Church members themselves in turn can also be split into various groups of persons with different attitudes and affinity to the Church. Of these in communicative terms, a breakdown might be of interest of the group of actively engaging members. This is because this group combines both consecrated and full-time staff members and also those who help as volunteers, those individually engaged and those organized in groups, the different types of supporters as well as "ambassadors of goodwill".

Traditionally, Catholic parishes refer in designing their offers to specific age groups or persons in different stages/at different turning points of life. Out of such considerations come for example the typical meetings for seniors and the devotions of the Rosary primarily frequented by these, and also school masses, altar boy and scout groups for children and adolescents as well as toddler groups for young mothers as acquisition events of the parish nursery. More advanced specifications of these offers are with a view to the progressive differentiation in society (cf. Chapter 1.4.3.2) and the partly conflicting mentalities and lifestyles of the approached groups in many a place rather an exception due to lack of personnel, but also due to poor understanding of the target groups and their needs. Hempelmann (2013) notes in this respect [195] "that, of all things, for the group of 40- to 50-year olds that is the best approachable and the most open for conversions, there are almost no adequate offers and ideas". For example, many parishes keep constant portfolios of offers with diminishing success for decades while paying no mind to what to actually achieve with and the future potential of such formats for the Catholic clientele of tomorrow. However, there is also a specific dilemma in designing church offers in that[196] "the Church must not adapt to the needs of the majority of its members who confess only as much as how they are struggling with the Christian tradition: it has to actually fulfil its orientation function. On the other hand though, it must also not focus only on its core audience if it is to remain a people's church."

Due to this, the Church, every diocese and every parish should individually analyze, examine, decide and review which themes and topics are suitable for what offers and for what target group and its particular individual environment, and what future potential in terms of evangelization these types of offers have with a view to retention and recruitment of members. Here a closer look might be helpful at the sc. milieus.

---

[195] HEMPELMANN, Heinzpeter (2013): *Gott im Milieu*. Ibidem, p.13.

[196] KUNZ, Ralph: Grenzen der Vermarktung – Marketing zwischen Ökonomisierung und Gemeindeaufbau. In: FAMOS (2006): *Kirche und Marketing*. Ibidem, p. 30, 31.

3.5.2 Milieu-specific Orientation of Church Action

With a view to the Church's mission of spreading the mission of salvation and faith and pastoral care in general and marketing and communication of church organizations in particular, it appears meaningful to explore the socio-economic attributes, the different value orientations, the particular lifestyles and not least also the communication and media preferences of the church target groups. For that, different research institutions and projects in the field of social sciences have devised sc. "milieu models" using which the increasing differentiation of the German population can be analyzed and operationalized.[197]

Principally, every milieu constitutes a self-referential system with its own dedicated codes and programs, and „though it represents a world that is open to the outside, it is semantically a distinct world. (...) Through strong flows of internal communication, every milieu reproduces and amplifies its subcultural logics and semantics. An actual mutual understanding between people from different milieus is not possible, or to a limited extent only",[198] which necessitates not just in the planning and implementation of church activities and offers, but also in communication a preferably specific targeting. In their analysis of how the Catholic Church in Germany is positioned and viewed in the different Sinus Milieus, Wippermann/Magalhaes (2005) conclude different milieu-specific perceptions of the Church: while in the upper social classes, the Church is regarded as a foundation of values and a carrier of high culture, the lower classes see the Church from a rather detached perspective as a charitable and social and/or existential saviour in need.

The Sinus institute of Heidelberg founded in 1978 today likely is the market leader in Germany in the field of social research of inequalities in particular with regard to market and consumer behaviour research but also in various social research topics. It provides a consistent and stable model over many years that given its long-term continuous use in a number of studies and many refinements should principally meet the quality criteria of scientific work. With the auxiliary tool of geographic data,

---

[197] For detailed treatises of the milieu models most commonly used in the church environment, refer for example to: WIPPERMANN et al. (2005), HERMELINK et al. (2008), EBERTZ (2009), SCHULZ et al. (2010), HÖFELSCHWEIGER (2011), CALMBACH et al. (2013, 2016), FÜRST (2013), HEMPELMANN (2013), SELLMANN (2013), EKD (2014), STELZER (2014).

[198] WIPPERMANN, Carsten, MAGALHAES, Isabel de: *MDG-Milieuhandbuch. Religiöse und kirchliche Orientierungen in den Sinus-Milieus® 2005. Zielgruppen-Handbuch.* München / Heidelberg: MDG / Sinus Sociovision, 2005, p. 8.

Sinus Milieus can be localized even down to individual street sections and used for example for direct marketing purposes.[199]

The Catholic Church has been making use of the Sinus institute repeatedly to determine the religious and church orientations of Catholics in Germany. Among the findings, Catholics generally can be found in all milieus, however with significant, both quantitative and qualitative differences as evident from the following visualization, also known as the "potato chart": [200]

Figure 3-4: Percentages of Catholics in the SINUS Milieus, Germany 2016

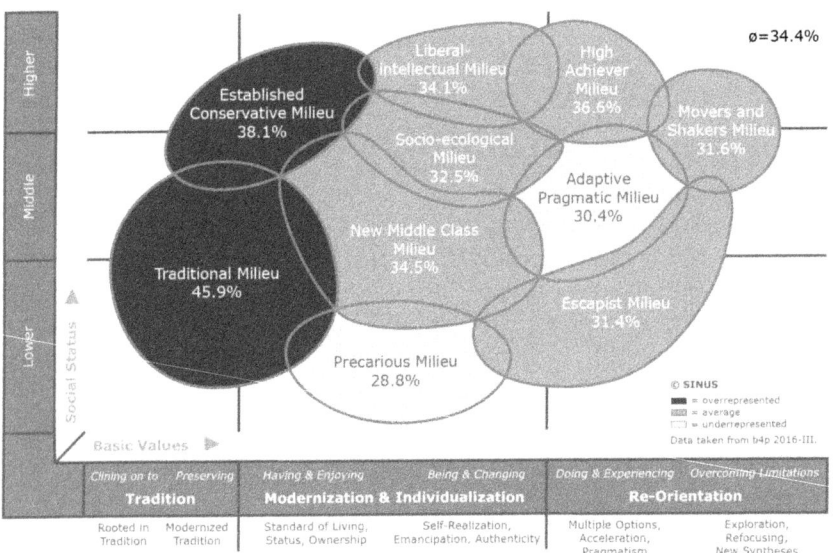

Different opinions on how after the German reunification, the eastern German milieus should be treated, gave rise in 1990 to the SIGMA institute the founder of

[199] SCHULZ, Rüdiger et al. (2010): *MDG-Trendmonitor*. Ibidem – as well as: SINUS-INSTITUT: *Sinus-Geo-Milieus*. [retrieved on 2018-04-30] Available from: https://www.sinus-institut.de/sinus-loesungen/sinus-geo-milieus/.

[200] Cf. SINUS-INSTITUT: *Sinus-Milieus*. [retrieved on 2018-04-30] Available from: https://www.sinus-institut.de/en/sinus-solutions/sinus-milieus/;
Data taken from B4P - BEST FOR PLANNING 2016 III. Data received on 2017-10-09 with kind permission of the Sinus institute from MDS-service@axelspringer.net. Potential in total: 30,190 cases, 69.56 m, 100%. Potential of sample: Catholics = 24.18 m. Used parameter: [Demography / Respondent / Religious community = Catholic] x [Qualitative Characteristics / Typology, Target groups = SINUS].

which previously had contributed to the development of the concept of social milieus and in particular of the first Sinus Milieu model.[201] As the SIGMA Milieus as well refer to a psychographic target group model, these naturally feature even despite different definitions of milieus and different detailed structuring in the social space certain similarities with the Sinus Milieus, which is also valid for the proportions of Catholics in the SIGMA Milieus.[202] For illustrative reasons, the over- and underrepresented SIGMA Milieus respectively in terms of the shares of Catholics are signified by colours otherwise typical of the Sinus Milieus:

Figure 3-5: Percentages of Catholics in the SIGMA Milieus, Germany 2016

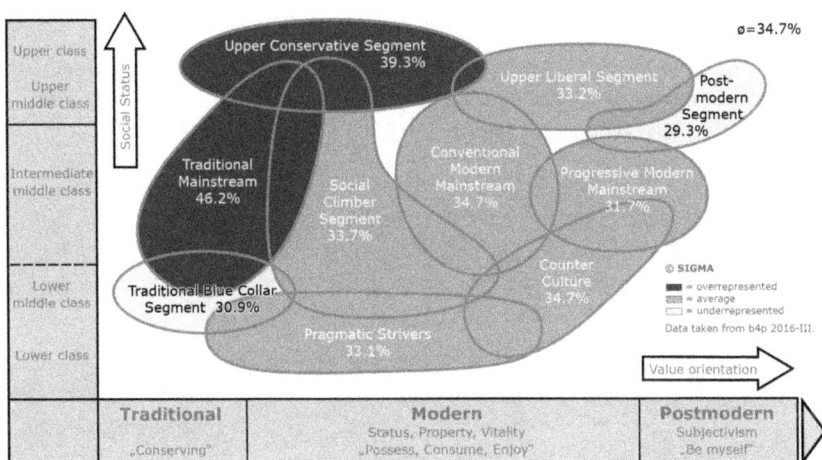

As the Catholic Church in dealing with the social milieus of its members has been preferring the Sinus Milieu model, here an outline only of the Sinus Milieus: [203]

---

[201] cf. SIGMA: *Über SIGMA*. [retrieved on 2018-04-30] http://www.sigma-online.com/de/ About_SIGMA/.

[202] SIGMA: *SIGMA-Milieus für Deutschland*. [retrieved on 2018-04-30] Available from: http://www.sigma-online.com/de/SIGMA_Milieus/SIGMA_Milieus_in_Germany/ Data taken from B4P - BEST FOR PLANNING 2016 III. Data received on 2017-10-09 from MDS-service@axelspringer.net. Potential in total: 30.190 cases, 69.56 m, 100%. Potential of sample: Catholics = 24.18 m. Used parameter: [Demography / Respondent / Religious community = Catholic] x [Qualitative Characteristics / Typology, Target groups = SIGMA].

[203] CALMBACH, Marc et al. (2013): *MDG-Milieuhandbuch 2013*. Ibidem, pp. 54-56.

Upper class milieus

- *Established Conservative Milieu* – The classical establishment: responsibility and success ethics; aspirations of exclusivity and leadership; class consciousness, tendency towards seclusion of the "entre nous" type

- *Liberal Intellectual Milieu* – The fundamentally liberal, enlightened educational elite with post-material roots; desire for a self-determined life; a broad array of intellectual interests

- *High Achiever Milieu* – Multi-optional, efficiency-oriented top performers with a global economic mindset and a claim to avantgarde in style and consumership; high level of IT and multi-media expertise

- *Movers and Shakers Milieu* – The ambitious creative avantgarde: mentally and geographically mobile, (digitally) networked both online and offline, and always on the lookout for new frontiers and new solutions

Middle class milieus

- *New Middle-Class Milieu* – The middle-class mainstream with the will to perform and to adapt: general acceptance of the social order; striving to become established at a professional and social level, seeking to lead a secure and harmonious existence

- *Adaptive Pragmatist Milieu* – The modern young core of society with a markedly pragmatic outlook on life and a sense of expedience: purposeful and prepared to compromize, hedonistic and conventional, flexible and security oriented; a strong need for anchoring and belonging

- *Socio-ecological Milieu* – With a critical stance to consumption/consumption awareness and with normative notions of the 'right' way of life: pronounced ecological and social conscience; globalization sceptics, standard bearers of political correctness and diversity

Lower-middle/lower class milieus

- *Traditional Milieu* – The security and order-loving wartime/post-war generation: rooted in the old world of the petty bourgeoisie or that of the traditional blue-collar culture: thriftiness, conformity and adaptation to the given necessities

- *Precarious Milieu* – The lower class in search of orientation and social inclusion, with strong anxieties about the future and a sense of resentment: faced with mounting social disadvantages; scant prospects of social advancement, a reactive attitude to life, keeping up with the consumer standards of the broad middle classes

- *Escapist Milieu* – The fun and experience-oriented modern lower class/lower-middle class: living in the here and now, shunning conventions and the behavioural expectations of the high-performance society

Based on the milieu-specific characteristics determined through interviews, the authors[204] of the MDG-Milieuhandbuch 2013 survey draw – in reference to their previous study from 2005 – comprehensive conclusions on the life philosophies and varieties and practices of faith of Catholics, on their forms of participation in church life including engagement as volunteers and not least about their perceptions of and expectations towards the Church and its communication. Holtkamp (2013) sums up the potential benefits of exploring the Sinus Milieu studies for parishes as follows: [205]

- The participants [in respective workshops] now know that they can motivate with their public relations work only some portions of their parish community.

- By having a look at the Sinus Milieus, one becomes sensitized to other milieus as well, but it also shows to what extent parish members are concentrated in few milieus.

- In order to appeal to various milieus, not just different media channels are needed but firstly also a factual discussion of pastoral goals and fields of action.

- Devising a parish communication concept is a more substantial effort than developing a new corporate design or updating the Internet presentation.

Putting the socio-economic milieu approach of the Sinus and SIGMA institutes into perspective, App et al. (2014) focus in their surveys and analyzes mainly on the communication styles and scopes as well as the underlying value orientations of Catholics. They correlate these with individual activity or passivity in communication, by doing which the consequences would have been drawn for the first time in milieu research from the media revolution and from the tectonic shifts in the sender and receiver roles over the past years.[206] In the resulting model of the "PRAGMA communication milieus", the following types of milieus are recognized:

---

[204] CALMBACH, Marc et al. (2013): *MDG-Milieuhandbuch 2013*. Ibidem.

[205] HOLTKAMP, Jürgen: Marketing für Pfarrgemeinden. In: FÜRST, Gebhard (ed.), HOBER, David, HOLTKAMP, Jürgen: *Katholisches Medienhandbuch: Fakten – Praxis – Perspektiven*. Kevelaer: Butzon & Bercker, 2013, pp. 319-210.

[206] APP, Reiner et al. (2014): *Zukunftshorizont Kirche*. Ibidem, p. 60.

- *Public Welfare Communicators* (strong in communication through a comprehensive media mix, high activity and engagement potential, strict social values)

- *Tolerance Activists* (a young milieu with a preference for digital, socially interconnected communication, value orientation on cohesion and openness)

- *Efficiency-oriented* (medium to fair use of media, targeted communication, technically and solution-oriented)

- *Individualist Activists* (high use of social media/online offers, leisure and experience-oriented, self-realization)

- *Individualist Consumers* (high but passive media use: private TV channels, social media mainly as a matter of pursuit of certain preferences)

- *Defensive Bourgeois* (passive media use, defensive retreat into the private sphere at high dynamics of value changes)

- *Passive Traditionalists* (classic print media and public service channels, strong safety orientation)

- *Conservative Activists* (strongly individualistic, selective use of media offers; conservative with a high differentiation and aggression potential)

The authors focus in their evaluations mainly on the "Public Welfare Communicators" the proportion of which in the Catholic population reaches a fairly substantial 20 percent as their high level of readiness to engage in civic matters would advance society and their communication strengths would shape public opinion. As a well-off, well-established and confident group seated in the middle of society, the Public Welfare Communicators are a highly significant asset for the Church in terms of both quality and quantity [207] "In the present day and age of a lack of priests, they [the Public Welfare Communicators] often are the peg that holds parish life together. What are the expectations of this milieu towards the Church and what framework conditions are vital for their readiness to engage thus is among the core questions of the future for the Church". Here the different "key influencer" types can be pointed out at this point already (see Chapter 3.6.3.3 – Word of Mouth and Viral Marketing) who have a function in word-of-mouth marketing.

---

[207] Ibidem, p. 66.

Complementary to the above outlined models of the Catholic milieus, now a brief look appears meaningful into the results of surveys among members of the Protestant Church in Germany. Schulz (2008) [208] defines on the basis of the fourth survey among members of the Protestant Church in Germany (IV. KMU) eight core dimensions that shape the interests and preferences of people not least towards the church:

- Both biological and mental age in terms of shutting oneself off/openness;
- A weak or strong orientation to tradition(s);
- A low/strong interest in communication and socializing;
- A high or low social status (e.g. income, education);
- Preference for simple or complex forms of experience;
- Preference towards orderly/spontaneous experience;
- Orientation to authoritative regulations/the individual;
- Preference towards a rural/urban residential setting.

Three of these life choice dimensions make acceptance of church offers and in particular access to specific groups in the population easier or more difficult, which was confirmed by the fifth KMU in 2014. Specifically "traditional orientation" and "affinity to education" as well as "interest in socializing" are the key determinants of success or failure of many church offers, and of attitudes of people towards the Protestant Church.[209]

Using the above dimensions, the Protestant Church identified among its membership six different types of lifestyles that are relevant to church work. These are "highly cultural-tradition oriented", "sociable and tradition oriented", "youth cultural-modern", "high cultural-modern", "do-it-yourself/modern" and "tradition oriented-ordinary". These lifestyles can be visualized in the social space in reference to Benthaus-Apel (2006) as follows:[210]

---

[208] SCHULZ, Claudia: Zielgruppenorientierung und Milieu-Überschreitung kirchlicher Arbeit. In: HERMELINK, Jan et al. (2008): *Kirche empirisch*. Ibidem, p. 297.

[209] SCHULZ, Claudia et al.: Dimensionen des Lebensstils. In: LISKOWSKY, Anne Elise, EVANGELISCHE KIRCHE IN DEUTSCHLAND: *Engagement und Indifferenz. Kirchenmitgliedschaft als soziale Praxis. Fünfte EKD-Erhebung über Kirchenmitgliedschaft.* Hannover: EKD, 2014, pp. 77-79.

[210] BENTHAUS-APEL, Frederike: Life-style-related patterns of church membership: results from the 4th Church Membership Study conducted by the Protestant Church in Germany (EKD). Frankfurt am Main: Campus-Verlag, 2016. [retrieved on 2018-04-30] Available from: http://www.ssoar.info/ssoar/handle/document/17436.

Figure 3-6: Lifestyles of Protestant Church Members in the Social Space (own graphic)
Percentages of "very closely connected to the church"

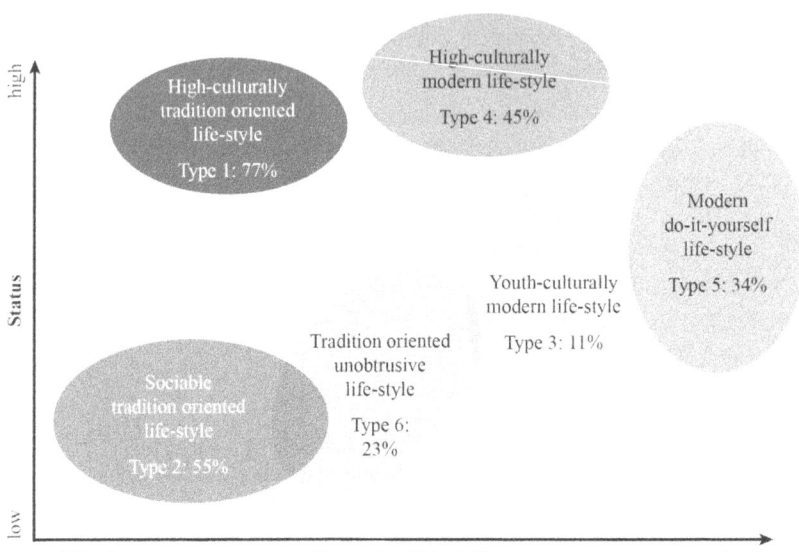

The similarities between the Protestant lifestyles with their positioning in the social space and the excessively used Sinus Milieus on the Catholic side come hardly as a surprise, which applies also to the fact that "the church members very closely connected to the Church typically include the two groups of older church members of the first and second lifestyle type".[211]

On a critical note regarding the use of studies on the basis of sociology of religion on members of church communities, it should be principally pointed out that these are frequently carried out by organizations and consultancies from the private sector that are primarily interested in commercial viability of their studies. Due to their respective business models and the existing competitive contexts in the consultancy markets, the assumptions, toolsets and conceptions such studies are built upon prevalently are kept confidential as business secrets.[212] That means such models are

---

[211] Ibidem, p. 2362, 2363.
[212] cf. HÖFELSCHWEIGER, Rainer: *Mitglied, wer bist Du? Eine kirchetheoretische Studie zur Differenzsensiblen Inklusion der religions-soziologischen pluralen Mitglieder evangelischer*

not really transparent or reproducible, and no authentic verification of reliability and validity by third parties is possible. In strictly scientific terms, such models – which applies at least to the Sinus Milieus but equally also to the three related approaches of "Sigma Milieus", "Delta Milieus" and "sociodimensions" – are of limited use as their fundamental design cannot be verified in detail.

Such studies become a real issue particularly where their buyers presume that by getting hold of the study it will actually enable them to successfully influence their customers or members in marketing-like efforts. The propensity for such 'holy grail' expectations completely detached from any sense of reality is additionally sustained by the large volumes of uncritical secondary and application literature.[213] Höfelschweiger (2011) concludes on this: "The absolute belief in the possibility of a market-style change counts accordingly to the axiomatic staple of membership studies from the marketing and sociological perspective. In that sense, such marketing and sociological analyses always go along inevitably with a certain measure of, partly self-imposed, claims of a universal panacea on part of their providers."[214] The possibility that the implementation of demands as derived from typologies of the different milieus for targeted milieu-specific forms of offers and communication may well remain without the projected success typically is obscured or not mentioned at all.

Providing that the insights from the milieu research principally result on part of the church and parish leaders in better sensitivity for and perception of the different typologies, lifestyles and needs of the church member milieus and that the offers, information and media channels of parishes are designed accordingly, the practical benefits of religion-specific milieu models prevail over their actual scientific transparency.

Kirchen. Leipzig: Evangelische Verlangsanstalt, 2011, p. 46, and other critical literary sources provided on p. 47.

[213] cf. EBERTZ, Michael N.: *Hinaus ins Weite. Gehversuche einer milieusensiblen Kirche.* Würzburg: Echter, 2008 – WIPPERMANN, Carsten, BDKJ / Misereor (Hg.): *Wie ticken Jugendliche? Sinus-Milieustudie U27.* Düsseldorf: Verlag Haus Altenberg, 2008 – EBERTZ, Michael N. (Hg.): *Milieupraxis: Vom Sehen zum Handeln in der pastoralen Arbeit.* Würzburg: Echter, 2009 – HEMPELMANN, Heinzpeter (2013): *Gott im Milieu.* Ibidem. – CALMBACH, Marc et al. (2016): *Wie ticken Jugendliche 2016?* Ibidem.

[214] cf. HÖFELSCHWEIGER, Rainer (2011): *Mitglied, wer bist Du?* Ibidem, p. 42.

3.6 The Church Marketing Mix

The AMA[215] defines marketing mix as follows: "Marketing mix refers to the mix of controllable marketing variables that the firm uses to pursue the desired level of sales in the target market. The most common classification of these factors is the four-factor classification called the 4 Ps: price, product, promotion, and place (...)."

In his elaborations on the range of marketing policy tools of service-oriented organizations that clearly include most church establishments, Bieberstein (2006) adds in reference to Anglo-Saxon literature to the classical 4Ps of the marketing mix a fifth material area of "people" (staff members) the core scope of which is human resources management including staff recruitment and personnel development ("internal marketing policies")[216]. Bruhn (2014) mentions in this respect the fifth "P" that signifies personnel policy:[217] "Service quality depends on the staff members. Their qualification, training and motivation hence is particularly important [for service marketing]." With a view to the provision of services in non-profit organizations, here as well the staff members, here however mostly volunteers, play a particularly important role.

Lichtsteiner (2015) speaks in his "Fribourg Management Model for Non-Profit Organizations" of "performance" as opposed to "product" and accounts in this way in addition to the provision of services that only relate to the product also for the service nature of an NPO (*Product-Service-Mix*, cf. Fig. 3-7) as well as for the extended product level (cf. Fig. 3-9, Chapter 3.6.1.2).[218] He further adds to his portfolio of marketing policy tools a sixth component, "politics", that comprises all forms of actively influencing the environment. With a view to socio-political relevance of the Church as a carrier of a number of healthcare, education and other types of facilities and given its "unpolitically political mode of work" (engagement in human rights, speaking up on behalf of the suffering and the poor and against violence – "guardian and protector function")[219], inclusion of this tool also in church marketing is entirely justified.

---

215 cf. AMERICAN MARKETING ASSOCIATION: *AMA Dictionary*. [retrieved on 2018-04-30] Available from: http://marketing-dictionary.org (search item "Marketing 4Ps")

216 BIEBERSTEIN (2006): *Dienstleistungs-Marketing*. Ibidem, pp. 374-389.

217 BRUHN, Manfred (2014): *Marketing*. Ibidem, pp. 35-36.

218 LICHTSTEINER (2015): *Das Freiburger Management-Modell*. Ibidem, pp. 225-228.

219 cf. BÖCKENFÖRDE, Ernst-Wolfgang: *Kirchlicher Auftrag und politisches Handeln. Analysen und Orientierungen*. Freiburg: Herder, 1989, pp. 112-115 / 128-132.

Figure 3-7: Components of the Marketing Mix in the NPO Sector according to Lichtsteiner (2015)

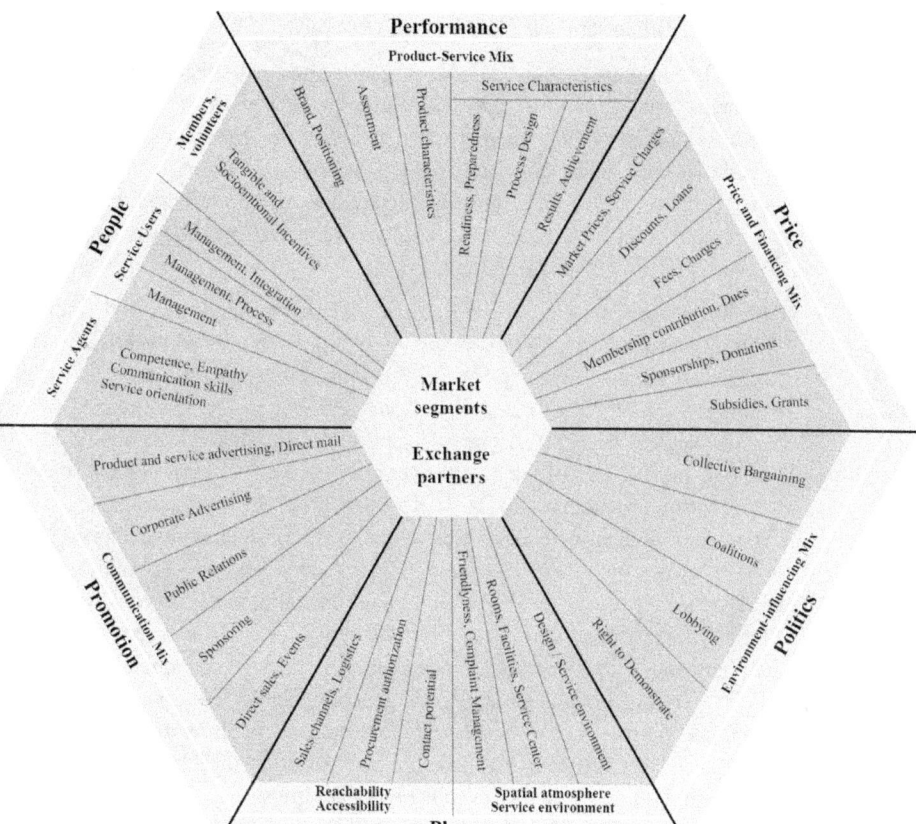

The US marketing manager Allan J. Magrath added to the classical 4Ps already in 1986 the three segments of "personnel", "process management" and "physical facilities"[220] that nowadays are recognized particularly in service marketing as the "7P". Parishes in particular should point their attention to exploring these additional marketing tools for the following reasons:

---

[220] MAGATH, Allan J., (1986) When Marketing Services, 4 Ps Are Not Enough. In: *Business Horizonts, Volume 29, Issue 3*, May-June 1986, pages 44-50.

- Firstly in service-oriented NPOs, planning and designing service processes and in particular how they are actually implemented and provided plays a particularly important role.[221]

- Secondly in particular in church organizations and facilities, unpaid volunteers and voluntary helpers have an especially vital function; on the one hand because they interact and deal with the parish members and outside persons and so carry and embody the spirit of the parish, and on the other because the positive mutual interactions of the staff members are essential in order for the services on behalf of the parish to be provided and delivered effectively and efficiently.

- Thirdly, church buildings in their aspect as centrally located and often culturally and historically significant structures are places of experiencing faith in an awe-inspiring and emotional way. Further they also – as for example the St Paul's Cathedral in London or the St. Peter's Basilica in Rome – signify a crucial part of the identity of a parish and the population of the respective part of the city or even the entire city. In this context, the US identity researcher Anastacia Kurylo (2012) defines two principal dimensions of identity[222], specifically the "place" in which a human being is born, grows up, marries, raises children, spends their old age and dies, and the "(identity) space" that is filled with the various roles an individual fulfils – as a citizen of the state, as neighbour, as co-worker, as a sports team member, as a mother or father to a family or a parish member. Church buildings and their environment hence generate identity-building moments for the people that need to be paid attention to in particular where dioceses or parishes over the course of reorganization efforts make a shift to the profane in, rededicate, sell or even raze the buildings.

On summing up all the previously outlined tools of the church marketing mix, the result for the needs of parishes is the following comprehensive system:

---

[221] BIEBERSTEIN (2006): *Dienstleistungs-Marketing*. Ibidem, p. 45 | LICHTSTEINER (2015): *Das Freiburger Management-Modell*. Ibidem, p. 49 f., 143 f. | SCHÜRMANN, Mathias: *Marketing. In vier Schritten zum eigenen Marketingkonzept*. Zurüch: vdf Hochschulverlag, 2011, p. 260.

[222] KURYLO, Anastacia: *Inter/Cultural Communication: Representation and Construction of Culture*. Los Angeles: SAGE Publications, 2013. pp. 118-120.

Figure 3-8: The 8 P of Parish Marketing (own graphic)

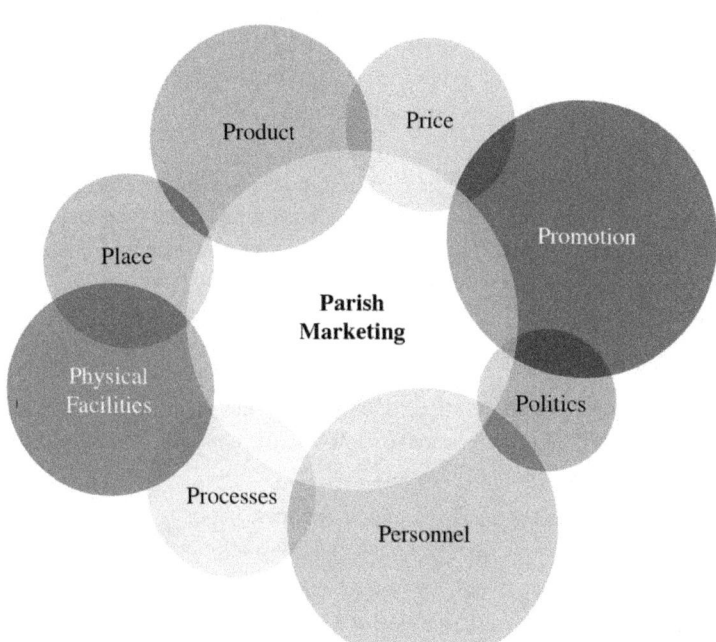

Due to the special nature of church products and services, and the focus points in communication in NPO marketing, the following observations explore the four classical marketing tools, with a particular focus on the segments of "product" and "promotion".

3.6.1 The Ecclesiastical "Product"

In his comments on the topic of church management, Thomé (1998) elaborates: [223] "The product with which the church (...) has been so successful to this day is faith, the meaning, the human sense of the transcendental. Such product, though it can be publically promoted with and, obviously, praised in propagandistic terms, nevertheless cannot be proven true with modern product communication means, nor positively verified for plausibility or have its effectiveness certified by laboratory tests. Having said that, the church justifiably insists on the inherent value of this

---

[223] THOMÉ, Martin: Unternehmen Orientierung. Probleme und Perspektiven eines Jahrtausend-projektes. In: THOMÉ, Martin (ed.): *Theorie Kirchenmanagement. Potentiale des Wandels.* Bonn: Lemmens, 1998. p. 17.

product that can manifest towards the individual as it can towards any human community, even the whole world". In contrast, Bucher (2007) concludes: [224] *"The church actually does not sell a "good". It does not sell anything as its message at its core comes free of charge, or put in theological lingo: grace. What it has there is to communicate is the God's grace, more specifically: the God's grace as a prerequisite to conversion."*

These conflicting quotes signify the special dimension of the original product of the church and of its "Product-Service-Mix".[225] Depending on the type and perspective of the theological interpretation of church activities and offers, there are a large variety of different concepts in pertinent church economic literature for a structured breakdown of these.

3.6.1.1 The Product Portfolio

Bruhn (2000) posits three dimensions of church services that can be determined from the expectations of the church members towards the church and within the context of which the specific church offers emerge:[226]

(1) Liturgical-catechetical services: prayer services, baptism, wedding and funeral ceremonies, religious education, guidance towards a religious life;

(2) Diaconal social services: meeting and education offers, pastoral care/counselling, opportunity for volunteer work, youth work, conveying fundamental ethical values, home visits, social integration;

(3) Cultural services: church music, preservation/maintenance of church buildings.

In her initial considerations on designing a survey on the brand profile of the Catholic Church, Giesen (2009) describes – in reference to the basic functions of the Church – four fields of activities of the Church[227] its offers including the at times fluent transitions between them can be subsumed under:

(1) Church services, pastoral care, endowment of sense/meaning and spirituality: liturgy, occasional services, catechesis, spiritual work and offers such as spiritual exercises, meditation, pilgrimages etc.;

---

[224]   cf. BUCHER, Rainer (2007): *Was geht und was nicht geht.* Ibidem.

[225]   cf. LICHTSTEINER (2015): *Das Freiburger Management-Modell.* Ibidem, p. 226.

[226]   BRUHN M., LISCHKA A.: Qualitätswahrnehmung und Zufriedenheit der Bevölkerung mit den Kirchen. In: BRUHN, Manfred et al. (2000): *Kirche und Marktorientierung.* Ibidem, p. 51.

[227]   GIESEN, Rut von (2009): *Ökonomie der Kirche?* Ibidem, p. 232 f.

(2) Social and civic engagement: Church social work, charities, daycare and assistance centers, healthcare, counselling centers;

(3) Upbringing and education: kindergartens, schools and tertiary education facilities run by the Church, religious classes and religious education for adults;

(4) Joint experience offers: meetings of societies, associations and initiatives, lectures, German Catholic congresses ("Deutsche Katholikentage"), parish celebrations, trips and theater visits organized by the parish, and much more.

With a stronger emphasis on the individual church member, Stolz (2006) recognizes in reference to the core parts of the church mission five types of concrete church goods that in themselves may have a stronger or less stronger religious tone to them:[228]

(1) The membership as such as a church good with the rights and obligations it entails, including social identity, paid for through membership fees in the form of money, time, one's active input or engagement and participation;[229]

(2) Individual positions such as volunteer functions remuneration for which comes in the form status, recognition or the satisfaction of doing something useful, and full-time jobs that as such also are rewarded financially;

(3) (Free of charge) services such as pastoral conversations, home visits or performance of holy rituals (occasional services: baptism, confirmation, Eucharist, confession, wedding ceremony, consecration, anointment of the sick);

(4) Collective activities in the community, socializing, joint activities and events such as church services, religious festivities, parish celebrations, the church choir, women's groups, spiritual meetings etc.;

(5) Public goods such as the large variety of social and charity services, development aid and disaster relief, missionary work but also conveying and preserving values such as engagement in human rights and on behalf of human dignity, advocating for

---

[228] STOLZ, Jörg: Kirchen im Wettbewerb. Religiöse und säkulare Konkurrenz in der modernen Gesellschaft, pp. 98-104. In: FAMOS (2006): *Kirche und Marketing.* Ibidem. – For comparison purposes, Stolz additionally also gives a sixth type, namely "goods" such as religious books, CDs and devotional objects the production of which however mostly is outsourced to external firms.

[229] This closely relates to "stewardship" described in Chapter 3.4.3 herein.

the suffering and the poor as well as renunciation of violence[230] ("the guardian and protector function of the church").

These various aspects of the church goods and services shall be further broken down in the following parts with a view to their specific benefits.

3.6.1.2   Faith as Ecclesiastical "Core Product"

According to Lichtsteiner (2015), every NPO – hence also including the church – pursues by virtue of its history and the context of its formation specific interests and values that ultimately boil down to its definition of mission.[231] On the backdrop of this context, an NPO offers a value system that is largely sustained also by those who join the organization as members and workers and act in accordance with this moral and ethical value system. From these collectively shared values, fundamental stances, norms and codes of conduct arise. In that sense the Catholic Church as well by virtue of its history and formation context builds on specific, namely Christian values that shape its mission, its purpose and hence ideally also the behaviour and actions of its members and their organizations. These values on the basis of a shared faith in Jesus Christ and his message of salvation

- Offer identification and identity;
- Give orientation and hence strength and the meaning of life;
- Promote trust and reduce fear and uncertainty;
- Facilitate respect for each other, awareness of guilt and forgiveness;
- By virtue of their collective nature, help counter loneliness,[232]
- Reinforce health behaviour, resilience and subjective sense of well-being;
- Boost satisfaction with life by virtue of serving others.

---

[230]   cf. POPE JOHN PAUL II.: Encyclical "Redemptor hominis" (1979). [retrieved on 2018-04-30] Available from: http://w2.vatican.va/content/john-paul-ii/en/encyclicals/documents/hf_jp-ii_enc_ 04031979_redemptor-hominis.html

[231]   cf. LICHTSTEINER (2015): Das Freiburger Management-Modell. Ibidem, p. 52 f.

[232]   German philosopher and theologian Rupert Lay (1996) explains in his lecture: "It was guilt, fear, search for orientation and loneliness that brought people to experience the Divine, not least also within social dealings and contexts. This experience ultimately leads up to a religiousness broken up into thousands of facets. But all religions also share precisely the one thing: they provide orientation, take away fear, release from guilt and, finally, lead human beings out of their loneliness." – DENZLER, Georg, JANSCHE, Rudolf, KÜNG, Hans, ROSENDORFER, Herbert: Der Ketzer Rupert Lay und das Versagen der Kirche. Sinnsuche in einer komplexen Welt. Düsseldorf: ECON-Verlag, 1996, p. 13 f.

Ultimately not just from the perspective of NPO marketing, of core importance for the spirit, development potential and continued survival of the church as an organization are the church members and their faith that promotes community building and invites joint action.[233] On consequently "breaking down" with Schürmann (2011) the previously outlined church products into the three product levels of

- *Core product* with its core values;

- *Formal product* with its direct added values, and

- *Extended product* with supportive and/or indirect added values,[234]

then especially faith itself can be deemed the church "core product" and the value orientation, search for meaning and the lifestyle of Christian love it gives rise to as "core values" (cf. Fig. 3-9, next page). This makes the church membership itself that is initiated by baptism and paid for by membership fees, or in Germany paid 'by imposition' via church tax a "formal product" of faith with multiple added values such as entitlement to receive further sacraments as well as to take on official tasks and functions.

Clustered around faith alongside church membership, further "formal products" firstly include those activities originally pertaining to the church that directly relate to its principal functions (basic church practice). Accordingly, these include practicing faith in terms of all types of religious services, in particular Eucharistic celebrations, administration of sacraments, pastoral care, spiritual guidance etc., as well as charitable activities of the church and of its members in their original sense of "loving service to others".

Among the added values attached to these formal services definitely is security; alongside the inner calm and stability generally provided by a religion, a vital security aspect alongside its initiation function is ritual celebration of important stages of and turning points in life in an exceptional, festive context. For example in confirmation, a young person gets reinforced in their faith and firmly attached to the community of believers. In the wedding ceremony, the spouses exchange the sacrament of marriage and so give each other in this way a security promise. Finally

---

[233] cf. Chapter 3.6.3.2 – Interpersonal Communication.

[234] SCHÜRMANN, Mathias (2011): *Marketing.* ibidem, pp. 146-149. – The term "product" is not broken down further in this Chapter but is used etymologically instead: coming from Latin "pro-ducere", it means "to bring forth", which comprises all types of tangible goods as well as intangible services.

also the anointment of the sick reinforces the seriously ill in their belief to be in, or will to entrust themselves to the hands of God.[235]

Figure 3-9: Ecclesiastical Product Levels (own graphic)

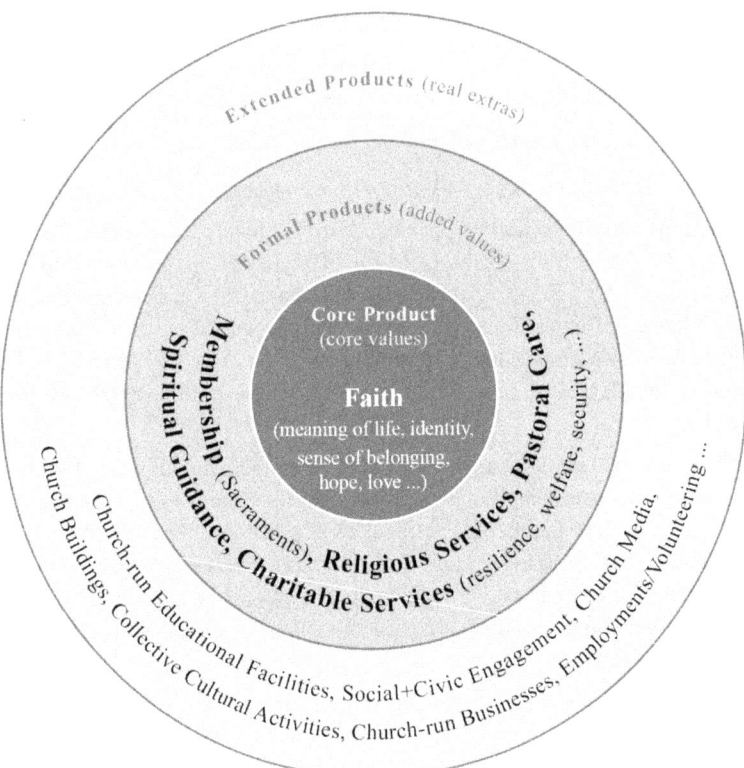

Finally as "extended products", all other dimensions of church services can be deemed the church as a service-oriented non-profit organization provides and offers both to its members and the public.

The question about the positive benefits (gratification) of their Church membership was answered by most Catholics in Germany[236] that they want to be guided at the

---

[235] cf. on this the remarks not least on the Catholic faith and sacraments at the internet portal KATHOLISCH.DE of the Catholic Church in Germany: *Unser Glaube.* (our faith) [retrieved on 2018-04-30] Available from: http://katholisch.de/glaube/unser-glaube

[236] cf. SCHULZ, Rüdiger et al. (2010): *MDG-Trendmonitor.* Ibidem, pp. 56-63.

turning points in their life by church rituals (68%), that belonging to the Church would be a family tradition (50%) and that they appreciate both the calm and the opportunity to reflect on matters (44%) as well as the sense of belonging to the community (44%). Worships and church celebrations appeal to well over a third of Catholics (35%), with substantial differences in the answers given by younger and older Catholics respectively (14% of the 16 to 29 year olds versus 54% of the above 60 year olds).

Here a critical note is due that the more a church offer, irrespective of its economic value or value to society, strays in its scope from the "core values", the more exchangeable and replaceable it gets. Specifically as concerns the positively appreciated "guidance through rituals" by the Church, it may be presumed that with the advancing secularization, this function is being increasingly taken over by "ritual guides" or "masters of ceremony" unrelated to the Church, who celebrate important rituals also without any references to religion or the Church. Not least because of this, obtaining services provided by the Church, and the authentic Christian motivation of the people providing the services are growing in importance. Fischer (2008) specifies:[237] "With its service capacities and their performance ability and with its material resources, the Church is principally capable of supporting its members, facilities and other parts of society as far as desired by these." All the services and benefits though do not represent a special quality that is unique to the Church in terms of a unique selling proposition as "Unselfish material support that does not directly serve strictly one's own selfish interests to players in need of resources [civil society] can also be provided by others as opposed to the various churches (…). The particularity of the church consequently is that its purpose is not in the activities of aid and support as such but in what makes it fundamentally different from other players: its faith-guided motivation that should be at the core of everything it does or decides not to." This presents church marketing with the challenge to present the charitable and social services of the parish and its establishments as far as possible with direct involvement of the individual providers of the services – pastoral workers, staff members, volunteers – which in turn opens up new possibilities of milieu-specific messages in marketing communication.

---

[237] FISCHER, Ralph (2008): *Kirche und Zivilgesellschaft*. Ibidem, p. 98 f.

3.6.2 "Price" and "Place"

3.6.2.1 Price Policy

Paying the "membership fee" is obligatory for members of the Catholic Church in Germany, on top of which the fee actually is levied and collected by third parties unrelated to the Church, specifically by tax authorities of the German federal states (cf. Chapter 1.3). This means a detachment of the services provided mainly by local churches and their local facilities from payment of individual member fees to the "official Church". Not least because of this, the marketing tool of "price" has very limited use as a lever in Germany to achieve any Church or parish marketing goals with, and only because many Catholic groups, establishments and associations additionally charge their own membership fees.

In spite of this, the Church must work and communicate with its price policies as "on the one hand, the price policy must signal towards its members what benefits they get for the church tax, their membership fees or for the donations they pay. On the other though, the price policy must also effectively communicate that the service a member gets is actually worth the price (church tax, fee, donation)".[238] The annual reports of the German Bishops' Conference give a comprehensive insight into how the tax and other types of income are used.[239]

Another price policy aspect are the expectations of church groups upon individual members to contribute their share in carrying and representing the principal values and goals of the respective church group, and to contribute to meeting the group's material or formal goals with their voluntary engagement within the meaning of stewardship outlined in Chapter 3.3 herein.

Special price policy challenges for churches arise particularly where the church members desire for certain services to be provided by their parish free of charge, or even automatically expect for the services to come free. Such situations happen for instance with occasional services such as baptisms, wedding and funeral ceremonies, in holding special masses or concerning the use of the parish property (real estate, equipment, vehicles etc.) for private purposes.

Finally, price policy also includes all the measures with which the church reduces the physical or psychic costs of its members.[240] Physical costs include for instance transport services to Sunday church services, or accompanying services where a warm welcome, friendly atmosphere and hospitality in events organized by the parish

---

[238] MÖDINGER, Wilfried (2001): *Kirchenmarketing*. Ibidem, p. 176.
[239] cf. SEKRETARIAT DER DEUTSCHEN BISCHOFSKONFERENZ (2017): *Katholische Kirche in Deutschland – Zahlen und Fakten*. Ibidem.
[240] MÖDINGER, Wilfried (2001): *Kirchenmarketing*. Ibidem, p. 177.

are meant to help newcomers overcome initial uncertainty and any reservations they may have, thus reducing the psychic costs of the church members.

3.6.2.2 Distribution Policy

As part of the restructuring efforts in the Catholic Church in Germany, a number of church facilities currently are being shut down and several parishes are being merged into larger pastoral units. This has far-reaching impacts on the acceptance and availability of the church and parish buildings that are to remain in use in the future as places where church activities are offered and take place.

In this respect there is a growing role of the sc. marketing agents. In religious contexts, these are often parents of the children and adolescents who participate in the events held by the parish, and further also cooperating institutions such as kindergartens and schools, sponsoring associations and mainly full-time and volunteering staff members as assessors and direct sellers of the church products and services. In particular the latter are to receive targeted training with a view to successful presentation and sale of the church offers and activities.

A relatively recent discipline in church distribution policy is online distribution[241] that closely relates to marketing communication and in which within the framework of Christian values, (parish-) specific services and products such as devotional objects, literature etc. are marketed directly via online shops, or indirectly via affiliate placements.

3.6.3 "Promotion": The Communication Mix of Parishes

While in media-based communication, the primary aim is (massive) spread of information about and boosting the significance of church and parish offers and topics, the interpersonal dimension of church communication is alongside the personal relationship with God and the experience of faith, mainly about mutual understanding, acceptance and interaction in the parish as well as about community building. With this in mind in the following parts, firstly the various different forms of media are explored and discussed. This is followed by an examination of interpersonal communication with a particular focus to its marketing variant, which is word of mouth.

---

[241] SCHÜRMANN, Mathias (2011): *Marketing*. Ibidem, pp. 197-199.

Figure 3-10: Types, Forms and Distribution Areas of Catholic Media

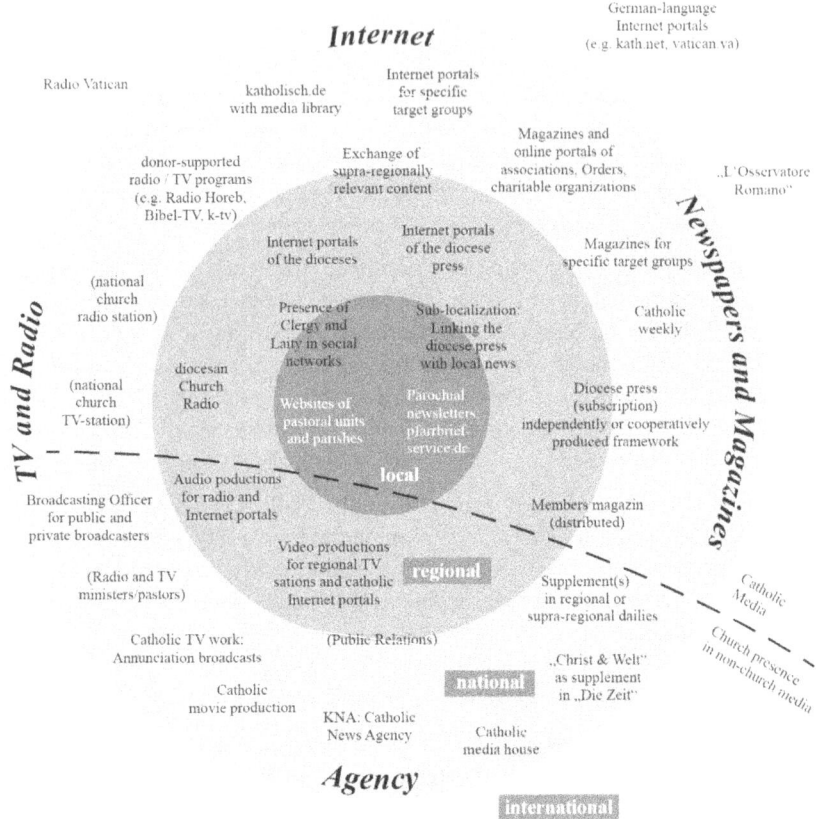

3.6.3.1 The Church Media Portfolio

Klenk (2013) performed a Delphi-method based survey among leaders and professionals in the field of church media as well as among external media experts on the outlook of Catholic media in their different distribution areas.[242] Figure 3-10 on the previous page exemplifies the large variety of Catholic media in Germany. Of these, Klenk correlated the key offers of church institutions or church publishing and media houses with quantitative data from the MDG-Trendmonitor survey on

---

[242] KLENK, Christian (2013): *Zustand und Zukunft katholischer Medien.* Ibidem, p. 352. – Details about the Delphi-method and the constitution of the panel of experts are provided on pp. 29 f. and 44 f.; a terminology of the "Catholic media" is given ibidem on pp. 61-65.

"Religious Communication"[243] and assigned them to the presently used Sinus Milieus as follows (cf. Chapter 3.5.2): [244]

Figure 3-11: Coverage of Ecclesiastical and Religious Media Related to the Sinus-Milieus (maximum coverages; © 2009 Klenk/Sinus)

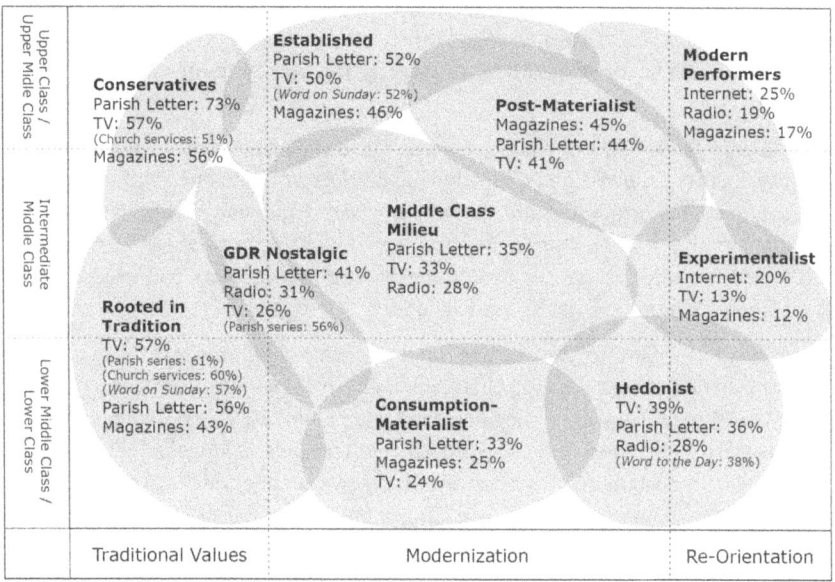

Based on expert opinions determined in a multilevel approach, for the mostly locally operating parishes and establishments of the Catholic Church the following scenarios and consequences can be summed up:

- *Parish letters and parochial magazines* – Parish letters and announcements of pastoral units are set to grow in significance into the future in particular within the context of a decline in importance of other religious print media:[245] "Parish letters, though as amateur journalism rarely comparable in content and visual style with publications of church publishing houses or with glossy magazines available at the newsstand, are actually the staple of

---

[243] SCHULZ, Rüdiger et al. (2010): *MDG-Trendmonitor*. Ibidem.
[244] KLENK, Christian (2013): *Zustand und Zukunft katholischer Medien*. Ibidem, p. 353.
[245] Ibidem, p. 110.

church media used by more Catholics (64%) than any other type of media, and are deemed the most important in terms of relevance." [246]

However, parish letters typically only reach active church members: "They are appreciated only by those who are principally interested in the Catholic Church and prefer print media, and by those who want to be informed on local events in church life."[247] Having said that, the makers of parish letters should receive more substantial support in terms of training offers, funding or the utilization of synergies across dioceses.[248]

- *Diocese press* – (Supporting) print publications of dioceses (diocese or church newspapers, "diocese press") likely will have been discontinued by 2025, or will continue only at significantly lower numbers of copies and a reduced number of titles.[249] In this context there has been an intense ongoing debate about the use of diocese titles as carriers and/or "shells" for parish letters and magazines of parochial unions and parish associations.

- *Radio/TV* – Due to the decline in importance and weight of the Church, contributions about the Church and church (proclamation) shows on radio and TV will be increasingly relegated from the public law broadcasting sphere to advertising-financed, often local dedicated channels. Alongside, all the radio and TV contributions produced by dioceses are collected in central Internet portals and remain available there (for example at katholisch.de).

Moreover, media experts deem developing new formats in the TV sphere as well as using contemporary language in radio proclamation shows an urgent necessity, at the same time however see as unlikely the launch of a church-run TV channel or regional dedicated channels. [250]

- *Internet – Full-time staff members of the Church need to receive training* in Internet use, although the Internet by now in the reception of church-related and religious topics only has been playing a marginal role. Nevertheless, parishes are to be supported in designing and running websites and apps to be developed and put in use for the mobile Internet. Potential types of content here include:

---

[246] Ibidem, p. 220 / SCHULZ, Rüdiger et al. (2010): *MDG-Trendmonitor.* Ibidem.
[247] CALMBACH, Marc et al. (2013): *MDG-Milieuhandbuch 2013.* Ibidem, p. 39.
[248] KLENK, Christian (2013): *Zustand und Zukunft katholischer Medien.* Ibidem, p. 369.
[249] Ibidem, p. 136 / p. 368.
[250] Ibidem, p. 272 / p. 370.

- *Homepage*: Presentation of parish life, of the variety of church offers and of contact partners (contact points) on modern webpages optimized for mobile devices;

- *Blog*: Information of current schedules, events and developments in the parish, in church establishments and church groups/ associations;

- *E-mail-newsletter* as a digital equivalent of print newsletters that are mostly published on a weekly basis (with content typically being church service schedules and current news[251]); acquisition of new subscribers (e-mail addresses) here is particularly through the homepage, blogs and social media.

• *Social networks/social media* – The use of social networks such as Facebook must be promoted even despite the currently still limited reach of church Facebook pages. Here the church representatives at all levels as well as in different church institutions must be more active in the networks than has been the case by now.[252]

According to Rinklake (2014)[253], the breakdown of media use structure of Catholic parishes in Germany looks as follows (see Fig. 3-12, next page): Despite a web penetration of nearly 83 percent, German Catholic parishes (still) appear to prefer the traditional print media, specifically "parish magazines" and "schedules of services/worships". This may be due to the age structure of the parishes, or of their members in full-time or volunteer functions charged with the tasks of communication and media presentation.

The publication of parish magazines on an auxiliary basis also in the PDF format in the Internet, and the supplemental mailing of schedules of service/worships as e-newsletters imply that Catholic parishes are well capable of creating and publishing static content through electronic means and channels; however, they lack the necessary media skills to generate and administer dynamic content (in particular user-generated content). Accordingly, this means a substantial need for improvement in this field.

---

[251] RINKLAKE, Thomas: *Befragung "Pfarrbriefservice.de"*. Nürnberg: xit GmbH, 2014, p. 9. [retrieved on 2018-04-30] Available from: http://www.pfarrbriefservice.de/file/ergebnisse-der-pfarrbriefbefragung-2014#download

[252] KLENK, Christian (2013): *Zustand und Zukunft katholischer Medien*. pp. 325-326 / pp. 370-371.

[253] RINKLAKE, Thomas (2014): *Befragung "Pfarrbriefservice.de"*, ibidem, pp. 14-15.

Figure 3-12: Media Usage of Catholic Parishes

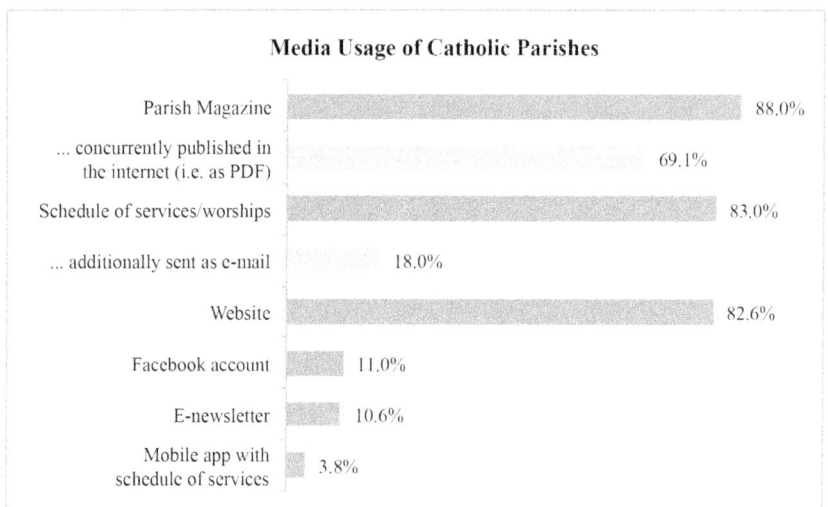

Still, as much as 11 percent of the parishes have a Facebook account, although the 2014 study did not investigate what priority is attached to this and to other social media and how the respective content is redacted and administered. However, the fact that merely 4.3 more percent plan to open up a Facebook account implies a fairly limited innovation capacity in this regard.

At the national and international level though, there are in the meantime fairly impressive online offers such as the news and information portal of the Catholic Church in Germany (katholisch.de), a comprehensive overview of online pastoral offers including personal online counselling and online guidance run by the Katholische Arbeitsstelle für missionarische Pastoral (Catholic Center for Missionary Pastoral) (internetseelsorge.de) or the global prayer network of the Pope (clicktopray.org).[254] From the results of a comprehensive analysis of media usage

---

[254] KAMP / Katholische Arbeitsstelle für missionarische Pastoral: *Internetseelsorge.de.* [retrieved on 2018-04-30] Available from: https://www.internetseelsorge.de/ | APOSTLESHIP OF PRAYER INTERNATIONAL, EYM (Eucharistic Youth Movement): Click to pray (clicktopray.org). [retrieved on 2018-04-30] Available from: https://clicktopray.org/de/

behaviour of US Catholics, the following topic preferences ensued for the partial area of online media that are particularly frequented mainly by the younger age groups:[255]

Figure 3-13: Catholic New Media Use in the United States 2012
> *If the Catholic Church had to focus on one area to improve its presence in the online, new media, or digital world, what should that be in your opinion? – Percentage responding as such:*

News: reporting on the activities of Church leaders and the Church's relationship with other institutions	**32%**
Media literacy: helping people discern reliable and competent Catholic sources develop positive conversations about the faith	**28%**
Catechesis, religious education: helping parents, catechists and teachers explain faith	**20%**
Evangelization: reaching out to non-Catholics and inactive Catholics	**11%**
Other	**9%**

Key in designing the concepts for church media is setting a targeted agenda, specifically defining concrete main topics that appeal not just to the older, mostly conservative audience of faithful to the church but also and in particular account for the existing landscape of steadily evolving target groups in the younger milieus, which, obviously, represent the Church's young blood. Here a note is due that specifically in the perception of younger age groups (16 to 29 year olds), the Church's acceptance, credibility and, most of all, problem-solving competence with a view to the question about the meaning of life and concerning moral problems and needs of the individual as well as problems in family life is fairly limited.[256]

The Allensbach Institute for Demoscopy (IfD Allensbach) determined in a dedicated survey a number of topics most Catholics in Germany are particularly interested in. Alongside common topical issues such as politics, sports, travel, economic news etc., the survey identified also topics more closely related to religious and church life of the respondents (cf. Fig. 3-14). Such topics can be principally recommended for editorial calendars of church media: [257]

---

[255] GRAY, Marc, GAUTIER, Mary: *Catholic New Media Use in the United States, 2012.* Washington, D.C.: Center for Applied Research in the Apostolate (CARA), Georgetown University, 2012, p. 85.

[256] SCHULZ, Rüdiger et al. (2010): *MDG-Trendmonitor.* Ibidem, pp. 75-79.

[257] SCHULZ, Rüdiger et al. (2010): *MDG-Trendmonitor.* Ibidem, p. 82.

Figure 3-14: Topics of Particular Interest to Catholics: An Overview

Topics the respondents are "particularly interested in"			
Politics	36%	Topics concerning the parish and what is happening in the parish	25%
Sports	35%	The meaning of life	23%
Schooling and education	34%	Economic news	23%
Nature and environmental protection	32%	Event tips and notifications	21%
Learning to think positively	31%	Contentious issues such as abortion, celibacy, women priests etc.	21%
Social engagement	29%	Household/gardening tips	21%
Travel, trip reports, holiday tips	29%	Everyday stories from and about people	19%
Training and education activities	27%	How to bring children closer to faith and the Church, religious education	18%
Statements and comments on topical issues	25%	Advice on upbringing and parenting	18%
Reports on people who have achieved something special (role models)	25%	Life counselling, how to better come to terms with life and its trials	17%

In all efforts of the Catholic Church and its parishes at defining and rejuvenating its media portfolio, alongside the church media channels increasingly also secular media offers have to be used – particularly when pursuing appeal to Catholics not connected to the Church (cf. Fig. 3-15, next page).[258] This is because such Catholics are substantially more interested in topics and issues of faith not explicitly related to the Church, such as inputs on "the meaning of life" or on "life counselling": "Contributions on these larger topics from the Church perspective apparently entail relatively better chances of reaching in this way also Catholics not connected to the Church", with interest in "the meaning of life" and "life counselling" being the strongest in the young, extremely individualistic and escapistically inclined milieu of Experimentalists. Figure 3-15 further also implies that these fundamental and discourse-setting topics primarily are discussed in private in the family and with friends as well as with pastoral workers, which is explored in more detail in the next chapter.

---

[258] Ibidem, pp. 122-127.

Figure 3-15: Preferred Information Sources of German Catholics 2009

Preferred Information Sources of the Catholics	(Especially/also) interested in the topic, in features –		
	'On the meaning of life'	'Life counselling, how to cope with the problems, that you have'	'Reports on church events and developments'
	n=1374 (66%=100)	n=1236 (59%=100)	n=1031 (50%=100)
Learning about this, looking for advice –			
In personal conversations with the family, with friends or acquaintances	75 %	90 %	41 %
In books	33 %	35 %	9 %
In worship, in mass	28 %	25 %	42 %
In conversations with the priest, other pastoral ministers or with active in the parish	29 %	29 %	36 %
In the Bible	25 %	19 %	6 %
From the daily newspaper, magazines	13 %	24 %	53 %
In general television program	15 %	19 %	35 %
From broadcasts on religion and church on television	15 %	12 %	42 %
From weekly newspapers or magazines, which often report on faith and church	4 %	5 %	12 %
From broadcasts on religion and church on the radio	7 %	6 %	23 %
On radio, in general radio program	7 %	8 %	18 %
Through the church newspaper, the diocese press	7 %	5 %	33 %
In the parochial magazine	9 %	10 %	53 %
On church websites	3 %	3 %	10 %
On websites of other providers	5 %	10 %	4 %
In forums, blogs, communities	3 %	8 %	2 %
At therapists / doctors	x	1 %	x

x = <0.5% | Base: Catholics from the age of 16 in total | Source: Allensbach Archive, IfD Survey 5266 (Oct./Nov. 2009)

3.6.3.2 Interpersonal Communication

In his treatises of media and society, communication theorist James Carey (2009) advocated two views on communication by differentiating between "communication as ritual" and "communication as transmission".[259] "Communication as ritual" means "construction and representation of shared convictions" as reflected for example by shared values, symbols, activities and cultural sensitivities of persons. In contrast "communication as transfer" refers, in an analogy to physical movement of goods, to the process of information transfer by (mass) media, which acts primarily as an enhancer of the spread and of the effects of messages.

A similar differentiation with regard to (religious) communication can be found in Ebertz (2013) who contrasts "Vis-à-vis communication in the form of rite and sermon" (gesticulation, facial expressions, verbal address) with communication that exceeds the scope of the former by using "propagation media".[260] The particular attribute of religious vis-à-vis communication is the spatial and temporal interconnection "between information, message and comprehension within the basic operation of communication", in which comprehension comes interactively and is precisely definable in terms of the point of time, place and recipients of the communication.

App et al. (2014) as well differentiates between a personal and a media dimension in church communication, associating the (inter) personal dimension particularly with "communication of faith": "Faith [is] conveyed, experienced and lived in a communication context and within a communication community. Consequently, the community-building aspect of the communication of faith is of principal importance to faith itself."[261]

This points to another, and important, aspect of interpersonal communication, which is the formation and promotion of community and of concerted action through

---

[259] CAREY, James W.: Communication as Culture, Essays on media and society. New York: Routledge, 2009, p.11.

[260] EBERTZ, Michael N.: Religion, Kommunikation und Medien. In: FÜRST, Gebhardt (2013): Katholisches Medienhandbuch. ibidem, p. 40 – Ebertz comments on a critical note on the types of logic used by "propagation media" that they may also misappropriate the visual, ritual and textual content of religions, as evidenced by advertising where it operates with religious notions via ironic presentation in everyday contexts, with the religious in cult-like presentation or even with the profane in cult-like presentation, and finally with sayings and mottos that express life wisdom transposed as product philosophy (p. 42).

[261] APP, Reiner et al. (2014): Zukunftshorizont Kirche. Ibidem, p. 102.

communication. This topic has been comprehensively explored by Habermas et al. (1981) and comprised in the "Theory of Communicative Action".[262]

Consequently while in the interpersonal dimensions of church communication, the key themes in addition to one's personal relationship with God and religious experience include mutual understanding, acceptance and interaction as well as community building[263], in media-shaped communication the primary emphasis is on (extensive) spread of information concerning the needs and/or offers of the church. Fig. 3-16 on the next page shows the relationships of German Catholics with the different direct and indirect representatives of their parishes that with a view to the interpersonal communication this entails is deemed an indicator of attachment to the parish.[264] The results imply that a fourth of all Catholics (25%) have a good relationship with their parish priest and another 19 percent with another priest.

On the whole, 44 percent of Catholics have good contacts with at least one official contact partner in their parish. Of these, 80 percent of those who identify as "faithful to the church" and still as much as 57 percent of the "critical church-connected" have goods contacts with at least one official church worker (cf. Fig. 3-16, next page). However, it seems already for Catholics who identify as belonging to the large segment of "ecclesiastically distanced Christians" that their personal communication typically is blocked, which is particularly true for the "not religious" Catholics.

In particular as regards communication with Catholics not connected to the Church and their environment, of particular importance is personally approaching the parish members on every possible occasion (cf. Chapter 3.4.1 – Retention and Recruitment of Parish Members). As far as the choice of topic(s) and the type and design of the used media resonate with the respective target group, this opens up a possibility for the parish of not just reaching with its offer the target group but also of the target group recommending it further.

---

[262] HABERMAS, Jürgen: *Theorie des kommunikativen Handelns*. Frankfurt/Main: Suhrkamp, 1981.

[263] Compare on this also the comments in Chapter 3.3.1 herein on homogeneity of a church target group.

[264] SCHULZ, Rüdiger et al. (2010): *MDG-Trendmonitor*. Ibidem, pp. 109-112.

Figure 3-16: Interpersonal Communication, Contacts with Parish Workers

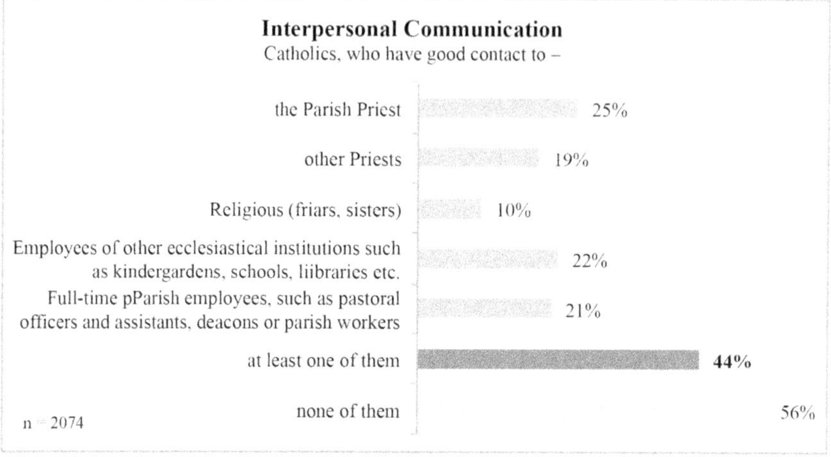

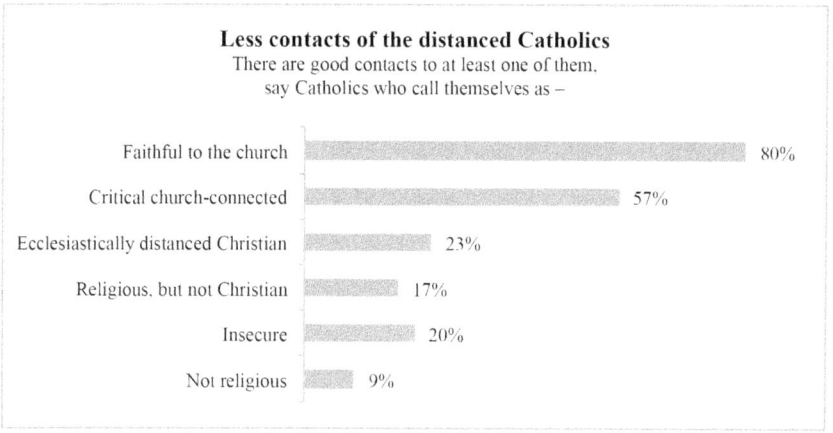

Figure 3-17: Interpersonal Communication, Contacts with Parish Workers

3.6.3.3   Word of Mouth and Viral Marketing

The Christian "Center for Church Communication" (CFCC) that has been running the worldwide known blog "churchmarketingsucks.com" in the US since the 1990s regularly collects data on the communication of parishes (Fig. 3-18, next page). In doing so, the findings already from 2005 clearly suggested that especially personal approach and a positively voiced invitation are attached particular importance in parish communication, all the more as about a fourth of the surveyed parishes have

been actively using this form of marketing already[265]: *"Another way to improve –
and one of the most cost effective methods – is the personal invitation, which was the
third most effective method, used by 24% of churches (and it was a write-in
response). While the marketing world is just discovering and exploiting word of
mouth marketing, it's something the church has been doing for 2,000 years."*

Figure 3-18: What's Working for Churches in the US. CFCC survey 2005

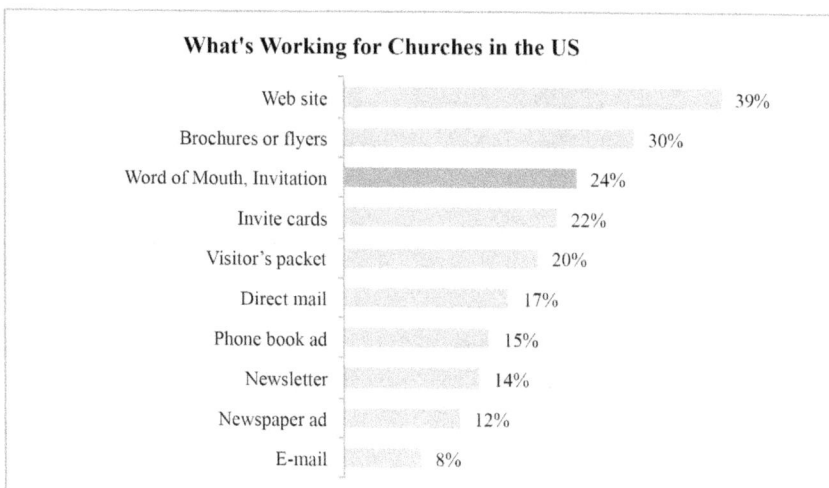

This implies a question as to how far word of mouth could be of interest also to the
Catholic Church in Germany and used systematically by the same both for
missionary and advertising/PR purposes.

Oetting (2009) defines word of mouth as "oral, person-to-person communication
between a perceived non-commercial communicator and a receiver concerning a
brand, a product or a service offered for sale".[266] Van der Lans (2010) narrows this
quite generic definition with regard to the online variant of word of mouth, which is
viral marketing: [267]

---

[265] CENTER FOR CHURCH COMMUNICATION: *Church Marketing Report. A casual look at the
marketing and communication practices of churches across the U.S.*. Los Angeles, 2005. p. 3
[retrieved on 2018-04-30] Available from: http://www.cfcclabs.org/ 2005/12/communications-
report/

[266] OETTING, Martin: Ripple Effect – How Empowered Involvement Drives Word of Mouth.
Wiesbaden: Gabler, 2009, p. 40.

[267] VAN DER LANS, Ralf et al.: A viral branching model for predicting the spread of electronic word-of-
mouth. In: *Marketing Science 2010, 29 (2)*, pp. 348-365.

"The term 'viral marketing' describes the phenomenon by which consumers mutually share and spread marketing- relevant information, initially sent out deliberately by marketers to stimulate and capitalize on word-of-mouth (WOM) behaviors. (...) viral marketing campaigns primarily aim to spread information, create awareness, and improve brand perceptions, which are non-economic goals." Or more briefly:[268] "Viral marketing refers to targeted triggering of word-of-mouth processes for purposes of marketing of companies and services."

In general, word of mouth/viral marketing consists of two components, which are the message and/or the product/service information that is to be spread orally or by phone, and the propagandists who spread the information by receiving, assessing and sharing it.

The key attribute of the respective message or piece of information at hand is its appeal and its value to the communication partners concerned, irrespective of whether these communicate personally, by phone, through WhatsApp etc. Berger (2013) identifies a total of six success factors that define 'contagiousness' of messages and by extension of products and services:[269] their social currency – the hoped-for increase of prestige within the own peer group –, their accompanying triggers in terms of stimuli or mnemonic hooks – novelty, extraordinariness, entertainment value, exclusivity ("insider knowledge") –, emotions – happiness, enthusiasm, joy vs. misfortune, disappointment, sadness –, a preferably broad public, their practical value, and framing stories. Hence the more 'contagious' a church message or church offer, the better the chances of success in terms of reaching the marketing goals pursued.

As for the "propagandists", Hinz et al. (2011) recommend:[270] "Marketers can achieve the highest number of referrals, across various settings, if they seed the message to hubs (high-degree seeding) or bridges (high-betweenness seeding). These two strategies yield comparable results and (...) are up to 8 times more successful than seeding to fringes (low-degree seeding). (...) According to these insights, marketers should pick highly connected persons as initial seeds if they hope to generate awareness or encourage transactions through their viral marketing campaigns since these hubs promise a wider spread of the viral message." Consequently for a church

---

[268] LANGNER, Sascha: Viral Marketing – Wie Sie Mundpropaganda gezielt auslösen und Gewinn bringend nutzen. 3rd extended edition, Wiesbaden: Gabler / GWV, 2009, p. 27.

[269] BERGER, Jonathan: Contagious. Why Things catch on. New York: Simon & Schuster, 2013, pp. 21-36.

[270] HINZ, Oliver, SKIERA, Bernd, BARROT, Christian, BECKER, Jan U.: Seeding Strategies for Viral Marketing: An Empirical Comparison. In: Journal of Marketing 2011, 75 (6), pp. 55-71.

community, the task arises to identify in its nearest and in the general environment precisely these types of users who are able as "hubs" with preferably large numbers of contacts and/or as "bridges" that interconnect various networks to quickly and comprehensively spread the information via the social media (seeding).

Controversially, but in a complementary manner the consultants with McKinsey&Company (2012) conclude that [271] "The environment where word-of-mouth circulates is crucial to the power of messages. Typically, messages passed within tight, trusted networks have less reach but greater impact than those circulated through dispersed communities .... That's why old-fashioned kitchen table recommendations and their online equivalents remain so important. After all, a person with 300 friends on Facebook may happily ignore the advice of 290 of them. It's the small, close-knit network of trusted friends that has the real influence."

Accordingly, the fact must be accounted for that apart from "high- degree or high-betweenness seeding", or alongside quantitatively oriented (mass) media communication with the aim of word-of-mouth, also the qualitative component in communication needs to be considered. This corresponds to the above outlined interpersonal dimension of church communication that is vital for parishes, which conveys faith and makes it an experience, and provides orientation and cohesion of the community.

The Word-of-Mouth Marketing Association (WOMMA, 2013) develops and expands the approach by Hinz that refers primarily to "seeding" by identifying "key influencers". [272] Key influencers are "a person or group of people who possess greater than average potential to influence due to attributes such as frequency of communication, personal persuasiveness or size of and centrality to a social network, among others." Using these criteria, a total of five different classes of individuals were defined the opinions and word-of-mouth involvement of which are particularly influential. Their characteristics applied to parishes can be outlined as follows:

• An *advocate* is a person that is formally independent from the institution, behaving generally in a supportive, promotive or even defending manner, which goes also for their argumentation, without getting for their involvement any reimbursement.

• An *ambassador* identifies with the precepts of the institution and declares this publically. They receive for their commitment and loyalty personal gratification or

---

[271] BUGHIN, Jacques, DOOGAN, Jonathan, VETVIK, Ole Jørgen: A new way to measure word of mouth marketing. In: *McKinsey Quarterly*, April 2010, p. 20.

[272] WORD-OF-MOUTH MARKETING ASSOCIATION: *WOMMA Influencer Guidebook - 2013*. Chicago, 2013, p. 6 [retrieved on 2018-04-30] Available from: http://womma.org/free-womm-resources/

reimbursement. They are strong team players with links to the institution that generate mutual benefits for both.

• A *citizen* is something of an 'everyman' in the social web who readily helps friends and acquaintances – however not necessarily institutions – and likely with above average influence in their social network.

• *Professionals/occupationals* are professionally highly regarded and well-anchored persons that by virtue of their occupation or position are able to exert influence upon others in their environment. Being university graduates, they are ready and willing to share their knowledge and experience.

• *Celebrities* use their popularity and public fascination with their person (celebrity status) for targeted influencing mainly of relevant media. Their special abilities and qualities however should match the type and targeted (current and/or potential) members of the institution.

All these classes of influencers - perhaps with the exception of the celebrities - are most likely to be found in every parish. That leaves as the task of the persons in charge of church communication to locate and identify these persons in the parish environment, and approach them with respective plea for support.

3.6.3.4 Event Marketing

As significant church events, the German Catholic Congress (Deutscher Katholikentag) and the World Youth Day (Weltjugendtag) shall be mentioned. The German Catholic Congress[273] is a multiday meeting of prevalently Catholic Christians that has been taking place since 1848 and is held since 1950 biannually on a rotational basis always in a different diocese. The event is organized by the Central Committee of German Catholics (ZdK). In contrast the World Youth Day is an international meeting for youth and young adults between 14 and 30 years of age from all over the world.[274] It dates back to the initiative of Pope John Paul II. who during the Holy Year of Salvation of 1983 invited youth initially for 1984 and 1985 to an international youth meeting in Rome and subsequently organized the first World Youth Day in 1986. In different host countries, in the meantime as many as millions of young people have been taking part in the concluding church services of the World Youth Day.

---

273 cf. ZENTRALKOMITEE DER DEUTSCHEN KATHOLIKEN: *Deutscher Katholikentag.* [retrieved on 2018-04-30] Available from: http://www.katholikentag.de
274 cf. DEUTSCHE BISCHOFSKONFERENZ, Arbeitsstelle für Jugendseelsorge: *WJT – Weltjugendtag.* [retrieved on 2018-04-30] Available from: http://www.wjt.de/

According to Klenk (2013), 95 percent of media professionals fully or rather agree with the statement that[275] "the Church should approach young people more consistently and actively via personal contact (youth and adult pastoral) and through events (such as the "Long Night of Churches")". This underlines the particular significance of event marketing as an interface for target group appeal through media-based and interpersonal communication. For this purpose, young event formats need to be developed that would fit the increasingly different expectations of the various milieus.

Ultimately, every religious service may be seen from a marketer perspective as an event with excellent multimedia mix, as church services consist depending on occasion and the visitor's individual perception of consoling, motivating, joyous, pensive or even irate words of address, a special and varied assortment of songs and music (classical church music, Gregorian chants, sacral pop), vivid play of colours (liturgical colours as seen e.g. on robes, plant and floral decorations), smells (plants and flowers, incense), light effects (candles, lighting) etc. It is no accident that people, including those distanced from the Church or the Christian body of thought, flock on various festive occasions in relatively substantial numbers in particular to Catholic churches. Especially for these core practices of the Catholic faith, it is vital to align both in language terms and conceptually as regards designing the rites to the lifestyle and experience worlds of the younger generations with their often entirely different perceptions.

---

[275] KLENK, Christian (2013): *Zustand und Zukunft katholischer Medien*. Ibidem, p. 89.

4 Objectives, Methodology and the Research Methods of the Dissertation

4.1 Objectives of the Scientific Effort

The present study aims to contribute to clarifying the question how to ideally design church communication to successfully approach church-connected groups in population with higher education, here on the example of Catholic Corporates, and to win these over for purposes of the Church.

The main objective of the examination thus is to explore the current state of communication of Catholic parishes with their graduate and student and members on the example of members of Catholic student associations under the umbrella of the Cartel Confederation of the Catholic German Student Associations (CV): how is the communication mix and the range of offers of the parishes perceived by these members? With what specific expectations, communication preferences and with what information behaviour these special members interact with their parish?

Further the examination is meant as a contribution on the relationship between religiousness and affinity to church of Catholic academics and their support potential for voluntary engagement in church contexts.

Finally from this, concrete areas are to be derived in need of action such as the need of communication to explain or promote parish offers and to design targeted church programs, as well as to recruit voluntary helpers from the ranks of Catholic Corporates.

4.2 Methodology and Research Methods

4.2.1 Examination Subject and Structure of the Dissertation

The examination subject of this thesis is marketing and marketing communication of parishes of the Roman Catholic Church in Germany with a view to its activities and offers and perception thereof by church-connected groups in population with higher education on the example of Catholic students and academics – members of Catholic associations.

For better comprehension of the role of the Roman Catholic Church in Germany in society, firstly its structure, its attributes and its unique form of financing in the global church context as represented by the "church tax" as well as the current challenges and issues this largest German community of faith is faced with (see Chapter 1 – The Roman Catholic Church in Germany) were outlined. Special focus in the effort was on the progressive, mainly demographically and socially driven decline in membership and its consequences for the organization of the Church facilities and establishments.

In the following Chapter 2, the comprehensive activities were outlined of the Catholic Church including its parishes and charitable and social facilities from a business economic viewpoint, highlighting their structural analogies and analogies in the scope of their operations with non-profit organizations and exploring the specific attributes of the Catholic Church in Germany as a socio-cultural non-profit organization.[276] The scientific status of this debate around the synthesis of the church and non-profit organizations (the church as a "socio-cultural non-profit organization") was explored in detail in reference to the Fribourg Management Model for Non-Profit Organizations. Finally, the insights gained from the examination were condensed with a view to church marketing communication.

Chapter 3 (Church Marketing) firstly dealt with clarification of church marketing as a term and presented successful concepts of church marketing communication using examples from the USA and Germany that was followed by a specification of church marketing objectives and bundles thereof and church target groups. Finally in reference to the classical "4Ps", the church marketing mix was outlined with a particular focus on the communication tools.

This Chapter 4 summarizes the objectives, methodology and research methods of this thesis and subsequently posits the hypotheses alongside the core question as to how to ideally design church communication in order to successfully approach Catholic Corporates.

The bundles of hypotheses are verified or rejected in the empirical part of this thesis (Chapter 5) by means of an online survey.

As regards the survey sample concept, this thesis builds on the notion of social capital and social engagement of German citizens: a key structural attribute of social capital

---

[276] LICHSTEINER, Hans et al. (2015): *Das Freiburger Management-Modell für Nonprofit-Organisationen.* Ibidem, p.19, and also: SALAMON, Lester M., ANHEIER, Helmut K. (1996): The International Classification of Nonprofit Organizations: ICNPO-Revision 1. Ibidem, p. 20.

is support of, or membership in, volunteer organizations (non-profit organizations, NPO). As the core determinants of social engagement in this respect, the level of education, affiliation with a particular social class, occupation, social integration, religiousness, gender and age apply of the voluntarily engaging person.

From a detailed analysis of these factors, the special role is derived of Catholic academics for social capital in Germany. Based on this in Chapter 5.2, this special role of Catholic academics is discussed on the example of members of the largest European confederation of academics (CV), and finally sustained with empirical evidence concerning their relationship with the Catholic Church, their perception of and communication with church establishments as well as their voluntary engagement.

Chapter 6 finally summarizes the conclusions with a view to the objectives of this thesis.

From the above discussion, the structure of this thesis thus looks as follows:

Figure 4-1: Dissertation Structure

①

The Roman-Catholic Church in Germany

Structure, Principal Features, Financing

The Problem: Ongoing Decline in Membership

②

Church and Business Economics

The „Third Sector": Non-Profit Organizations

The Catholic Church as Socio-Cultural NPO

NPO Marketing, NPO Communication

③

Church Marketing

Origin of Church Marketing, Definitions, Samples

Objectives/Target Groups of Church Marketing and Marketing Communication

Church Marketing Mix and Communication Mix

④

Objectives, Methodology and Research Methods of the Dissertation

Research Question and Deriving of the Hypotheses

⑤

Results and Discussion

Quantitative Survey among Catholic Academics and Students

Presentation and Discussion of the Results

Recommendations, Further Research questions

⑥

Conclusion

4.2.2 Methodology and the Research Methods

The actual exploration of the thesis subject took place in two phases:

In the first explorative phase, there was research of scientific literature on the topics given in Fig. 4-2. Initially, a systematic research was performed of German publications by churches or by church-related sources on business economic, marketing and communication topics. Among the findings, there is a substantially larger volume of available scientific literature in the Protestant environment as compared to the Catholic side, not least because the Protestant Church in Germany has been performing empirical surveys among its members ("KMU") in about ten year-intervals already since 1972. The respective evaluation results and practical and theological interpretations of these are readily made available to the general public.[277]

Figure 4-2: Research of Literature

Topic	Relevance Criteria
Church: religion, faith, religious community, the parish, the church community	- Business economics, management, coaching, human resources - Brand, marketing, communication, information, distribution, media - Scientific merit of the publication or contribution
Marketing: brand, communication, advertising and promotion, working with the press and the public, PR, public affairs, media, the Internet	- Relevance of the publication to the church - Case examples of religious or social relevance, or relevance to the church or NPOs
Society: pluralism, differentiation, secularization	- Leaving the church, evangelization and new evangelization, mission - Social milieus
Social capital: voluntary engagement and engagement in social matters, voluntary functions, volunteer organizations and non-profit organizations	- Relevance of the publication to the church - Marketing, communication, promotion to recruit new members, fundraising - Socio-economic factors; income, level of education, religiousness, milieu

---

[277] VETTER, Martin: Ein halbes Jahrhundert KMU. In: *Praktische Theologie*, Volume 51 (3), 2016, pp. 133-140.

Due to the lack of sufficient scientific literature specifically on Catholic marketing and communication themes, the domestic scope of the examination was extended by the English (UK and the US) language areas. Not least by virtue of the US missionary movement in the mid-1960s, this particular language area boasts a comprehensive pool of pertinent scientific literature on the topic of 'parish growth' alongside a broad variety of practical guides[278]. In this sense, pertinent marketing literature was searched for contributions of relevance to the church.

From the rich variety of charitable and social activities of the church and the groups of persons acting in support of the church, complex relationships became exposed between religiousness and affinity to the church, and between socio-economic factors on the one hand and voluntary engagement of different groups in population on the other. Due to this, changes in German society particularly concerning social capital were researched.

The information collected in the research of literature was further extended over the course of interviews with certified professionals on the above topics plus the subjects of sociology, civic associations and associations of Catholic academics.[279] The respective questions aimed primarily at identifying church concepts on the topic of "Marketing and Communication"[280] and on the role of academic target groups in church life and activities of the church[281].

---

[278] cf. Chapter 3.3.1 herein.

[279] Here the author would like to express gratitude to the following experts for their invaluable support (in alphabetical order):

Bräkling, Elmar, Prof. Dr.; University of Koblenz, Gen. Business Admin., esp. Procurement and Logistics

Dörnemann, Michael, Msgr. Dr.; Canon of the Diocese of Essen, Germany

Frericks, Georg; Business Consultant with MDG GmbH, Munich, Germany

Grütering, Michael, Dr.; former Student's Priest / Dean em., Wuppertal/Germany

Ottawa, Marco; Head of Secondary and Special Research Market Research, Telekom, Bonn/Germany

Rietz, Christian, Prof. Dr.; University od Education Heidelberg/Ger., Educational and Social Sciences

Speck, Manfred; President of KAD (Catholic Academic Work Germany), Bensheim/Germany

Štarchoň, Peter, Prof. Mgr., PhD.; Comenius University Bratislava/Slowakia, Faculty of Management

Thomé, Martin, Dr.; European Research Organizations, Federal Ministry of Education and Research, Bonn/Germany

Weiskorn, Richard; Secretary of the CV, Bad Honnef/Germany

Wiggins, Jonathon L., Ph.D.; CARA Research Associate, Georgetown University, Washington/USA

[280] cf. Chapter 3.3.4 (Parish Development on the Example of German (Arch-)Dioceses), 3.4.3 (Stewardship, Providing Systematic Support), and 3.5.2 (Milieu-specific Orientation of Church Action)

[281] See in particular Chapter 5.1.1.3 (Milieu-specific Classification of Catholic Academics)

In the second descriptive phase, the insights gained from secondary research with a particular focus on surveys examining religious and church-related issues as well as pertinent issues of sociology and the sociology of religion, parish surveys, studies among members of German and US churches as well as national and transnational studies on religiousness and concerning value orientations in general.

Respective selection criteria primarily included scientific merit of and quality of the samples used in the studies. Examples of such studies include the various surveys by the Allensbacher Institut für Demoskopie, the MDG-Trendmonitor survey on "Religious Communication", the German Survey on Volunteering (Deutsche Freiwilligensurvey) and not least surveys among members of the dioceses of Essen, Münster und Rottenburg-Stuttgart[282].

From these principal stages of the work, the theoretical part of the thesis ensued as well as the research question provided in the following Chapter 4.2.3 alongside the derived hypotheses.

In follow-up to the theoretical part and the hypotheses, finally an empirical study was devised on the relationship of current and prospective academics with their faith and the Catholic Church as well as on their opinions about the offers of and communication with their parishes.

For the purpose, Catholic academics and students from a variety of professional fields and occupations were surveyed on their religiousness and affinity to the Church, on information and communication by their parishes as well as on their views on life of their parishes. These included in particular those persons who had experienced an additional socialization phase in the Catholic environment via membership in confessional student associations during their studies and were voluntarily engaging in church, social and other general society contexts.

---

[282] cf. INSTITUT FÜR DEMOSKOPIE ALLENSBACH (1992): *Kirchenaustritte*, ibidem. | SCHULZ, Rüdiger et al. (2010): *MDG-Trendmonitor*, ibidem. | TESCH-RÖMER, Clemens et al. (2016): *Der Deutsche Freiwilligensurvey 2014*, ibidem. | EBERHARDT, Tim et al.: *Zufriedenheitsstudie "Katholiken des Bistums Münster"*. Münster: Münster Research Institute, 2015 | BISTUM ESSEN: *Kirchenaustritt hat viele verschiedene Gründe*. [retrieved on 2018-04-30] Available from: http://zukunftsbild.bistum-essen.de/die-bistums-projekte/die-bistumsprojekte/initiative-fuer-den-verbleib-in-der-kirche/kirchenstudie/ergebnisse-stimmungsbild-und-interviews/ | APP, Reiner et al.: *Zukunftshorizont Kirche: Was Katholiken von ihrer Kirche erwarten. Eine repräsentative Studie*. Ostfildern: Grünewald, 2014.

For these reasons, the online survey focused on members of the Cartel Confederation of the Catholic German Student Associations ("Cartellverband", abbreviated: "CV") that was founded already in 1856.[283]

More detailed information on the survey method (how the data were obtained, the sources used, evaluations methods, interpretation of results etc.) is provided in Chapters 5.1.2 to 5.1.4 of this thesis.

The terms 'Catholic Corporates', 'CV-member(s)' and 'CVer(s)' used in the following chapters are meant as synonyms for the exclusively male individual members of CV-affiliated student associations. These in turn split into 'Active' students and graduated 'Seniors'.

4.2.3 Research Question and Derivation of the Hypotheses

The present study discusses and answers the following research question:

**"How must church communication be ideally designed in order to
successfully approach Catholic Corporates?"**

From this research question and the theoretical elaborations on the nature and business economic classification of the Roman Catholic Church in Germany as well as on the church marketing mix and communication mix, special hypotheses ensued that are listed in three thematically nested groups in the following parts and operationalized for the empirical survey in Chapter 5.

Due to lack of specific professional literature and studies on the subjects of "parishes / (marketing) communication / target groups with substantial resources", the final decision about the hypotheses was made rather in an exploratory/heuristic manner. Due to this, a final statistical evaluation of the hypotheses in the prevalently descriptive discussion of the results of this study is refrained from.

4.2.3.1 *Hypotheses on Religiousness and Affinity to Church*

There is no generally binding definition of the term "religiousness". In the sense of "belief in a higher power or a god", religiousness of a person is determined by their cultural and/or social environment and their pertinent possibilities to develop within

---

[283] The online survey was first tested using a questionnaire survey on a focus group and subsequently condensed in content. Its evaluation ultimately served to verify the posited hypotheses. More details on the survey method are provided in Chapter 5.1.2. f.

that context a personal conception of the world and of oneself[284]. This may, though not necessarily, happen within a community of faith as a person may well be religious or a believer without being connected to a community of faith and its culture.

In the Catholic Church, religiousness of its members manifests *inter alia* by regular, church-imposed participation in worship. The frequency of attendance at church services further also is deemed an indicator of readiness and/or potential for voluntary engagement[285]:

HR1: The prevalent part of Catholic Corporates regularly participate in church services.

By virtue of their membership in Catholic student associations, young men undergo over the course of their studies an additional, Catholic socialization phase. However, in particular late adolescence and/or the age group around 20 years of age is deemed the potential starting point of an alienation from the Church[286]. Through an additional Catholic socialization in this age, Catholic Corporates may exhibit closer affinity to the Church than other Catholics:

HR2: Catholic Corporates are above-average faithful to the Church.

Based on religiousness and affinity to the Church, also tendencies of Catholic Corporates to leave the Church are smaller than in other Catholics:

HR3: The prevalent part of Catholic Corporates have not yet been considering leaving the church.

4.2.3.2 Hypotheses on Information and Communication

Where Catholic Corporates count among regular churchgoers, the classical, "church typical" information channels as well as oral announcements in worship (publicandum), notices on announcement boards at church buildings and parish letters are the primarily perceived means of communication:

HK1: The classical church media constitute the primarily perceived information channels for Catholic Corporates.

By virtue of their studies, students and academics are familiar with targeted research of information. Given this, Catholic Corporates that are attached to the Church get

---

[284] See on this topic among others: PICKEL, Gert: *Religionsmonitor. Religiosität im internationalen Vergleich.* Further POLLACK, Detlef, MÜLLER, Olaf: *Religionsmonitor. Religiosität und Zusammenhalt in Deutschland.* Gütersloh: Verlag Bertelsmann Stiftung, 2013.

[285] BENNETT, Matthew R.: Religiosity and Formal Volunteering in Global Perspective. In: HUSTINX, Lesley, VON ESSEN, Johan, HAERS, J. / MELS, S. (ed.): *Religion and Volunteering. Complex, Contested and Ambiguous Relationships.* Cham: Springer International Publishing, 2015, p. 87.

[286] INSTITUT FÜR DEMOSKOPIE ALLENSBACH (1992): *Kirchenaustritte.* Ibidem, p. 8.

their information on activities and offers of their parish prevalently in own effort and in a targeted (proactive) manner:

HK2: The prevalent majority of Catholic Corporates get their information on church activities and offers proactively.

As a result of information research and processing of information having been revolutionized by the Internet and given the rise of networking of people through mobile communication technologies and social media, Catholic Corporates have been preferring electronic and online communication channels over the classical church media:[287]

HK3: The communication mix of parishes does not match the communication preferences of Catholic Corporates.

For Catholic Corporates who are particularly attached to the Church and get their information on church matters in own effort, a high communication readiness may be presumed concerning matters of the Church and parishes. This implies that:

HK4: The prevalent part of Catholic Corporates actively informs third parties on the events organized by the parish.

Given their affinity to the Church, their interest in information and their communication readiness, Catholic Corporates should be able to comprehensively assess church offers and the life of parishes. From this it may be posited that:

HK5: Catholic Corporates are comprehensively informed on the specific activities and offers of their parishes.

The prevalent affiliation of academics with higher social classes (milieus)[288] gives rise to their stringent quality requirements on the education and other schemes provided by parishes. The generally rather low-threshold offers of parishes might be unlikely to meet this requirement. That means:

HK6: The expectations of Catholic Corporates as regards offers of their parishes are not fully met.

The services of the Catholic Church primarily focus on the needs of handicapped people or of those in need of help and less on the special – often intellectual –

---

[287] 72.8 percent of men with tertiary education use in their voluntary engagement the Internet: cf.: TESCH-RÖMER, Clemens (ed.), SIMONSONS, Julia, VOGEL, Claudia: *Freiwilliges Engagement in Deutschland. Der Deutsche Freiwilligensurvey 2014.* Berlin: Deutsches Zentrum für Altersfragen (DZA) / Bundesministerium für Familie, Senioren, Frauen und Jugend (BMSFSJ), 2016. – Table annex, Table 11-10, p. 132: Percentages of persons using the Internet for their voluntary activities in a time comparison by gender, age and education.

[288] See Chapter 5.1.1.3 as well as CALMBACH et al. (2013): *MDG-Milieuhandbuch 2013.* Ibidem, p. 95 ff.

interests of the generally socially and economically better positioned members of the population such as academics.[289] From this it follows that:

HK7: Catholic Corporates desire in offers of their parishes in particular specific education and discussion events.

Shrinking membership and the resulting mergers of parishes and church closures instil particularly in traditionally and conservatively-oriented environments uncertainty that manifests in a higher need of informative communication and an urge to be given perspective. This means a new need of communication:

HK8: The expectations of Catholic Corporates as regards communication of Church content and Church aims are not fully met.

4.2.3.3 Hypotheses on Voluntary Engagement

The "double" Catholic socialization of members of CV-affiliated student associations in their childhood and during studies goes along with comprehensive knowledge of and experience with Church establishments and organizations. From this with a view to the generally high engagement potential of Catholics[290], it follows that:

HF1: Catholic Corporates are above-average ecclesiastically engaged.

HF2: Catholic Corporates strive also in their engagement in student associations for close cooperation with the Church and/or their parish.

The Christian general attitude goes along *inter alia* with a particular affinity for those in need and handicapped persons. As most academics in Germany have better professional and financial standing than other population groups, they bring in also in the Church environment their social contribution. This implies that:

HF3: Catholic Corporates engage in Church contexts mainly in matters of charity projects and social service projects.

Due to affiliation of Catholic academics with their particular social environment (milieu), their voluntary engagement may be assumed to be driven mainly by the motivation to actively shape society, manifesting in cultural and political engagements:

HF4: Alongside honorary offices in the Church, Catholic Corporates mainly assume cultural and political tasks.

---

[289] cf. Chapter 3.5.2.

[290] OFFE, Claus, FUCHS, Susanne: Schwund des Sozialkapitals? Der Fall Deutschland. In: PUTNAM, Robert D. (2001): *Gesellschaft und Gemeinsinn*. Ibidem, p. 417, p. 445.

In reference to the bundling of the hypotheses according to topics, subsequently the questions were devised for the empirical survey that builds upon the theoretical part and the hypotheses of this dissertation:[291]

A fundamental prerequisite to successful communication is affinity in terms of interest in or even affiliation of the target group to be approached with the institution initiating the contact or engaging in promotional activities[292]. This resulted in the first part of the questionnaire that is elaborated on in detail in Chapter 5.1.4.1 (Questions on Religious Orientation and Practice).

Along the same lines, communication may only succeed where the communicated content is relevant, i.e. appealing and valuable (see Part 3 of the questionnaire in Chapter 5.1.4.3: Evaluation of the Parish Life) and pertinent information mainly is conveyed by those media that are preferred by the target group approached and hence ideally used extensively and on a proactive basis[293]. The perception of the media used and the specific preferences towards these were explored in the second part of the questionnaire and mutually correlated (see Chapter 5.1.4.2: Information and Communication of the Parish).

The socio-economic factors of a target group, its affinity for a certain topic or institution as well as pertinent communication are the key determinants of the form and intensity of a potential voluntary engagement, which was addressed in the fourth part of the questionnaire, "Voluntary Engagement" (Chapter 5.1.4.4).

---

[291] See Chapter 5.1.4 (The Online Questionnaire). Also includes more detailed information on how the individual questions were derived and how the sets of questions are logically structured.

[292] cf. Chapter 3.5: Ecclesiastical Target Groups.

[293] See Chapter 3.6.3.1: The Church Media Portfolio, here in particular Figures 3-14, 3-15 and 3-11.

5 Results and Discussion

5.1 Quantitative Survey of Catholic Academics and Students

To verify the hypotheses of this thesis, an online survey of Catholic students and academics was performed.

5.1.1 Concept of the Random Sample

5.1.1.1 Catholic Academics as a Relevant Target Group

The Catholic Church has always been ascribing great weight to science; today, there are Catholic theological faculties at eleven state universities in Germany. Further also there is a Catholic University (Eichstätt), three diocesan theological faculties run by the Church, and five monastic tertiary education institutions. To train teachers of religion, there are 34 Catholic theological institutions and tertiary education facilities available nationwide in Germany. In the field of science and research, the Catholic Church runs several societies and supports via the Cusanuswerk diocesan scholarship foundation and the Catholic Academic Foreign Service (KAAD) about 1,500 highly talented students and graduates. Alongside "as Catholic establishments in the spheres of universities and science, there is particularly the presence of Catholic university/student parishes and student associations". [294]

Though Catholic student associations and other academic confederations are officially recognized on part of the Church as "Catholic establishments", their multilateral and often excellent networking interconnections within society and the socio-economic status of these church members with higher levels of education – hence their activatable/usable potential as well as that of their associations for charitable and social activities – is not being used by the Church and its parishes. The remarks of diocesan officials on the future of Catholic associations to the tune of "These social forms lack any greater appeal anymore", even though their themes would still continue to be important, only confirm this[295].

---

[294] GERMAN BISHOPS' CONFERENCE: *Science and higher Education.* [retrieved on 2017-12-22] Available from: http://www.dbk.de/en/katholische-kirche/katholische-kirche-deutschland/aufgaben-kath-kirche/bildung-wissenschaft/hochschule/

[295] cf. WULLHORST, Heinrich: Leuchtturm oder Kerzenstummel? Die katholischen Verbände in Deutschland. Paderborn: Bonifatius Verlag, 2017, p. 11.

Hence in the following parts, the relationship is explored between socio-economic factors, the "social capital" and voluntary engagement of Catholic academics and the special potential is outlined of this target group.

5.1.1.2 Social Capital and Voluntary Engagement of Catholic Academics

The term "social capital" generally is used by sociologists in describing and evaluating the conception of social groups and the relationships and interactions among and within those, and/or among their members.

The term is ascribed to US school inspector Lyda Judson Hanifan (1920) who explained [296]: "We do not refer to real estate or to personal property or to cash, but rather to that in life which tends to make these tangible substances count for most in the daily lives of a people; namely, good will, fellowship, sympathy, and social intercourse among the individuals and families who make up a social unit (...) The individual is helpless socially, if left to himself. Even the association of the members of one's family fails to satisfy that desire which every normal individual has of being with his fellows, of being a part of a larger group than the family. If he comes into contact with his neighbours, there will be an accumulation of social capital, which may immediately satisfy his social needs and which may bear a social potentiality sufficient for the substantial improvement of life in the whole community." Hanifan emphasizes in this respect both the individual and the community-wide benefits of social capital: „The community as a whole will benefit by the cooperation of all its parts, while the individual will find in his associations the advantages of the help, the sympathy, and the fellowship of his neighbour ..."

Hanifan's early insights and his concept failed to gain a broader recognition in the decades that came thereafter. The number and the variety of themes of scientific contributions on social capital only started rising from about 1995 as sociologist and political scientist Robert David Putnam[297] concluded on the basis of his comprehensive body of research work of more than 20 years he did in Italy the erosion of the US social capital and consequently was seriously questioning the future of US democracy and civil society.[298] Pertinent scientific contributions that have seen exponential growth since Putnam's publications of 1995 testify to comprehensive variations in relevant attributes of civil society that constitute the

---

[296] HANIFAN, Lyda Judson: *The Community Center*. New York: Silver, Burnett & Company, 1920, p. 78.

[297] PUTNAM, Robert D., LEONARDI, Robert, NANETTI, Raffaella: *Making Democracy Work: Civic traditions in Modern Italy*. Princeton: University Press, 1993.

[298] PUTNAM, Robert D.: Turning In, Turning Out: The strange Disappearance of Social Capital in America. In: *Political Science and Politics XXVIII/4*, 1995, pp. 664-683.

landscape of social capital over space and time, affecting in the process the health status of democracies and parishes alike as well as of individuals themselves.[299] Putnam (2001) confirms Hanifan's early insights with a view to both private, or "internal", and public, or "external" benefits of social capital and concludes that social capital can be a private and public good at the same time.

For a detailed analysis of social capital, the key aspect is that it combines three elements:[300]

a)   Density and reach of community life outside the family;

b)   Mutual social trust of members that arises as a result of volunteering and other active involvement, and finally

c)   The orientation to the community values and norms of mutual support (reciprocity) this gives rise to.

An important structural feature of social capital is support of, and/or membership in, volunteer organizations. These may include for example sports or cultural associations, or groups and establishments of Catholic parishes, but also student associations, academic societies and confederations.

As for engaged individuals who join their forces in volunteer organizations, the most important determinants of their social engagement are their level of education, social class, occupation, social inclusion, gender and age.[301] With a view to the objectives of this thesis, of particular significance that warrants a more detailed investigation is the social capital of persons who have become as students members of a student association and, on the basis of this special Catholic and social socialization instance and/or as academics, socially active in their social environment.

The data processed by Westle/Gabriel (2008) from a study by the Konrad Adenauer Foundation imply[302] that in volunteer organizations, in particular working men engage up to 65 years of age with A-level equivalent (German Abitur), or university graduates, and coming from the upper middle class or upper-class social environment. This conclusion has been principally confirmed by the German Survey

---

[299]   PUTNAM, Robert D.: *Gesellschaft und Gemeinsinn*. Ibidem, p. 20.

[300]   WESTLE, Bettina, GABRIEL Oscar W. (ed.): *Sozialkapital. Eine Einführung*. Baden-Baden: Nomos, 2008, p. 12.

[301]   KUNZ, Volker, WESTLE, Bettina, ROSSTEUTSCHER, Sigfrid: Sozialkapital in Deutschland. In: WESTLE, Bettina et al. (2008): *Sozialkapital*. Ibidem, p. 51.

[302]   Ibidem, p. 62.

on Volunteering 2014 according to the results of which men up to 65 in vocational training or education, or in gainful employment already, with "Abitur" or "FH-Reife" (a form of academic degree from technical colleges in Germany), or university graduates, volunteer to a significantly higher degree than other groups in the population.[303]

Positive correlations between household income and/or the labour market status and the readiness to voluntarily engage in associations as well as between formal education and social capital, and between completed education and the readiness to engage have been proven numerous times already since the 1950s.[304]

In addition to these socio-economic determinants of social capital, Offe/Fuchs (2001) state the positive correlation between religious orientation, plus the extent of religious engagement, and social capital, and conclude with a particular reference to the Roman Catholic Church that "the Catholic religious doctrine imprints on believers (to an undeniably higher degree than most Protestant varieties of Christendom) an ethic of compassion, as well as an active interest in the well-being of fellow believers in a parish. (...) Religious engagement generally is a very strong predictor of membership in associations in the social sphere and also resonates with the theological emphasis on the duty of a practicing Christian to serve fellow human beings."[305] Many studies that have been presented in this context since the 1990s refer to the "Conviction and Community Theory" by Wuthnow (1991), according to which religious affiliation and religiousness affect social engagement and volunteer work in two different ways, specifically through the believer's conviction, and through their community, which is identifiable with a parish, that acts accordingly..[306]

In his empirical examination of the relationship between religious attitudes and engagement in volunteering initiatives, Hoof (2010) reaches *inter alia* the conclusion that those who get involved in the church as volunteers bring along a high level of

---

[303] TESCH-RÖMER, Clemens et al.: *Freiwilliges Engagement in Deutschland. Der Deutsche Freiwilligensurvey 2014*. Ibidem, pp. 438-441 ff.

[304] OFFE, Claus, FUCHS, Susanne: Schwund des Sozialkapitals? Der Fall Deutschland. In: PUTNAM, Robert D. (2001): *Gesellschaft und Gemeinsinn*. Ibidem, p. 417.

[305] Ibid., p. 445.

[306] See KLÖCKNER, Jennifer: *Freiwillige Arbeit in Gemeinnützigen Vereinen: Eine vergleichende Studie von Wohlfahrts- und Migrantenorganisationen*. Wiesbaden: Springer Fachmedien, 2015, p. 210, under reference to WUTHNOW Robert: Acts of Compassion: Caring for Others and Helping Ourselves. Princeton: Princeton University Press, 1991, p. 121 ff.

religiousness, meaning that they deem religion an important factor in their life and that they regularly participate in church events.[307]

Bennett (2015) confirms these findings at the international level in that he under a comprehensive secondary research effort evaluated the data of a total of 165,625 persons of many different confessions in 113 countries and supplied on this basis a proof that "people who attend a religious service in the past week are nearly twice (1.87 times, exp (0.625)) as likely to volunteer relative to those who do not attend a religious service (...) This suggests that the difference between the religious and the non-religious is to a certain extent due to service attendance".[308] His auxiliary assumption that the growing variety in religions as observable mainly in highly differentiated societies as a result of immigration and pluralism also is associated with a higher rate of voluntary engagement only has been confirmed to an extent in the multinational Religionsmonitor survey by the Bertelsmann Foundation.[309]

Under the German Survey on Volunteering (FWS) 2014, 28,690 phone interviews were performed and evaluated. On the basis that positive correlations between education/income/religion and social capital can be deemed certain, the FWS 2014 results can be summarized with the following selection of statements with a view to social capital of Catholic academics also including gender-specific differences:

a)   43.6% of the resident population in Germany aged 14 and older engage as volunteers.

b)   The volunteering ratio has risen by about ten percentage points over the past 15 years; since the last survey in 2009, there has been a dynamic growth observable mainly in the young part of the population.

c)   Women volunteer at 41.5 percent less often than men with 45.7 percent, however the share of female volunteers has been on the increase. In the tops spots in voluntary engagement, there are the age groups of between 14 and 29 and between 30 and 49 year olds.[310]

---

[307] HOOF, Matthias: Freiwilligenarbeit und Religiosität. Der Zusammenhang von religiösen Einstellungen und ehrenamtlichem Engagement. Berlin: LIT-Verlag Dr. W. Hopf, 2010, p. 312.

[308] BENNETT, Matthew R.: Religiosity and Formal Volunteering in Global Perspective. In: HUSTINX, Lesley et al.: Religion and Volunteering. Ibid., p. 87.

[309] cf. TRAUNMÜLLER, Richard: Religiöse Vielfalt, Sozialkapital und gesellschaftlicher Zusammenhalt. (Religionsmonitor) Gütersloh: Verlag Bertelsmann Stiftung, 2014.

[310] TESCH-RÖMER, Clemens et al. (2016): Der Deutsche Freiwilligensurvey 2014. Ibidem, p. 85.

d) The key fields of voluntary engagement are sports and physical activity (43.7%), culture and music (19.2%), social activities (15.1%), schools and kindergartens (13.7%) as well as church and religion (12.3%).[311]

e) Organized volunteering services are the most prevalent in the age group of between 18 and 29 year olds with high education. In this particular group, one in ten persons has participated in such services.[312]

f) Members of the Catholic Church and of the Protestant Church volunteer more frequently as compared to Muslims and non-denominational persons.

g) Men and persons with higher or high education are more likely to be ready to volunteer and accordingly are more frequently members in associations or charitable organizations.[313]

h) More than a fourth of the resident population in Germany above 14 years of age (26.3%, men more frequently than women) provide material support in their social neighbourhood outside their family.

i) Persons with high education provide support to their neighbours and their friends and acquaintances more frequently than persons with medium or lower education, nevertheless with less average amount of time spent.[314]

j) More than a fourth of all volunteers has a managing or supervisory role, with men still engaging in managerial or supervisory activities substantially more often than women in 2014.

k) There is a local aspect to volunteering: voluntary engagement in Germany mainly is directed at one's region of residence.[315]

l) Persons with higher education prevail in preparatory and administrative activities, in networking as well as in pedagogic supervision of or guidance to groups of persons.[316]

m) Volunteers with high education engage as compared to those with lower or medium education more frequently on behalf of children and adolescents. Also of persons with higher education, a comparatively high number indicate to engage on behalf of another, not further specified target group.[317]

---

[311] Ibidem, p. 110.
[312] Ibidem, p. 175.
[313] Ibidem, p. 233.
[314] Ibidem, p. 251.
[315] Ibidem, p. 295.
[316] Ibidem, p. 306.
[317] Ibidem, p. 321.

n) More than a half of volunteers spend with their activity up to two hours weekly. Men indicate more weekly hours than women. Men and older persons indicate more often than average to be volunteering daily or several times a week.[318]

o) Almost a fourth of volunteers engage in an activity that requires special training or education. Men in this respect engage in activities that necessitate a specific qualification substantially more often than women.

p) Two fifths of all volunteers have already taken part in training events one or more times as part of their engagement, thereof a higher share of men than women. (...) In doing so, volunteers with higher education benefit the most from the skills and competences acquired in this way.[319]

q) Men are recruited more frequently by leaders in organizations than women. In contrast, a higher share of women than men have found their way to volunteering through experience in the family, or in own initiative.[320]

r) Both the attained level of education in school and of vocational on-the-job education causally relate to voluntary engagement. The highest proportions of volunteers are among persons with completed technical college or university education (54.1%).[321]

s) Persons who find their financial position very good engage at 50.0% almost twice as much than persons who view their financial standing as very poor (26.9%), with the assessed socio-economic variables having cumulative effects.[322]

t) For people with high education, constraints of daily life, poor subjective health and poor satisfaction with life have a much less pronounced effect on the probability of volunteering.[323]

u) Irrespective of their education and financial, social and health resources, people who deem as important the values of "solidarity" or "creativity"

---

[318] Ibidem, p. 329.

[319] Ibidem, p. 349.

[320] Klöckner (2016) elaborates on this: "Only confessional volunteers in dedicated organizations who visit a church or mosque more often than average have come to their volunteering more frequently through leaders in organizations". For other volunteers, this direct approach effect has not been confirmed; cf. KLÖCKNER, Jennifer (2016), ibidem, p. 417.

[321] TESCH-RÖMER, Clemens et al. (2016), ibidem, p. 429.

[322] Ibidem.

[323] Ibidem, p. 455 as well as p. 464: "In the group of severely restricted persons with high education, the volunteering ratio is at 36.9% substantially higher than in the group of persons without a medical condition, but with low education (31.3%)."

volunteer relatively more often while people who appreciate the value of "security" volunteer relatively more rarely.[324]

v) Socially well-anchored people volunteer relatively more often, with trust in other people being more significant for engagement of the younger and older age groups as opposed to middle-aged persons.

w) In religious associations and state-run or municipal establishments, there are relatively more often contact persons for volunteers than in other types of organizations.[325]

x) Individually organized voluntary engagement has grown much more substantially than engagement in societies and associations. Church-related and other religious engagement has grown relatively fairly in comparison.[326]

y) In western Germany, the volunteering ratio in 2014 was at a total 44.8 percent while in eastern Germany at 38.5 percent. In both parts of the country, men volunteer more frequently than women, and students and persons with higher education relatively more often in terms of proportions than persons with medium and lower education.[327]

From the results of the German Survey on Volunteering 2014, it additionally follows that religiously-oriented men with high or higher education in direct comparison with women

• Have a higher readiness to engage in volunteering (g), and

• Actually volunteer more frequently (c);

• Join volunteer organizations more frequently (g);

• Provide more often material support in their social neighbourhood (h);

• Engage substantially more often in managerial and supervisory functions (j) and in this respect

• Are rather recruited by other persons/leaders than they become active in own initiative (q);

• Spend with their volunteering several hours a week (n), and

• Volunteer more often than average daily or several times a week (n);

---

[324] Ibidem, p. 475.
[325] Ibidem, p. 513.
[326] Ibidem, p. 523.
[327] Ibidem, p. 559.

- Carry out more frequently an activity that requires special qualifications (o), and finally

- Participate more often in training and education pertinent to their voluntary engagement (p).

This breakdown of voluntary engagement according to gender is relevant for purposes herein in as much as most student associations and confederations thereof have exclusively male membership, which allows to draw conclusions on the social capital of these social groups and organizations. For more detailed insights into the social group Catholic academics, the following chapter deals with milieu-specific classification of Catholic academics.

5.1.1.3 Milieu-specific Classification of Catholic Academics

In the 1960s, sociologist Mario Rainer Lepsius posited as the cause of the steady voting behaviour of Germans during the era of the German Empire (1871-1918) and the (interwar) Weimar Republic (1918-1933) four "social-moral milieus", namely the conservative-Protestant, the liberal-Protestant, the social-democratic and the Catholic milieu.[328] Specifically the Catholic milieu defined primarily through life and engagement of its members in their local parishes and so featuring strong inner cohesion forces was in his views practically the antipode at the time to the "godless" social-democratic milieu. After the "cultural war" between the German Empire headed by Imperial Chancellor Otto von Bismarck and the Catholic Church under Pope Pius IX. centered around the separation of church and state came to an end, the internal cohesion forces of the Catholic milieu gradually weakened. The consequent outlawing and/or subjugation in the Nazi era of the associations and societies that were vital for the cohesion in the Catholic milieu finally meant its dissolution. Despite a brief revitalization of the Catholic milieu with its landscape of societies and associations after World War II in response to both Nazism perceived as "godless" and to the "Cold War" with the communist states of the Eastern Bloc, the integrative power and influence of the Catholic milieu then was steadily dissipating over the course of the social upheavals of the 1960s, which rendered the old milieu structures soon meaningless. With the advent of the Sinus Milieus in early 1980s- and the SIGMA Milieus in early 1990s (see Chapter 4.2), today there are much more

---

[328] Comprehensive treatises of the trends in milieus in Germany can be found for example in: LEPSIUS, M. Rainer: Parteien und Sozialstruktur. In. LEPSIUS, Mario Rainer: Demokratie in Deutschland: soziologisch-historische Konstellationsanalysen; ausgewählte Aufsätze. Göttingen: Vandenhoeck & Ruprecht, 1993 | ANGENENDT, Arnold, DAMBERG, Wilhelm: Geschichte des Bistums Münster: Moderne und Milieu. Münster: Dialogverlag, 1998, p. 322 ff. | KLÖCKER, Michael: Religionen und Katholizismus, Bildung und Geschichtsdidaktik, Arbeiterbewegung; ausgewählte Aufsätze. Frankfurt am Main: Verlag Peter Lang, 2011.

varied options for analyses both from the perspectives of marketing and the sociology of religion.

For example a targeted evaluation of the database of the largest and representative market media survey in Germany, the "Best 4 Planning" (b4p 2016 III) survey by the Axel Springer, Hubert Burda Media and Gruner & Jahr publishing houses and the Bauer media groups facilitates a comparative analysis of social affiliations of Catholics and Catholic academics/students in terms of social groups not least with a view to the Sinus and SIGMA Milieus (cf. Fig. 5-1 and 5-2, next page). Here a general note is due that under the SIGMA Milieu definitions, there is a higher concentration of Catholics observable in the upper milieus. For students including Catholic students, these are naturally concentrated in the 'younger milieus', though the smaller number of cases for this particular target group does not permit any more detailed conclusions.[329]

Figure 5-1: SINUS Milieus in Different Population Groups of Germany 2016

SINUS Milieu	Men	Catholic Men	Male Academics	Male, Catholic Academics	Male Students	Male, Catholic Students
Established-Conservative Milieu	9,5 %	11,3 %	18,3 %	22,8 %	1,8 %	3,4 %
Liberal-Intellectual Milieu	7,1 %	7,5 %	16,4 %	18,4 %	1,3 %	2,5 %
High Achiever Milieu	8,5 %	8,8 %	13,2 %	14,1 %	2,4 %	3,1 %
New Middle Class Milieu	14,3 %	15,4 %	10,4 %	12,7 %	9,8 %	6,2 %
Movers and Shakers Milieu	8,9 %	7,7 %	11,9 %	9,7 %	36,1 %	43,3 %
Escapist Milieu	16,6 %	15,4 %	10,1 %	6,7 %	25,5 %	21,3 %
Social-Ecological Milieu	6,9 %	6,2 %	8,6 %	6,1 %	6,5 %	7,5 %
Traditional Milieu	9,7 %	12,7 %	3,4 %	4,4 %	1,1 %	3,9 %
Adaptive Pragmatic Milieu	9,1 %	7,5 %	4,8 %	3,5 %	13,2 %	5,7 %
Precarious Milieu	9,1 %	7,2 %	2,7 %	1,4 %	2,2 %	2,2 %

---

[329] B4P - BEST FOR PLANNING: b4p 2016 III [SIGMA data retrieved on 2017-08-23, own research] Available from: http://www.b4p.media/online-auswertung/ – SINUS-data received with kind permission of Sinus-Institut from MDS-service@axelspringer.net – Potential in total: 30,190 cases, 69.56 m, 100%; Potential of samples: Men: 14,767 cases, 34.03 m, 48.91% / Catholic men: 4,867 cases, 11.21 m, 16.12% / Male academics: 2,675 cases, 6.16 m, 8.86% / Male, Catholic academics: 798 cases, 1.84 m, 2.64% / Male students: 620 cases, 1.43 m, 2.05% / Male, Catholic students: 184 cases, 0.42 m, 0.61%; Used demographic parameters: [Gender = male] [Religious community = Catholic] [Education = study] [Occupation = student].

Figure 5-2: SIGMA Milieus in Different Population Groups of Germany 2016

SIGMA Milieu	Men	Catholic Men	Male Academics	Male, Catholic Academics	Male Students	Male, Catholic Students
Social Climber Segment	22,6 %	21,7 %	29,4 %	25,9 %	1,9 %	–
Upper Liberal Segment	7,2 %	6,8 %	19,8 %	22,8 %	0,6 %	–
Upper Conservative Segment	10,7 %	12,4 %	18,8 %	22,7 %	–	–
Postmodern Segment	10,2 %	8,9 %	11,2 %	11,0 %	60,4 %	57,7 %
Progressive Modern Mainstream	11,4 %	9,7 %	11,5 %	10,1 %	32,2 %	38,2 %
Conventional Modern Mainstream	7,9 %	8,4 %	6,0 %	6,4 %	0,7 %	–
Traditional Mainstream	7,2 %	9,8 %	0,5 %	0,5 %	–	–
Pragmatic Strivers	11,6 %	11,3 %	1,7 %	0,4 %	–	–
Counter Culture	7,5 %	7,5 %	0,5 %	0,2 %	4,3 %	4,1 %
Traditional Blue Collar Segment	3,7 %	3,6 %	0,6 %	–	–	–

Still, some milieu-specific conclusions can be drawn for male Catholic academics and students that can be paired with the following insights from the MDG-Sinus-Milieuhandbuch 2013 survey: [330]

- Relative to the entirety of all Catholic men, Catholic academics are substantially overrepresented in the Upper Liberal SIGMA Milieu with 22.8% (as compared to 6.8% for the former). A similar conclusion applies for the corresponding Liberal Intellectual Sinus Milieu at 18.4 vs. 7.5 percent, which overall has the largest share of university graduates.

- In the Upper Conservative SIGMA Milieu, Catholic academics also are substantially overrepresented at 22.7 percent versus 12.4% of all Catholic men. Here also the proportions in the Established Conservative Sinus Milieu are similar at 22.8% vs. 11.3%.

- In the Social Climber SIGMA Milieu that cuts across social levels, there is more than a fourth (25.9%) of Catholic academics vs. 29.4% of all male academics.[331] It may be presumed that the majority of these persons are located in the overlap between the Upper Conservative and Social Climber Segments of the SIGMA Milieus. No direct assignment is possible here to a specific Sinus Milieu, however

---

[330] cf. CALMBACH, Marc et al. (2013): MDG-Milieuhandbuch 2013. Ibidem, pp. 69-71: conservative established milieu, p. 79, 117: philosophy & the meaning of life, pp. 84, 122-123: faith & religion, pp. 95-96, 134: participation in church life, pp. 107-109: liberal-intellectual milieu.

[331] Yet in the previous year of 2015, the target group of "Catholic academics" was notably underrepresented in the Social Climber Segment with merely 20.7% as opposed to 25.4% of all academics; cf. B4P - BEST FOR PLANNING: b4p 2015 III [data retrieved on 2017-07-16, own research].

there are similarities with the status-oriented portions of the Established
Conservative Sinus Milieu as well as with the upper portions of the Socio-
ecological Sinus Milieu that is ascribed a high level of formal education; almost
a third of its members have an A-level equivalent or are university graduates.

- Another 11 percent of Catholic academics are located in the Postmodern SIGMA
  Milieu that corresponds to portions of the Sinus Milieu of High Achievers who
  frequently are higher education graduates.

- A majority of 57.7 percent of all Catholic students are located in the Postmodern
  SIGMA Milieu. This converges with the Movers and Shakers Sinus Milieu that
  includes 43.3 percent of all Catholic students, and which has the largest share of
  high school graduates.

- Another 38.2 percent of Catholic students are assignable to the Progressive
  Modern Mainstream Milieu (SIGMA); merely 4.1% are located in the Counter-
  Culture SIGMA Milieu. Here the Escapist Sinus Milieu in comparison counts a
  solid 21.3% of the Catholic students, which implies that the majority of them may
  be located in the overlap with the Movers and Shakers Milieu, in any case though
  in the middle class.

On visualizing the percentage shares of Catholic academics in the Sinus und Sigma
Milieus respectively in corresponding hues of grey and on projecting in reference to
Otte (2004) both the milieu models over each other in the social space,[332] the result
is the following outline of where Catholic academics are located (see Fig. 5-3 on the
next page): Accordingly, male Catholic academics can be located in the better
earning upper classes throughout, from the traditionally oriented to post-modern
value orientations. This contiguous presence may relate not least to the "tendency
towards homogenization" under which particularly in the "upper class/segment,
mentalities significantly move together and become mutually aligned.[333]

In contrast, no above average concentration of Catholic academics is observable in
the traditional, conservative segment.

---

[332] cf. OTTE, Gunnar: *Sozialstrukturanalyse mit Lebensstilen. Eine Studie zur theoretischen und
methodischen Neuorientierung der Lebensstilforschung.* Wiesbaden: VS Verlag, 2004 – Otte
performed a synoptic analysis a large number of milieu models from science and marketing research
and devised from that the "Model of Integrative Typology of Life Choices" that integrates the insights
of similar milieu studies. In 2015, Stelzer/Heyse relaunched Ottes's model using the b4p database:
STELZER, Marius, HEYSE, Marko: *Typologie der Lebensführung.* [retrieved on 2017-12-07]
Available from: https://lebensfuehrungstypologie.wordpress.com/ubersicht/.

[333] HEMPELMANN, Heinzpeter (2013): *Gott im Milieu.* Ibidem, p. 67.

Figure 5-3: Catholic Male Academics in the Sinus and SIGMA Milieus (own graphic)

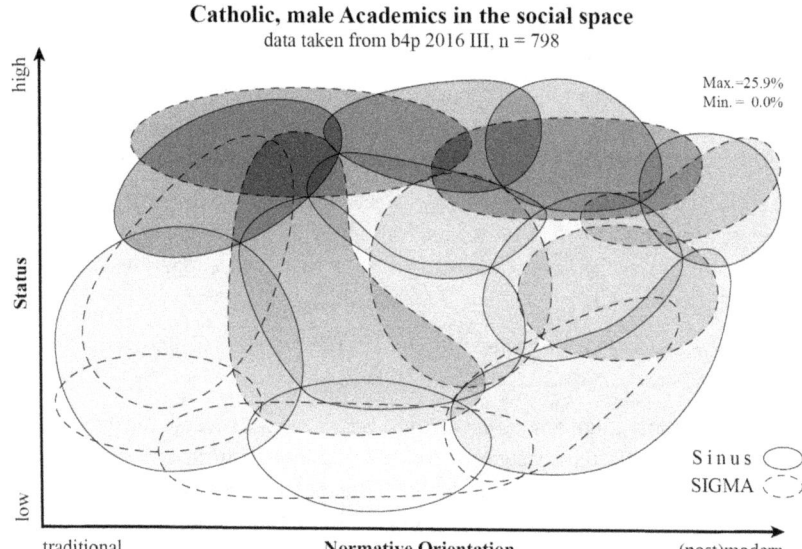

Catholic, male Academics in the social space
data taken from b4p 2016 III, n = 798

On the whole on the basis of identified analogies in the locations of Catholic students and academics in the Sinus and SIGMA Milieus respectively as well as in reference specifically to the results of the German Survey on Volunteering 2014 and conclusions of the MDG-Milieuhandbuch survey on upper class milieus[334] the following insights apply:

a) Catholic academics frequently are positioned in the socially upscale upper-class milieus (Established Conservative, Liberal Intellectual, High Achievers) with correspondingly high status, wealth and living standards.

b) The fundamental attitudes of graduate and studying Catholic academics span depending on age and preferences in life the range from traditional to post-modern.

c) Performance orientation, individual responsibility, higher incomes and a strong interest in church life and church events are the prominent features that qualify Catholic academics from the Upper Conservative Milieu as volunteers in particular for management and organizing tasks. These must be approached by leaders/officials personally to recruit them for such tasks.

---

[334] See CALMBACH, Marc et al. (2013): *MDG-Milieuhandbuch 2013*. Ibidem, pp. 42-44.

d) The options of academics of exerting influence and of participating in the parish and pertinent establishments, recognition of their mostly sustained and true commitment as well as the boost to prestige that goes along with volunteer functions play a significant role.

e) Alongside individual responsibility, particularly important to Catholic academics from the Liberal Intellectual Milieu is the possibility of exerting influence including political influence, and of a structural change.

These specific target group attributes may be accounted for and used by parishes and their establishments in their communication with members and marketing communication proactively in order to generate sustained support (*time, talent, treasure*, cf. Chap. 3.4.3.

5.1.1.4   *Sociological Particularities of Catholics Organized in Confessional Student Associations and Academic Confederations*

Student associations count among the earliest organizations of Catholic citizens and also among those with the strongest membership. Since their advent in the second half of the 19th century and their heyday in Wilhelmine Germany (i.e., the German Empire under Emperor Wilhelm II from 1890 until World War I), student associations originally were construed as the typical form of student organizations and as powerful and influential socialization instances.

After World War II, a number of previously outlawed or dissolved student associations again enjoyed the freedom of new formation. "By the mid-1950s, reconstitution of the association landscape finally was complete; in those years again as many as 30 percent of all male students were incorporated again."[335]

But the cultural change after World War II and ultimately the western German student movement of the 1960s ("the '68 movement") with its escalated conflict between the German war generation and the coming post-war generation with its emancipatory and anti-authoritarian protests brought about sweeping societal changes as a result of which traditional and conservatively grounded societies both in the population at large as well as in the church and university spheres met with growing rejection. As a result by the mid-1970s, only as few as two percent of students were incorporated. Since the 1980s and the German reunification of 1990,

---

[335] ANGERMANN, Eric / GLÖCKLER Lena: Die Geschichte der Korporationen in der Moderne. Ein Abriss, p. 47. In: FACHSCHAFTSRAT DER PHILOSOPHISCHEN FAKULTÄT DER UNIVERSITÄT GÖTTINGEN (ed.): *Studentenverbindungen gestern und heute. Kritische Perspektiven auf Korporationen in Göttingen und Deutschland.* Göttingen: Aktiv Druck & Verlag, 2017.

student corporations again have better appeal that ultimately boils down also to positive trends in their membership.

The Katholische Akademikerarbeit Deutschlands (Catholic Work of Academics Germany, KAD) is an umbrella organization and a network of the 14 major German academic and student confederations and as such has meanwhile a total of about 60,000 individual members.[336]

The most influential member of KAD and the largest Catholic academic confederation in Europe at about 30,000 male members, thereof approx. 4000 students, is the Cartel Confederation of the Catholic German Student Associations (CV). The CV holds in excess of 125 student associations from the principal university locations in Germany as well as in Fribourg (Switzerland), Rome (Italy), Strasbourg (France), Gliwice (Poland), Leuven (Belgium), Tokyo (Japan) and Dschang (Cameroon).[337] Its about 30,000 members are in addition to their life-long membership in their respective parent CV-affiliated student associations in many places organized in local associations – sc. local CV circles – as well as in profession-specific groupings up to informal CV rounds. The more comprehensive the extent of organization of the respective grouping, the more sustained and professional its local operations with a view to compiling its own schedule of events or the assumption of voluntary social tasks.

The second largest confessional confederation of academics under the KAD umbrella is the Cartel Confederation of the Catholic German Student Societies (KV), which has about 16,000 members in some 80 student associations, followed by the oldest Catholic academic confederation, which is the Verband der wissenschaftlichen katholischen Studentenvereine Unitas (Confederation of Scientific Catholic Student Societies, UV, brief: Unitas) that has in more than 45 associations, including with exclusively female membership, about 7000 members.

Kurth (2004) differentiates student corporations and associations principally according to whether they distinguish themselves by showing colour (for instance on hats and/or chest straps in the association colour), academic fencing (fencing of students), have a particular explicitly proclaimed political mission, whether they are organized under an umbrella confederation and according to what exclusion and

---

[336] cf. KATHOLISCHE AKADEMIKERARBEIT DEUTSCHLANDS (KAD): *Webseite des Akademiker-Dachverbands.* [retrieved on 2017-12-07] Available from: http://www.k-a-d.de/

[337] cf. CARTELLVERBAND: *Webportal "Cartellverband.de"* [retrieved on 2018-04-30] Available from: https://www.cartellverband.de/

inclusion criteria they apply, meaning whether membership is attached to confessional, gender-specific, nationality-specific, or ethnic or cultural criteria:[338] "All student associations share an emphasis on history and traditions, the principle of getting bound for life, more or less pronounced elitist conceptions, frequently coupled with protectionist mechanisms, the Comment [339], the Convent principle [340] and a hierarchic structure."

All the CV-affiliated associations and their individual members have aligned their valuesets and their activities to the four principles of the cartel confederation:[341] Catholicity (Latin: *religio*), scientific character (*scientia*), friendship for life (*amicitia*) and homeland (*patria*) in the sense of preserving cultural roots and the free democratic order of Germany as well as an active involvement at all levels of society at large.

The examination primarily of student associations gives ideal insights into the conceptual worlds of academically educated Catholics in the different phases of life – as students, as young and then established professionals and as retireds, or old-age pensioners. Specifically the members of student associations organized under the CV umbrella that are examined in detail herein are by requirement male, all Catholic, wear association-specific colours, reject student fencing, and are perhaps politically engaged, but do not proclaim either on behalf of their association or of the cartel confederation a political position.

They all have had from the crib a Christian Catholic socialization. By virtue of their studies and in particular through their membership in a Catholic student association, they have undergone an additional and highly formative socialization phase. This is because in this phase of life, an individual is "incorporated and socialized"[342] in

---

[338] KURTH, Alexandra: *Männer – Bünde – Rituale. Studentenverbindungen seit 1800*. Frankfurt am Main: Campus Verlag, 2004, p. 39.

[339] The "Comment" is the entirety of internal and external rules of behaviour on the basis of a shared set of values. cf. MAI, Paul et al.: *CV-Handbuch*, 3rd extended edition. Regensburg: Gesellschaft für Studentengeschichte und studentisches Brauchtum, 2000.

[340] "Convents" are democratic assemblies of a part or all members to rule on all matters of the student associations under strict confidentiality obligations regarding the topics discussed (Convent secret). See the same, ibidem.

[341] cf. CARTELLVERBAND: *Wesen der CV-Verbindungen*. [retrieved on 2018-04-30] Available from: https://www.cartellverband.de/studentenverbindungen/wesen-der-cv-verbindungen/ – Details s. MAI, Paul et al. (2000): ibidem, p. 175 f.

[342] PETERS, Stephan: *Elite sein. Wie und für welche Gesellschaft sozialisiert eine studentische Korporation?* Marburg: Tectum Verlag, 2004, p. 283. – Under his little objectified examinations into the socialization of the individual within the "Kösener und Weinheimer Senioren-Convent(s-Verband)" (an umbrella confederation of the oldest student associations in German speaking areas including Switzerland and Austria), Peters devised a "socialization model of the membership"(pp.

accordance with the perceived values and pursued goals and principles of the respective corporation and sent after their graduation as "Seniors" into society. In particular an incorporation and socialization during the time of study – in a CV-affiliated association additionally with strong linkage to the Catholic Church – ensures strong inner cohesion and accordingly comprehensive support in matters of student and professional life as well as in personal and personality building matters.

Here at least one further principle comes in additionally to the religious, societal and economic principles of Catholic student associations that reinforces cohesion in mutual dealings of their student members and promotes a sense of belonging of graduates to the association or academic confederation even after completion of studies, change of location and start of professional career; it is the principle of getting bound for life, or the principle of life-long membership, in a male society that cuts across occupations and generations.

The largest European academic confederation, the CV, states on this in the updated 2015 version of its social policy principle statement:[343]

"The associations under the CV umbrella are the primary place in which fellow members of the confederation educate each other to the spirit of our principles, and in order to bring forth mature personalities who are aware of their responsibility before God and the people and capable of social engagement. (...) Out of our Catholic faith, we want to design our own life and our community that binds us together.

But out of this faith, we also want to engage in society. Because we are convinced that a democratic state and societal system depends on prerequisites it cannot provide for itself alone. As such an essential prerequisite, we deem the Christian faith and the Christian culture of our country. It has substantially shaped our convictions of human dignity and of the freedom of the individual, and of an economic system that is principally based on personality, solidarity and subsidiarity."

Already since the end of the 19th and the beginning of the 20th century, academics with student association backgrounds have been shaping the political, economic and

---

282-286) that – on the provision of a thorough, individual and critical revision and adaptation to case-specific circumstances – could be applicable to socialization processes in other student associations as well.

[343] cf. CARTELLVERBAND: *Charta '15. Gesellschaftspolitische Grundsätze des CV*. p. 4-5 [retrieved on 2018-04-30] Available from: https://www.cartellverband.de/cartellverband/wer-wir-sind/charta-2015/

social developments in Germany. In the following part, some examples are provided of the most prominent Catholics from the major academic confederations.[344]

Politics:

- Konrad Adenauer (1876-1967), German Chancellor and Federal minister (KV)
- Joachim Herrmann (1956-), Bavarian Minister of the Interior (CV)
- Dr. Klaus Kinkel (1936-), former Federal minister and Vice-Chancellor (CV))
- Heinrich Lübke (1894-1972), German Federal President (CV)
- Reinhold Mitterlehner (1955-), former Austrian Vice-Chancellor (ÖCV)
- Franz-Josef Strauß (1915-1988), Bavarian Prime Minister, Federal minister (CV)
- Dr. Edmund Stoiber (1941-), former Bavarian Prime Minister (CV)

Church:

- Prof. Dr. Jòsef Bilczewski (1860-1923), Archbishop, canonized (CV)
- Clemens August Graf von Galen (1878-1946), Cardinal, blessed (CV)
- Dr. Reinhard Marx (1953-), Chairman of the German Bishops' Conference (CV)
- Dr. Eugenio Pacelli (1876-1958), Pope Pius XII (CV)
- Prof. Dr. mult. Joseph Ratzinger, (1927-), Pope em. Benedict XVI (KV, CV)
- Dr. Robert Zollitsch (1938-), former Chairman of the German Bishops' Conf. (CV)

Media:

- Dr. Alfred Biolek (1934-), talk show host, TV producer (ÖCV)
- Dr. Klaus Doberschütz (1932-), former government speaker and head of the Press and Information Office of the German Federal government, holder of the German Federal Cross of Merit (Bundesverdienstkreuz) (CV)
- Thomas Gottschalk (1950-), actor, talk show host/presenter (CV)
- Dr. Claus Kleber (1955-), journalist, TV presenter (CV)

Economy:

- Dr. Rainer Dulger (1964-), entrepreneur, President of Gesamtmetall (CV)
- Dr. Paul-Otto Faßbender (1946-), Chairman ARAG insurance group (CV)
- Dr. Norbert Rollinger (1964-), Management Board of R+V Versicherung (CV)
- Prof. Dr. Norbert Winkeljohann (1957-), Chairman pwc Germany (CV)

---

[344] See MAI, Paul et al. (2000): *CV-Handbuch*. ibidem. pp. 527-606, as well as: WEISKORN, Richard (ed.): *Gesamtverzeichnis des CV 2015*. Bad Honnef: CV-Sekretariat, 2015 | List of Politicians: cf. WIKIPEDIA: *Liste der korporierten Bundestagsabgeordneten*. [retrieved on 2018-04-30] Available from: https://de.wikipedia.org/wiki/Liste_der_korporierten_Bundestagsabgeordneten

Science:

- Dr. Jürgen Aretz (1946-), former state secretary, member of the University Council of the University of Eichstätt-Ingolstadt (UV, CV)
- Prof. Dr. Theodor Berchem (1935-), multi award-winning Romanist philologist, former President of the University of Würzburg and of the German Academic Exchange Service (DAAD), holder of the German Federal Cross of Merit (CV)
- Prof. Dr. Hans-H. Bolt (1960-), Management Board of the Jülich research center (CV)
- Prof. Dr. Eberhard Jochem (1942-), internationally recognized energy scientist, holder of the German Federal Cross of Merit (CV)
- Prof. Dr. Hubertus Strughold (1898-1986), pioneer in space medicine, holder of the German Federal Cross of Merit (CV)
- Dr. Bernd Freiherr von Droste zu Hülshoff (1938-), former Secretery General of the UNESCO World Heritage Convention, founder of the UNESCO World Heritage Centre (CV)
- Prof. Dr. Anton Zeilinger (1945-), leading quantum physicist, President of the Austrian Academy of Sciences, member of the US National Academy of Sciences (ÖCV)

Not just the examples of these prominent personalities but also and in particular the social capital of Catholic academics, their specific milieu affiliation and the Catholic student associations as an additional socialization instance they all go through all suggest comprehensive engagement of Catholic academics – particularly with a view to the needs and purposes of the Church and its parishes.

5.1.2   Outline of Chosen Data Collection Methodology

With the aid of the provider of professional survey software "umfrageonline.com", an online survey consisting of 33 questions was performed over the period from October to November 2016.

The structure and scope of the online questionnaire was optimized on the basis of a prior test survey. Under the pretest on the occasion of annual general meeting of the Cartel Confederation of Catholic German Student Associations (CV) held on 26th to 29th May 2016 in Würzburg, Germany, representatives of students and of senior members of the 126 associations affiliated to CV as well as representatives of CV organizations were given a total of 250 printouts of the questionnaire. Of the questionnaires distributed under the label of the CV-Academy,[345] it was possible to fully evaluate 175 copies, amounting to a participation of exactly 70 percent. The test survey questionnaire that mainly comprised choice-based questions explored church and demographic attributes, posed questions on religious orientation and practice as well as on the respondents' current parish and life of the parish. Based on the insights gained from the pretest, the final online questionnaire was designed and implemented that was then actually used.

The surveying method to use and the design of both the test questionnaire and the online questionnaire as well as the topic of the target groups to approach were discussed on 12 April 2016 as part of an expert interview with Mr. Marco Ottawa – Head of Secondary and Special Research, Market Research, Telekom Deutschland GmbH, Bonn (Germany), and Lecturer at the Technical University of Cologne, Faculty of Information and Communication Sciences, who gave a positive assessment of all the aspects.

The online questionnaire was distributed primarily via the closed group of members of the CV confederation, the largest confessional confederation of academics in Europe, subscribing to the XING social business network (www.xing.de). The group comprised at the time of the survey 2434 persons. The members of the group contacted by automatic e-mails under the label of the CV-Academy were informed on the purpose of the survey, invited to participate in the same and asked to forward the links to the survey to students and academics they personally knew.

By virtue of this, a secondary distribution occurred of the study not least via the Facebook fanpage of the "CV-Vorort"[346] as well as through a number of e-mail distribution lists. Here a note is due that a part of the primarily contacted target group may have been contacted and/or reminded again about the survey through these secondary channels. Though double participation in the survey thus could not be entirely excluded, it was unlikely given the specific topic and the large volume of the survey questions.

---

[345] The CV-Academy is the non-profit educational institution of the CV. For further information see: CV-AKADEMIE: Die CV-Akademie. [retrieved on 2018-04-30] Available from: https://www.cv-akademie.de/die-cv-akademie.

[346] The "CV-Vorort" is the executive committee of the CV student confederation in which all the CV-affiliated student associations are represented with the elected boards of their student members (in German: "Aktivitas"). The name of the private Facebook group is "Cartellverband der Katholischen Deutschen Studentenverbindungen (CV)" (Cartel Confederation of Catholic German Student Associations). See: CV-VORORT: Facebook-Fanpage des Vorstandes des CV-Studentenbundes. [retrieved on 2018-04-30] Available from: https://www.facebook.com/DerVorort/

5.1.3 Total Sample, Structure of Analysed Groups

The study covers essentially all Catholics who are willing to actively participate in shaping the Church community and the life of the Church. Even though given the online surveying method, parts of the older age groups in the population were excluded from participation, these however may be neglected due to their lower potential to shape the future.

The primarily surveyed sample though included male Catholic students and active or retired academics who had experienced through membership in a confessional student association (corporation) during their studies an additional Catholic socialization phase and were voluntarily engaging in church, social and other general society contexts. Though corporative organizations[347] had their prime mainly in the era of Germany under Kaiser Wilhelm around the turn of the 19th and 20th century, student associations in many places still are deemed even today a typical form of student organizations and not least powerful and influential socialization instances, members of which have been consistently shaping the political, economic and societal developments in Germany.[348]

Given this, the online survey focuses on individual members of the Cartel Confederation of Catholic German Student Associations (CV) founded in 1856. CV is among the oldest academic associations and comprised already in the early 20th century more than 30 member associations. Today, CV is the largest confessional confederation of academics in Europe counting around 30,000 individual members in 8 countries, 126 member associations and about 250 local circles, and as such represents the Catholic corporative organizations of Germany.

---

[347] In contrast to the pre-modern German structure of society defined by social classes by virtue of occupation or origin, "corporations" were already functionally oriented or specialized and accordingly formally structured. Their members had to meet certain admission criteria and to commit themselves to specific goals, tasks, mentalities and traditions.

The self-concept of student corporations is, as a rule, based on ideal and/or religious principles to which the common thinking and action is aligned. Among these, in particular the "Lebensbund" principle is to be mentioned, meaning lifetime membership of the "corporates" in their association, provided that they do not voluntarily leave or are not excluded from their corporation by a majority decision of the members' meeting ("Convent").

In Germany there are currently about 1000 student associations that are organized in about 30 confederations; most of them 'show colour', meaning that their members wear a band/sash in the colours of the association and a student cap, the so-called "couleur".

Cf. CARTELLVERBAND: *Was ist eine Studentenverbindung?* [retrieved on 2018-04-30] Available from: https://www.cartellverband.de/studentenverbindungen/was-ist-eine-studentenverbindung/

[348] See Chapter 1.1.1.

The terms "Catholic Corporates" and "CVer(s)" used in the following are meant as synonyms for members of CV-affiliated student associations. These in turn split into 'Active' students and graduated, professionally active or retired 'Seniors'.

In total in the online survey, 694 male Catholics with student and/or academic background were surveyed about their Christian faith, their views on church offers and on communication by their parishes, amounting to a participation of 28.5 percent of the persons contacted via XING.

In order to guarantee best quality of the results to the extent possible, only datasets were considered in the evaluation that were answered all along up to and including the last mandatory question. This because this particular question 30 (of 33) was meant to verify the gender of the exclusively male members of the CV-affiliated student associations. Thus a total of 469 students and academics organized in CV (67.6% of all the respondents) were included in the evaluation of the study.

Where over the course of the evaluation, a comparison of the results for the group of CV-organized students with the group of CV-organized alumni/academics appeared meaningful, the sample totalling 469 individuals was broken down according to provided information on current membership status in the original or initial association. This allowed a comparison of the information provided by the 98 'Actives' with that given by the 370 'Seniors'.[349] The respective percentage values were not weighted.

The collected data were evaluated/analysed using the IBM SPSS Statistics software, Version 24.

5.1.4   The Online Questionnaire

The online questionnaire the (translated and commented) print version of which is attached in Annex b) of this thesis is structured after an introductory note into a total of six parts that are explained hereinafter:

5.1.4.1   Questions on Religious Orientation and Practice (4 questions)

In order to ensure that only Catholic persons could participate in the survey, firstly the question was posed about religious denomination. Those among the participants who indicated being "not Catholic" were then redirected straight to the final page of

---

[349] A direct mutual comparison of the results for students ('Actives') and academics ('Seniors') only is made where there were significant differences between the two groups (asymptotic significance (2-sided)/chi-square according to Pearson).

the online questionnaire. A repeated attempt to participate in the survey directly thereafter was prevented by means of a cookie.

Individual religiousness of the participants and their affinity to the Church was explored through three proven closed questions on their own assessment of their religiousness, their participation in church services and their affinity to the Church and/or tendencies of leaving the Church. For the sake of ultimate comparability of the survey results with other representative studies, equally also time-tested items were employed.[350]

5.1.4.2   Information and Communication of the Parish (5 questions)

Via this branching section that consisted of one dichotomous and four multiple choice questions, an inventory check was performed of the perception and active use of and preferences concerning church communication channels and media.

Using the same 16 answer options throughout a total of three questions, plus a field for additional own answer options, the subjective perception, active use of media and information preferences of the participants were explored and mutually correlated.

The 16 items provided as predefined answer options included traditional church communication channels as well as "new media" in the broadest sense and "announcing" elements such as recommendations by word of mouth or personal invitation. The composition of the 16 predefined items as elements of the church communication mix referred to comprehensive studies in German and US literature[351] while accounting for the results of the test survey outlined in chapter 5.1.1.

---

[350]   Question 2 uses as answer scale the six Catholic segments of "faithful to the church; critical church-connected; ecclesiastically distanced Christian; religious, but not Christian; unsecure; not religious" according to Allensbacher Institut für Demoskopie, cf. INSTITUT FÜR DEMOSKOPIE ALLENSBACH bzw. SCHULZ, Rüdiger et al. (2010): *MDG-Trendmonitor*. ibidem. p. 52.

Question 3 explores the frequency of attendance at church services based on a Likert scale version used globally by the CARA institute. cf. CARA – CENTER FOR APPLIED RESEARCH IN THE APOSTOLATE: Parish Life Survey Compilation of Questions. Washington D.C.: Georgetown University, 2014.

[351]   Regarding the church communication mix, see: GERHARD, Joachim, MATTHIS, Karsten: *Öffentlichkeitsarbeit praktisch in Kirche und Gemeinden*. Göttingen: Vandenhoeke & Ruprecht, 2008 | HOLTKAMP, Jürgen: *Fremde Welten entdecken. Marketing für, Pfarrgemeinden Verbände und Vereine*. Munster: Dialog-Medien, 2010, p. 84 ff. | SCHULZ, Rüdiger et al. (2010): *MDG-Trendmonitor*. Ibidem, p. 87: Informationsquellen der Katholiken im Überblick, p. 93: Nutzung und subjektive Beurteilung der verschiedenen Informationsquellen | KLENK, Christian (2013): *Zustand und Zukunft katholischer Medien*. Ibidem. | LICHTSTEINER, Hans (2015): *Das Freiburger Management-Modell*. Ibidem, p. 226: NPO-Marketing Mix | CENTER FOR CHURCH COMMUNICATION (2005): *Church Marketing Report*. Ibidem., p. 3 | GRAY, Mark M., GAUTIER, Mary L.: *Catholic Media Use in the United States, 2011*. Washington, D.C.: Center for Applied Research in the Apostolate (CARA), Georgetown University, 2011.

The key focus of this section was on proactive information behaviour of the respondents both in terms of own information research and as regards active forwarding of church relevant information to others.

5.1.4.3 Evaluation of the Parish Life (4 + 2 questions)

The life and work of a parish manifests on the one hand in its specific offer of social and charity events and activities as well as in its communal and liturgical attributes. Consequently, both the aspects of parish life were surveyed separately on the basis of rating scales using 14 and 12 items[352] respectively in addition to which there was finally for both a question on personal priorities. This total of four questions was embedded into a multiple-choice question on the home diocese and into an open question about ideas for events and activities specially designed for academics.

5.1.4.4 Voluntary Engagement (5 + 4 questions)

Believing Christians, in particular Catholic men with academic background, engage more frequently and intensively than other population groups in voluntary social and charity work [353]. Based on this, firstly the possibility was surveyed of a potential engagement in the Church. Voluntary engagement in a student association was surveyed by means of a yes/no question as well as the current member status, the respective Catholic umbrella organization and the contact (Likert scale) of the student association with the local parish.

Subsequently the voluntary engagement of the participants in different areas of life was investigated with 14 proven items[354] (multiple choice questions) and its intensity explored by means of an invitation to indicate up to three special engagements of one's own choice. Where here at least one special engagement was indicated, two further multiple-choice questions followed for the participant on the scope of tasks within the special engagement (11 items) and on the motivations for their special engagement (8 items.

5.1.4.5 Academic Attributes

To explore the academic and professional background of the study participants, subsequently four multiple choice questions (single choice) were included. The section concluded with an open question on the core focus points of the work of academic confederations.

---

[352] The items offered by questions 11 and 13 are based on: CARA – CENTER FOR APPLIED RESEARCH IN THE APOSTOLATE (2014): *Parish Life Survey Compilation of Questions.*, ibidem.

[353] cf. chapter 1.1.1 herein.

[354] TESCH-RÖMER, Clemens et al. (2016): *Der Deutsche Freiwilligensurvey 2014.* Ibidem, pp. 122-147 and pp. 420-423.

5.1.4.6 Demographic Data

Complementary to the collected data on professional background according to Point 6.4.5., finally the remaining demographic data were explored, with a question about income left out in this respect.

5.2   Presentation and Discussion of the Survey Results

5.2.1   Demographic Data

All the 694 participants in total in the online study were initially asked whether they were baptised Catholic (97.4%), joined or rejoined the Church (–), converted to the Catholic faith (1.6%) or were not Catholic (1.0%). Within the sample of 469 all male Catholic CVers, four participants (0.9%) joined the Catholic faith by conversion.

In terms of the age groups represented, peculiarly the age groups of 20 to 30 year olds and those between 45 and 59 years of age had the strongest showing. The average age of the respondents was at 47.1 years:

Figure 5-4: "In which year you were born?" (Question 31)

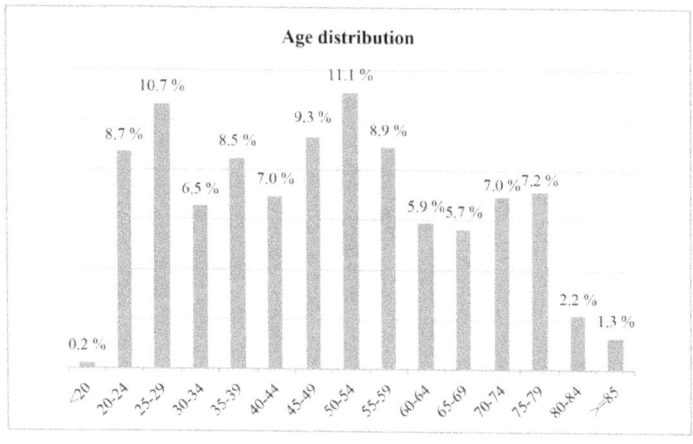

On average, more than a half (55.5%) of the CVers were married, another 5.8 percent lived unmarried with their partner and 31.7 percent were single/unmarried. A look at the specific evaluation [355] of marital status for 'Actives' and 'Seniors' respectively reveals a relationship between age/phase of life and marital status. Of the professionally active and retired academics, a total of 72.1 percent lived in a

---

[355] The breakdown of the sample of the 469 CVers into Actives and Seniors was made based on answers to question 18, through which 98 Actives and 370 Seniors were identified; one indication was missing.

marriage, including remarried. This share is significantly above the German average of 59.4 percent in 2016.[356]

Figure 5-5: "Which marital status best applies to you?" (Question 32)

	All CVers	Actives	Seniors
Married	55.5 %	5.2%	68.6%
Single, never married	31.7 %	80.2%	19.1%
Unmarried cohabiting	5.8 %	14.6%	3.5%
Divorced and remarried	2.4 %	0.0%	3.0%
Divorced	1.7 %	0.0%	2.2%
Widowed	1.3 %	0.0%	1.6%
Living separated	1.1 %	0.0%	1.4%
Widowed and remarried	0.4 %	0.0%	0.5%

The majority of the approached persons came from regions in Germany with the highest population density (North Rhine-Westphalia and Bavaria) and from dioceses with traditionally the largest shares of Catholics in total population (cf. Fig. 5-6 as well as Fig. 5-7 on the next page).[357]

Figure 5-6: "Please enter the postcode of your place of residence" (Question 33)

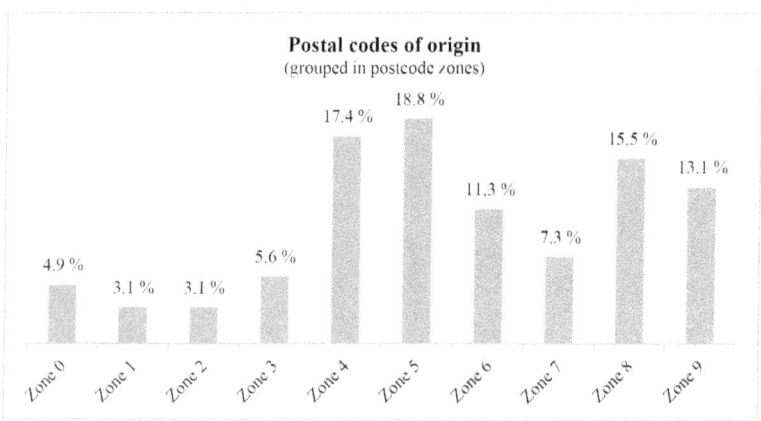

[356] Marital status of male Catholics with academic degree: cf. B4P – BEST FOR PLANNING: b4p 2016
       III [retrieved on 2017-02-16] Available from: https://online.mds6.de/mdso6/b4p.php / | Own research
       results: Single 28.4%, Married 59.4%, Divorced 5.9%, Widowed 6.3%. Used parameters:
       [Demography / Respondent / Gender = male, Religious community = Catholic, School/Professional
       education = Study] x [Demography / Respondent / Family / Marital Status].

[357] Own graphic, designed on the basis of: https://de.wikipedia.org/wiki/R%C3%B6misch-
       katholische_Kirche_in_Deutschland#/media/File:Roman_catholics_germany_2012_de.svg
       [retrieved on 2017-06-08]

Figure 5-7: "To which (arch-)diocese belongs your parish" (Question 10)

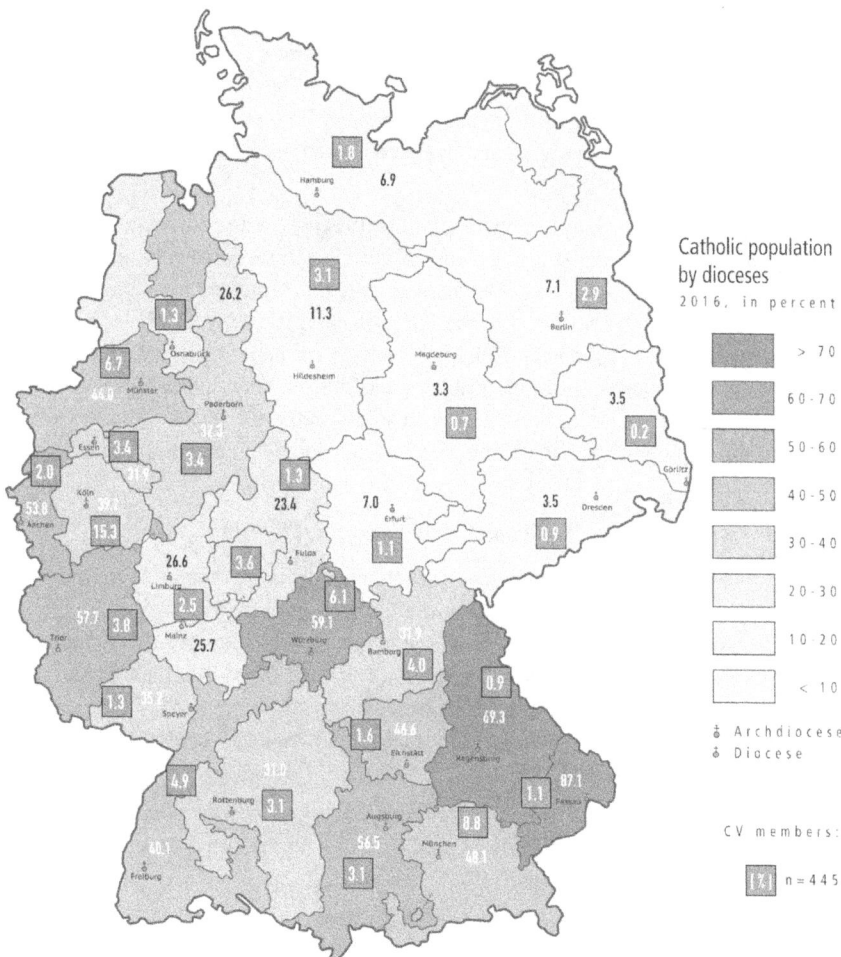

5.2.2 Religious Orientation and Practice

By now in respective examinations such as the SINUS studies commissioned by the Catholic Church or in surveys by the Allensbach Institute for Demoscopy, both the attributes of "religiousness" and "affinity to church" have been not consequently treated separately[358] while in contrast in the annual Protestant membership studies, the attributes have been analysed and evaluated strictly separately since many years already.[359]

Determination of religious orientation and affinity to church of the CVers was surveyed in the present study through a total of three mutually conditioning questions: Initially with the aid of an answer scale that was used in a commissioned representative study performed by the Allensbach Institute for Demoscopy (IfD) already in October/November 2009, [360] self-assessment was explored of the approached CVers on their religiousness and affinity to church and correlated with the representative results of the Allensbach study. Subsequently the frequency was determined of attendance at church services and any tendencies of leaving the Church.

5.2.2.1 Self-Assessment: Religious Orientation and Affinity to Church

Based on the results of the IfD survey, respective values were quantified for the male portion within the different segments of the Catholic population and compared with the self-assessments of the CVers from the present study (Fig. 5-8, next page). Of the surveyed Catholic students and academics, a total of 63.3 percent referred to themselves as "faithful to the church". Consequently, the sample of CVers exhibits a significantly more pronounced religiousness and affinity to church than average male Catholic population (11.9%).

Further about a fifth (22.2%) of the surveyed Catholic Corporates indicated being "critical church-connected", while merely 10.4 percent referred to themselves as "ecclesiastically distanced Christians".

Thus overall, about 85 percent of the surveyed CVers may be deemed "connected to church", which is almost double the average for male Catholics in Germany according to the 2009 Allensbach survey. Also in that survey, 37.7 percent of

---

[358] See CALMBACH, Marc et al.: (2010) *MDG-Trendmonitor* / (2013) *MDG-Milieuhandbuch 2013.* Ibidem.

[359] HÖFELSCHWEIGER, Rainer (2011): *Mitglied, wer bist Du?* Ibidem, p. 46.

[360] Sociodemographic structures of the various Catholics segments / Allensbacher Archiv, IfD survey 5266 (Oct./Nov. 2009), chart 22, see: SCHULZ, Rüdiger et al. (2010): *MDG-Trendmonitor.* Ibidem. p. 52 | Own calculation: All participants (n = 2074) x Percentage in Catholic segment [%] x Percentage of men [%] = number of Catholic men per segment.

respondents referred to themselves as ecclesiastically distanced Christians, and as many as 8.4 percent indicated being not religious – compared to 10.4 and 1.9 percent respectively for the CVers.

Figure 5-8: "How would you describe yourself most?" (Question 2)

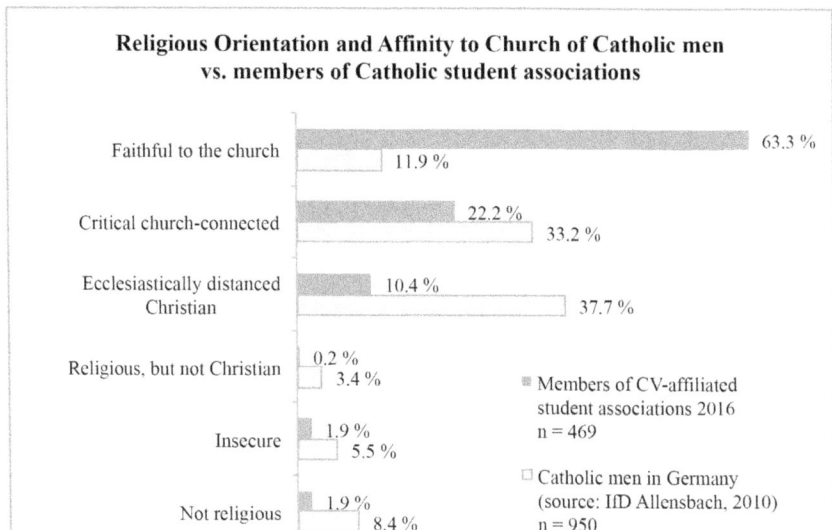

Though the Allensbach study was performed already in October 2009, its results that are representative of German Catholics can be used here as reference values.[361] As regards the 63.3 percent of the "faithful to the church" indications by the CVers, the value for the Catholic average in direct comparison is 11.9 percent:

⇨   **Hypothesis HR2 can be deemed confirmed.**

5.2.2.2   Attendance at Church Services

In general, attendance at church services is used as one of the key indicators of religiousness and affinity to church of Christians. Further with respect to willingness to voluntarily engage in social or charity work, it was verified that a certain regularity

---

[361]   A current survey is likely due to the progressing secularisation of the bulk of German Catholics rather to confirm a declining religiousness and a growing distance from church than the opposite.

and frequency of attendance at church services significantly increases readiness for voluntary engagement.[362]

Figure 5-9: "Apart from weddings, baptisms, funerals and other special occasions: How often do you attend church services?" (Question 3)

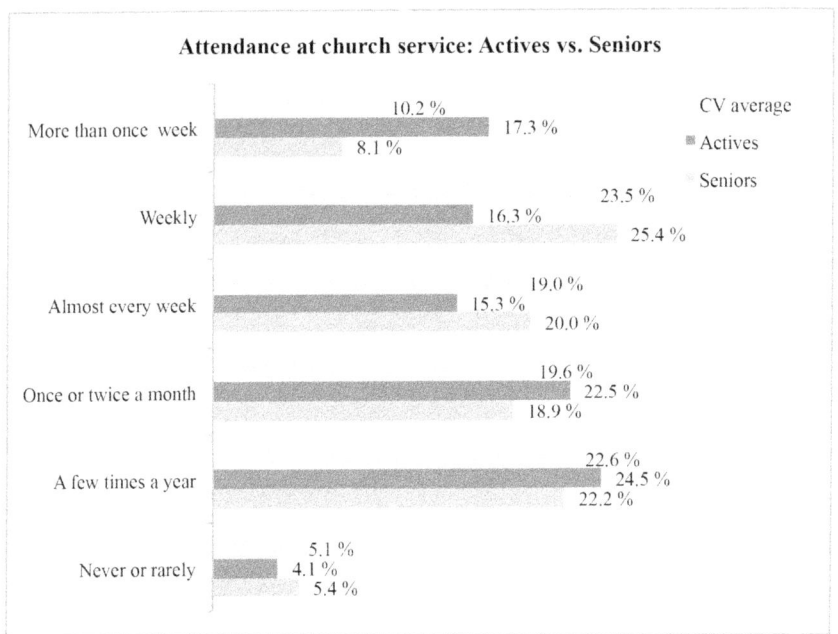

A peculiar aspect with regard to the collected data on the frequency of attendance at church services, as much as a third of the surveyed CVers (33.7%) attended church services at least once a week [363] and another 19 percent "fast jede Woche" (almost every week) (Fig. 5-9). This means that more than a half of the Catholic Corporates (52.7%) participated in church services regularly – not including special occasions and festive holidays.

This result was primarily shaped by the frequency of attendance at church services of the 370 "Seniors", even though almost a fifth of the "Actives" (17.3%)

---

[362] BENNETT, Matthew R.: Religiosity and Formal Volunteering in Global Perspective. In: HUSTINX, Lesley et al.: *Religion and Volunteering.* Ibidem, p. 87.
[363] Summarized answers "More than once a week" (10.2%) and "Weekly" (23.5%).

participated in church services several times a week. Given the 52.7 percent of regular churchgoers, it can be concluded that:

⇨ **Hypothesis HR1 can be deemed confirmed for the surveyed Catholic Corporates overall, in particular however for the Seniors in the CV-affiliated associations.**

5.2.2.3   Thoughts about Leaving the Church?

The question "Have you ever thought about leaving the Church?" was answered by 80.2 percent of the CVers overall with a "No". This result is mainly shaped by the statements of the CV-organised Seniors, 82.2 percent of which claimed never having considered leaving the Church. But even of the Actives, the same was indicated by 72.4 percent of the respondents (Fig. 5-10):

⇨ **HR3 can be deemed confirmed.**

On correlating the answers of the CVers to this oft-posed 'church leaving question' with the answers of approached Catholics from more recent diocese surveys (Fig. 5-10), only limited similarities can be concluded.

Figure 5-10: "Have you ever thought about leaving the church?" (Question 4)

Leaving the church?	CVers	Actives	Seniors	CV[364] pretest	Diocese R.-Stuttgart	Diocese [365] Münster
No	80.2%	72.4%	82.2%	84.0%	76.0%	56.2%
Yes	19.8%	27.6%	17.8%	16.0%	24.0%	43.8%
n =	469	98	370	175	> 4,000	995

For example according to the results of the PRAGMA study named after the homonymous institute that was commissioned by the diocese of Rottenburg-Stuttgart in 2015,[366] 76 percent of all the Catholics in that diocese "had not been seriously considering leaving the church". The satisfaction-focused study of the diocese of

---

[364]   Results of the pretest for this study among managers of CV associations, questionnaire see Annex a).

[365]   EBERHARDT, Tim (ed.): *Zufriedenheitsstudie „Katholiken des Bistums Münster"* (presentation for press interview, 2 March 2015). Münster: Münster Reasearch Institute, 2015, p. 17 | Own calculation: n = 995, answer "Leaving the church is basically out of the question for me"; results cumulated, netted of "Don't know/not specified".

[366]   APP, Reiner (2014): *Zukunftshorizont Kirche.* Ibidem, pp. 45-51.

Münster performed in the same year by the Münster Research Institute[367] (in collaboration with Prof. Dr. Dr. h.c. mult. Heribert Meffert) draws a conclusion that for 55.9 of the respondents "leaving the Church essentially was not an option". Another 22.5 percent of the participants indicated that they had "thought about leaving once or twice already, however it is rather not an option". Unfortunately the offered answer scale in the survey contains not clearly worded answer options to the generally dichotomic question of "Have you ever been toying with the idea of leaving the Catholic Church?". Hence in total, about half of the respondents in the diocese of Münster had thought about leaving the Church and/or had already taken respective decisions.

5.2.3 Academic Attributes and Occupation

The majority of the surveyed students and academics had a university degree in the form of a diploma or a Master's degree (39.2%, see Fig. 5-11). 14.9 percent of the study participants had passed a final state examination for example in medicine or law. Further also 24.5 percent – a near quarter of the total of the respondents – had successfully obtained their doctorate or qualified as a professor.

Figure 5-11: "What is your highest educational achievement by now?" (Question 25)

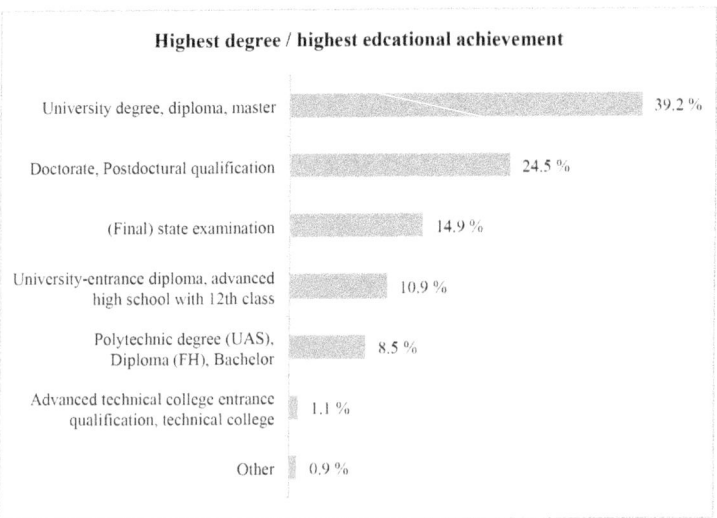

---

[367] EBERHARDT, Tim (ed.), MEFFERT, Heribert, KENNING, Peter: *Zufriedenheitsstudie "Katholiken des Bistums Münster"* (presentation for press interview, 2 March 2015). Muenster: Münster Research Institute, 2015.

Merely 8.5 percent of the respondents had a polytechnic degree (University of Applied Sciences) in the form of an FH-diploma or Bachelor's degree. Most of the still studying CVers had an A levels equivalent (German Abitur) or similar qualification (10.9%), only a small part of them were still studying on the basis of an advanced technical college certificate or a similar qualification (1.1%).

The prevalent part of the respondents (42%) completed or were still doing their studies in the field of social sciences (Fig. 5-12). As the OECD applies a very broad interpretation of this segment of cultural sciences and includes in these *inter alia* also economic sciences, educational and law sciences, no conclusive statements can be immediately drawn from the indications on scientific education of the respondents.

Figure 5-12: "In which field of science have you mainly studied or are you currently studying?" (Question 26)

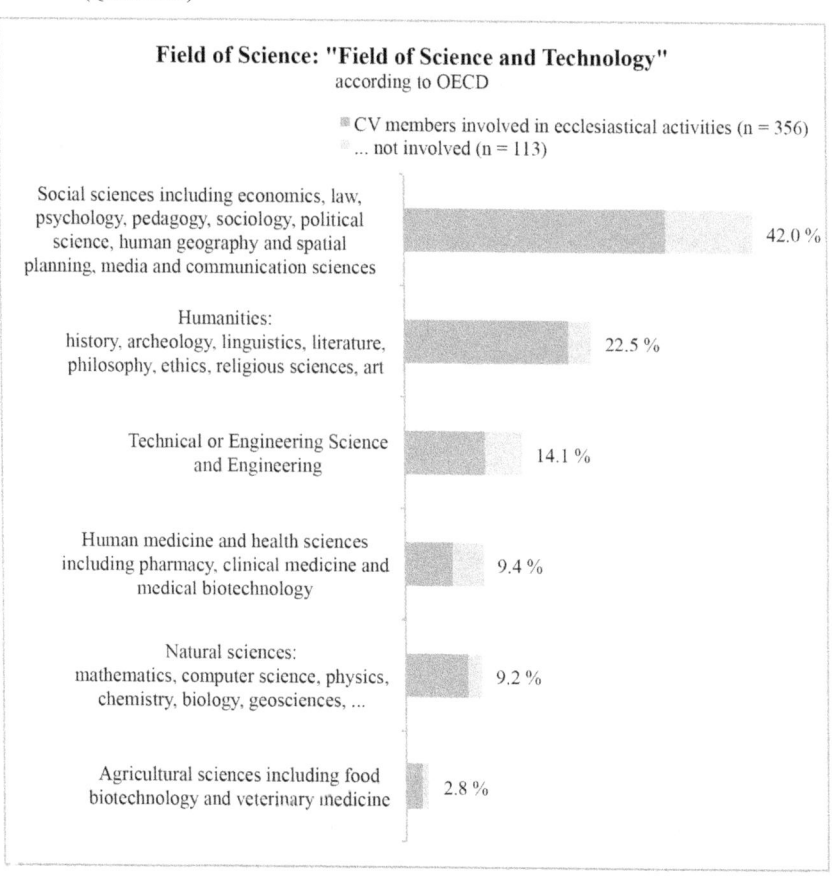

A more detailed look at the collected data however implies that the number of persons engaged in church is particularly high mainly among the CVers with education in human and natural sciences, and particularly small among those from the field of medicine (Fig. 5-12). This statement however would have to be verified for example through appropriate interviews with focus groups to make it reliable.

Among the professionally active academics however, the fields prevail of law and economics (Fig. 5-13); for example about a quarter (25.6%) of the respondents were active in the field of "business organization, accounting, law and administration". About one is seven was working in the sector of "health, social affairs, teaching and education" (14.6%) or in "linguistic, literary, intellectual, social and economic sciences, media, art, culture and design" (13.9%). Another 11.4 percent were active in the professional fields of "commercial services, trade, marketing/sales, the hotel industry and tourism".

An in-depth analysis of the indications on the fields of studies and professional occupation reveals a clear prevalence in the intersection of education in social sciences (including economics, law etc.) with the fields of business / law / administration as well as commercial activities. Further also there is a strong presence of the fields of healthcare / medicine and of humanities / arts.

Figure 5-13: "In which professional field are you currently mainly active?" (Question 27)

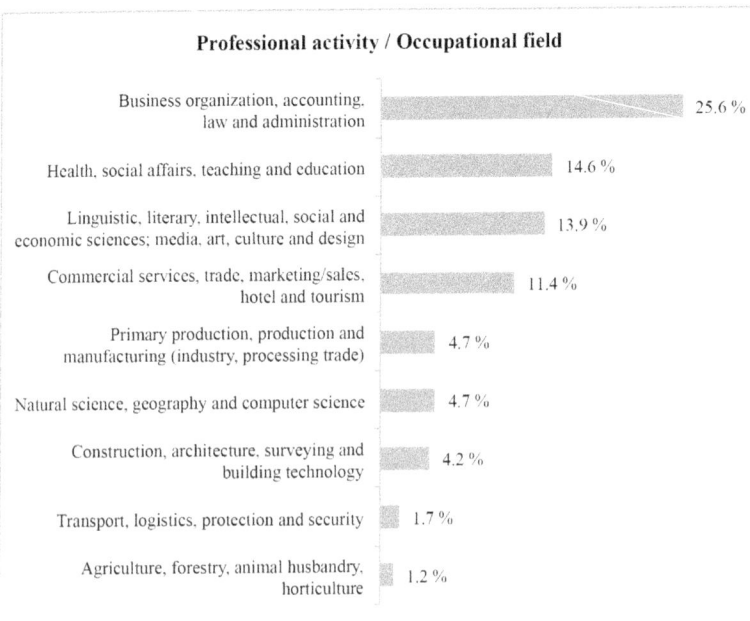

5.2.4   Information from and Communication with Parishes

In this part of the present study, perception was explored of the communication and information channels systematically used by parishes (communication mix)[368] and their alignment with information preferences of the respondents. In the process, it was ultimately important to determine whether the respondents proactively, meaning independently and in a targeted manner, sought information on the news and various offers of the parish and through what channels this preferably happened and/or to what extent the respondents informed their environment on the events organised by the parish.

From Figure 5-14 (next page), it follows firstly that in the parishes of the approached CVers the systematically used means of communication appeared to be mainly print media: according to the indications made, the bulk of media communication by the parishes consisted of print information on church information boards as well as regularly published flyers and brochures.

Among the non-print exceptions were oral announcements in church services (to get which however one must be physically present), the in the meantime nearly ubiquitous websites and recommendations by word of mouth.

Nevertheless with a view to the surveyed Catholic students and academics, it may be positively concluded that these mainly perceived the "classical church communication channels.

⇨   **Hypothesis HK1 thus can be deemed confirmed.**

The question whether they get their information on the offers of their parish in own effort/by themselves as well was answered by 68.4 percent of the respondents with a "yes", as substantially shaped by the answers of the Seniors (72.6%). In comparison of the CV-affiliated Actives, only 52 percent gave the same positive answer, somewhat weakening the statement mainly with respect to the younger respondents. Nevertheless, a high level of interest overall can be concluded in the life of the parishes. This means that:

⇨   **Hypothesis HK2 can be deemed generally and in particular for the CV-affiliated Catholic academics confirmed.**

---

[368]   See bibliographical references in Chapter 5.1.4.2.

Figure 5-14: "Which communication channels/media are systematically used by your parish to inform members?" (Question 5)

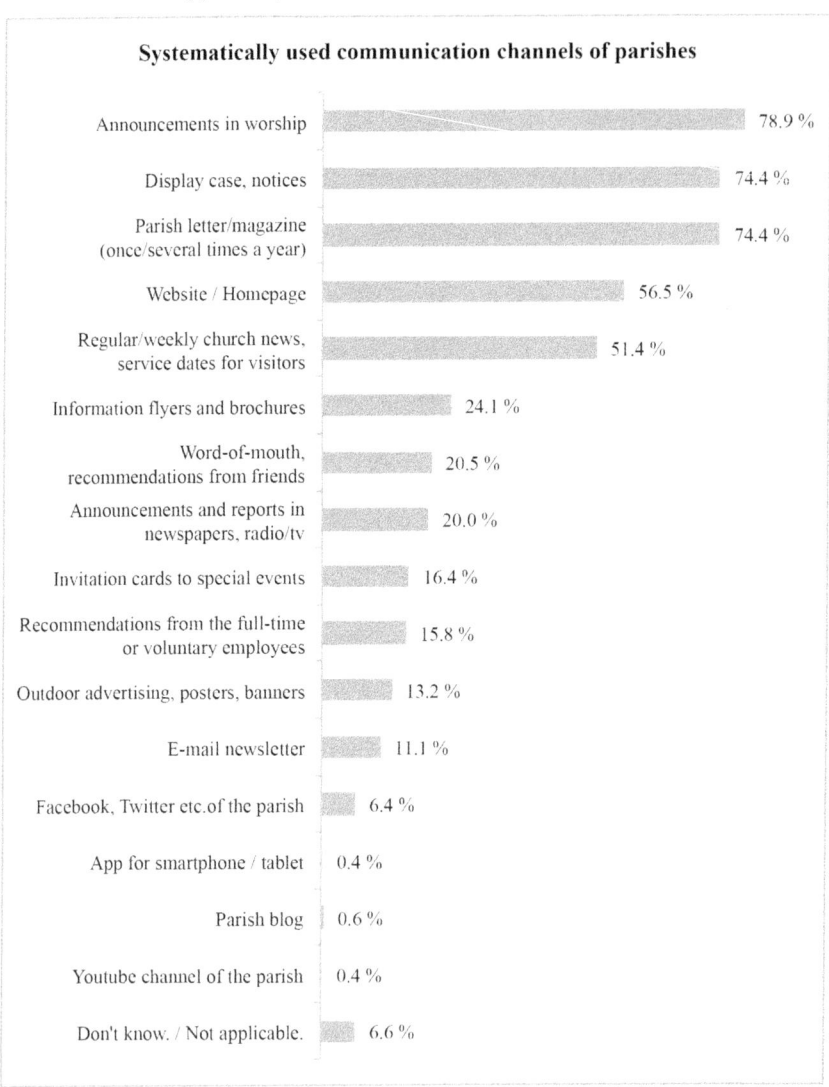

Systematically used communication channels of parishes

Announcements in worship	78.9 %
Display case, notices	74.4 %
Parish letter/magazine (once/several times a year)	74.4 %
Website / Homepage	56.5 %
Regular/weekly church news, service dates for visitors	51.4 %
Information flyers and brochures	24.1 %
Word-of-mouth, recommendations from friends	20.5 %
Announcements and reports in newspapers, radio/tv	20.0 %
Invitation cards to special events	16.4 %
Recommendations from the full-time or voluntary employees	15.8 %
Outdoor advertising, posters, banners	13.2 %
E-mail newsletter	11.1 %
Facebook, Twitter etc.of the parish	6.4 %
App for smartphone / tablet	0.4 %
Parish blog	0.6 %
Youtube channel of the parish	0.4 %
Don't know. / Not applicable.	6.6 %

Those 68.4 percent of the CVers who according to their indications in answering the previous question were getting their information on the offers of their parish in own effort were additionally asked which information channels they used most (Fig. 5-15, next page).

On the whole a total of 55 percent of the respondents primarily used parish letters and magazines. 43.8 were visiting the parish website, slightly more than a third (36.6%) were reading the weekly news of the parish and service dates for visitors, and about every fourth (24.7%) perused information notices in the display cases. Further also 14.4 percent of them paid attention to recommendations and word of mouth of their friends and relatives. All other information sources were rather insignificant:

Figure 5-15: "If you mainly get information in your own effort/initiative: Which information channels or parish media do you use most often?" (Question 7)

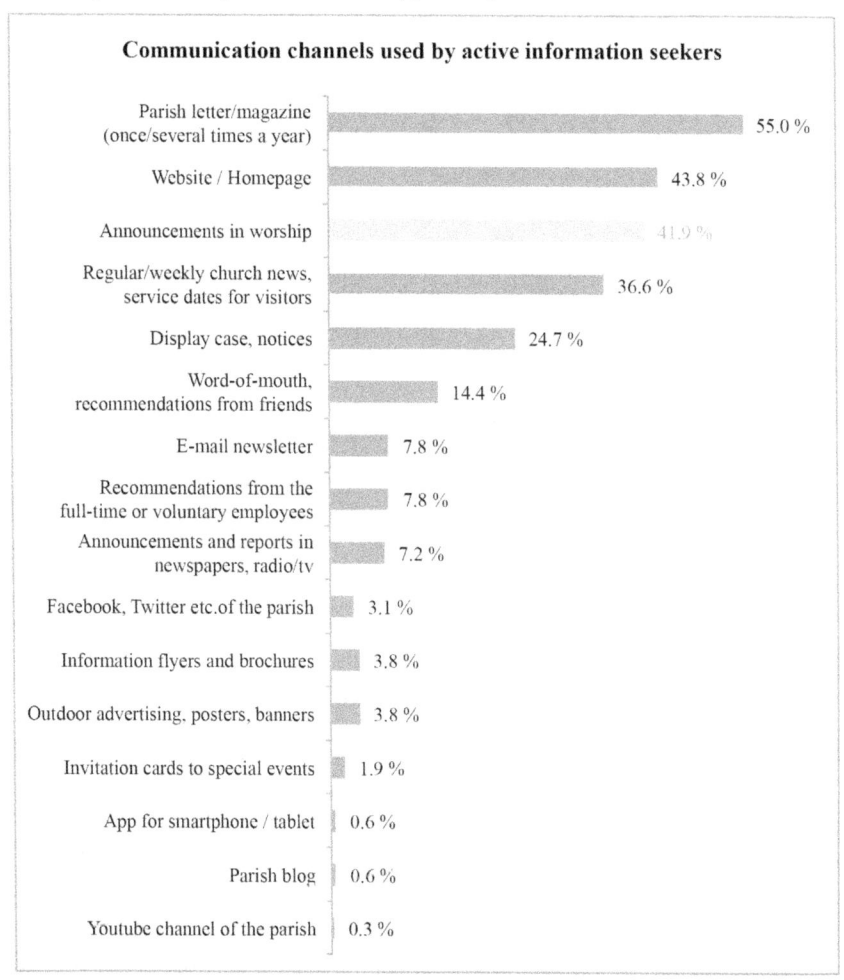

Communication channels used by active information seekers

Parish letter/magazine (once/several times a year)	55.0 %
Website / Homepage	43.8 %
Announcements in worship	41.9 %
Regular/weekly church news, service dates for visitors	36.6 %
Display case, notices	24.7 %
Word-of-mouth, recommendations from friends	14.4 %
E-mail newsletter	7.8 %
Recommendations from the full-time or voluntary employees	7.8 %
Announcements and reports in newspapers, radio/tv	7.2 %
Facebook, Twitter etc.of the parish	3.1 %
Information flyers and brochures	3.8 %
Outdoor advertising, posters, banners	3.8 %
Invitation cards to special events	1.9 %
App for smartphone / tablet	0.6 %
Parish blog	0.6 %
Youtube channel of the parish	0.3 %

Finally on correlating the parish media that get used in the perception of the CVers (Fig. 5-14) with the indicated information preferences of these Catholic Corporates, a significant discrepancy becomes evident between church communication and this particular target group:

Figure 5-16: "Which communication channels/media are systematically used by your parish to inform members?" (Question 5) in correlation to "How would you like to be informed about appointments, events and offers of your parish?" (Question 8)

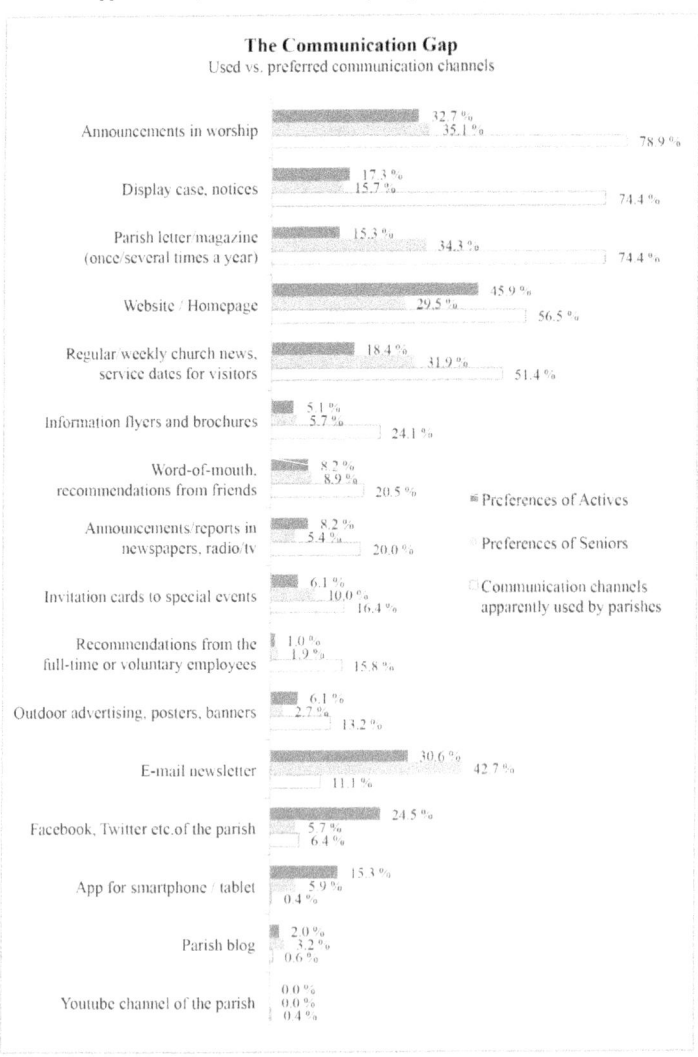

This discrepancy mainly manifests concerning the use of e-mail newsletters (42.7% versus 11.1%), of social media (24.5% vs. 6.4%) or an app (software application). In these fields the communication preferences of the Seniors as those of the Actives only are fulfilled to a very limited extent by the parishes.[369] In addition, the extensively used "classical church media" are, measured by the communication preferences of the Catholic Corporates, far too overrepresented.

Consequently in communication of parishes with Catholic Corporates, there appear to be still substantial areas in need of improvement, in particular with a view to the use of electronic means of communication and social media. And, in particular the latter are the preferred communication channels of the coming generation. Thus it follows that:

⇨   **Hypothesis HK3 can be deemed fully confirmed.**

In order to explore the proactive communication behaviour of the surveyed CVers not just with respect to research of information but also as regards actively forwarding information to others, the CVers were asked on these aspects separately:

Figure 5-17: "Do you inform others about interesting parish events, do you pass on information?" (Question 9)

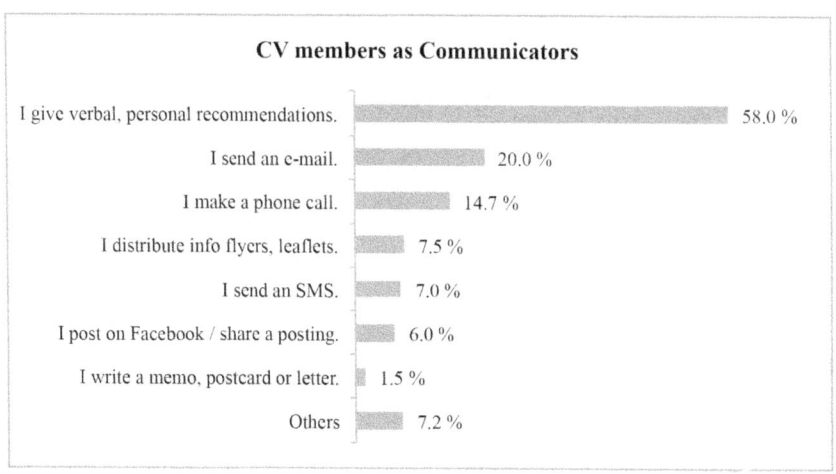

CV members as Communicators

I give verbal, personal recommendations.	58.0 %
I send an e-mail.	20.0 %
I make a phone call.	14.7 %
I distribute info flyers, leaflets.	7.5 %
I send an SMS.	7.0 %
I post on Facebook / share a posting.	6.0 %
I write a memo, postcard or letter.	1.5 %
Others	7.2 %

---

[369]   Question 5, "Which communication channels/media are systematically used by your parish to inform members?" (please choose all applicable answers.) in correlation to Question 8, "How would you like to be informed about appointments, events and offers of your parish?" (please choose a maximum of three questions). Results divided by Actives and Seniors.

More than a half of the Catholic Corporates (58%) gave verbal and personal recommendations on events of interest organised by the parish, so engaging in active word of mouth. A fifth of the respondents (20%) were sending pertinent e-mails, and as much as 14.7 percent made respective phone calls, which qualifies in pertinent research as "electronic word of mouth"[370].

Perhaps through targeted activation of word of mouth and/or personal recommendations, it might be possible to open up new, hitherto unused opportunities for communication of parishes, which nevertheless warrants firstly a detailed investigation. Irrespective of this, it can be concluded that:

⇨ **Hypothesis HK4 can also be deemed confirmed.**

5.2.5 Evaluation of the Parish Life

As regards evaluation of this part of the questionnaire, a note is due that those participants in the study who indicated in answering the question about the frequency of their attendance at church services "never or rarely" were not given these questions on the evaluation of the parish life. This because it can be presumed that someone who never or seldom attends church services is hardly capable of assessing the life of the parish. Overall in this aspect, a total of 445 answers (94.9%) were evaluated.

5.2.5.1 Activities and Offers

At first sight, the parishes score in the assessment of their offers by the Catholic students and academics very good (Fig. 6-15 on the next page). For example, as many as 65.8 percent evaluate the bulk of the programs and activities as "good" or even "excellent". Similarly in a positive vein are viewed the volunteering opportunities (65.7%) and offers of services in the field of pastoral care (62%).

Further also about a half of the surveyed CVers deem as very good to excellent the aid and relief actions of their parishes for those in need (55.6%), offers for the elderly (49.9%) as well as offers for families with small children and for young parents (48.5%).

Slightly more reserved are the views on and evaluation of the topics of youth work (41.2%), religious education for children and young people (35.5%) or events for contact promotion (35.2%):

---

[370] On the term of "electronic word-of-mouth", see: OETTING, Martin: *Ripple Effect: How Empowered Involvement Drives Word of Mouth.* Wiesbaden: Gabler, 2009.

Figure 5-18: "Please rate the following offers of your parish:" – sorted by "Good/Excellent" (Quest. 11)

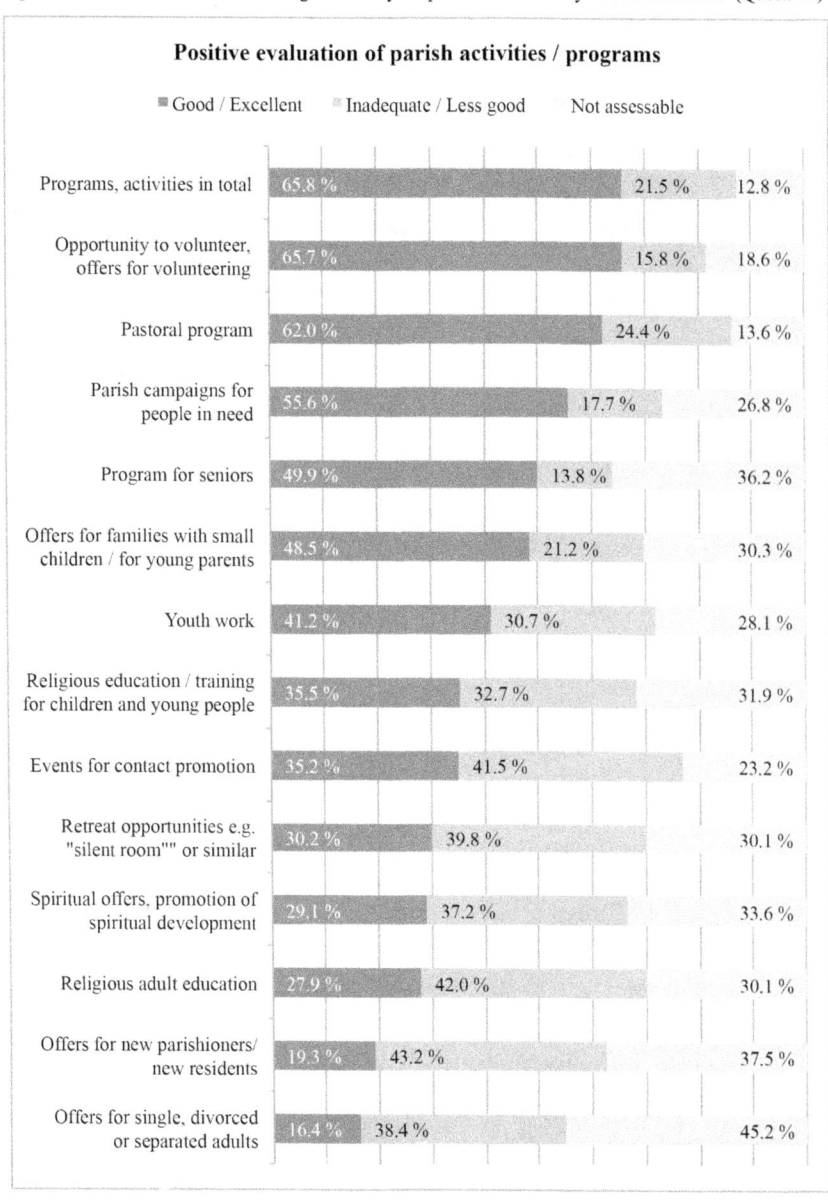

Positive evaluation of parish activities / programs

▪ Good / Excellent   ▫ Inadequate / Less good   Not assessable

	Good/Excellent	Inadequate/Less good	Not assessable
Programs, activities in total	65.8 %	21.5 %	12.8 %
Opportunity to volunteer, offers for volunteering	65.7 %	15.8 %	18.6 %
Pastoral program	62.0 %	24.4 %	13.6 %
Parish campaigns for people in need	55.6 %	17.7 %	26.8 %
Program for seniors	49.9 %	13.8 %	36.2 %
Offers for families with small children / for young parents	48.5 %	21.2 %	30.3 %
Youth work	41.2 %	30.7 %	28.1 %
Religious education / training for children and young people	35.5 %	32.7 %	31.9 %
Events for contact promotion	35.2 %	41.5 %	23.2 %
Retreat opportunities e.g. "silent room"" or similar	30.2 %	39.8 %	30.1 %
Spiritual offers, promotion of spiritual development	29.1 %	37.2 %	33.6 %
Religious adult education	27.9 %	42.0 %	30.1 %
Offers for new parishioners/ new residents	19.3 %	43.2 %	37.5 %
Offers for single, divorced or separated adults	16.4 %	38.4 %	45.2 %

On sorting the results presented above the other way round, specifically by the more reserved to negative ratings and the number of times the "not assessable" option was chosen, the result is an entirely different take on the situation (Fig. 5-19):

Figure 5-19: "Please rate the following offers of your parish:" – sorted by "Inadequate/Less Good"

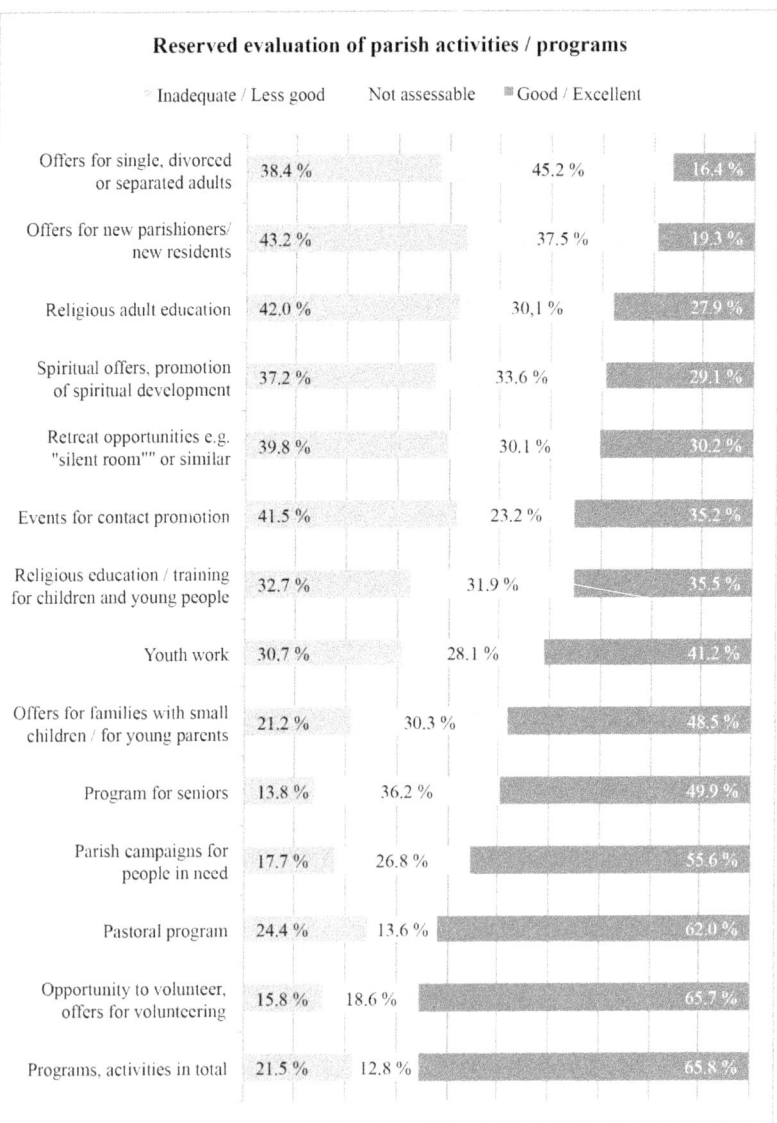

Reserved evaluation of parish activities / programs

Inadequate / Less good   Not assessable   ▪Good / Excellent

	Inadequate/Less good	Not assessable	Good/Excellent
Offers for single, divorced or separated adults	38.4 %	45.2 %	16.4 %
Offers for new parishioners/ new residents	43.2 %	37.5 %	19.3 %
Religious adult education	42.0 %	30,1 %	27.9 %
Spiritual offers, promotion of spiritual development	37.2 %	33.6 %	29.1 %
Retreat opportunities e.g. "silent room"" or similar	39.8 %	30.1 %	30.2 %
Events for contact promotion	41.5 %	23.2 %	35.2 %
Religious education / training for children and young people	32.7 %	31.9 %	35.5 %
Youth work	30.7 %	28.1 %	41.2 %
Offers for families with small children / for young parents	21.2 %	30.3 %	48.5 %
Program for seniors	13.8 %	36.2 %	49.9 %
Parish campaigns for people in need	17.7 %	26.8 %	55.6 %
Pastoral program	24.4 %	13.6 %	62.0 %
Opportunity to volunteer, offers for volunteering	15.8 %	18.6 %	65.7 %
Programs, activities in total	21.5 %	12.8 %	65.8 %

Of course, one can argue about the allowability of the approach to directly connect via such sorting the negative assessments with the "not assessable" answers. This because of the polarising presentation, the "not assessable" indications that do not necessarily contain negative evaluation are treated as such.

However, within the context of the efforts of parishes for an attractive presentation and ultimately for "successful marketing" of their activities and offers towards the Church's different target groups, the "not assessable" offers may well have negative impacts. This is because a lack of awareness about the availability and/or scope of such offers precludes them from being perceived as attractive and ultimately their effective "sales". At the very least though, the particularly strong presence of the "not assessable" indications points to a likely need of more intensive information and communication efforts that can be addressed by the parishes with targeted measures.

Figure 5-20: "On which offer should the parish focus the most?" (Question 12)

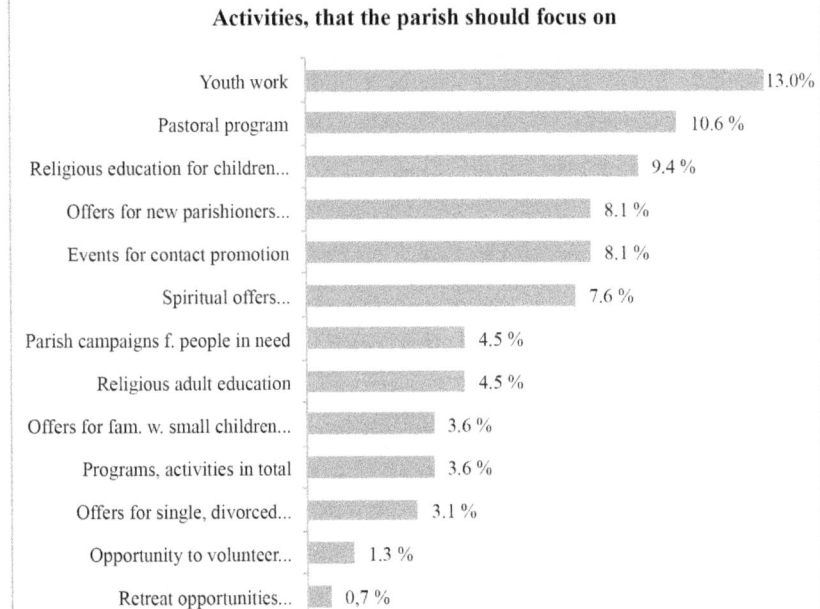

For example in this respect, efforts in the fields in particular need of attention by parishes from the viewpoint of the CVers (Fig. 5-18) such as 'youth work' or 'religious education/training for children and young people' should be sufficiently well known in terms of scope instead of being judged as "not assessable" by almost a third (28.1% for youth work and 31.9% for religious education for children respectively, cf. Fig. 5-19) of this surveyed group of church-connected Catholics.

The same applies regarding 'offers for new parishioners and new residents' as an aspect of particular importance for continued membership and hence for continued existence of the parish, or to 'events for contact promotion' of parishioners among each other, which were both assessed by more than 40 percent of the respondents negatively, or given a "not assessable" verdict by as much as a third (37.5%) and fourth (23.2%) respectively of the participants (cf. Fig. 5-19).

Figure 5-21 on the following page breaks down the "not assessable" indications of the CVers according to Actives and Seniors; in general, the Actives appear, judging by the higher presence of the "not assessable" indications, less informed on the offers and activities of their parishes as compared to the Seniors. Given the found information deficiencies, it may be concluded as a result that:

   ⇨ **HK5 can be deemed falsified.**

Along the same lines, it can be concluded that the expectations of the academically educated CVers as concerns training and education offers of parishes – 'religious adult education' as well as 'religious education/training for children and young people' – were not being fully met. Both the education offers were viewed by 42.0 and 32.7 percent respectively of the CVers as "less good" and "inadequate" while 30.1 and 31.9 percent respectively gave here the "not assessable"-indication. The same applies concerning offers for singles and aliens (new parishioners, new residents): these were assessed negatively by 38.4 and 43.2 percent respectively of the CVers while 45.2 and 37.5 percent respectively were unable to assess them. Consequently, this means that:

   ⇨ **HK6 can be deemed confirmed.**

The open question about which events specially tailored to academics could be successfully offered by parishes yielded as answers a total of 202 constructive comments and ideas by a third of the CVers (33%). By analysing word usage frequency in the answers on eliminating all the conjunctions, prepositions, auxiliary verbs etc., there were 64 found instances of mentioning "discussion" events and synonymous events, as well as 40 instances of the word "lecture".

Thus on accounting for the critical stances regarding 'religious adult education' and 'religious education/training for children and young people' as evident from Fig. 5-19, it follows that:

⇨   **HK7 can be deemed confirmed.**

Figure 5-21: "Please rate the following offers/programs of your parish:" analyzed by "Not assessable" (Question 11)

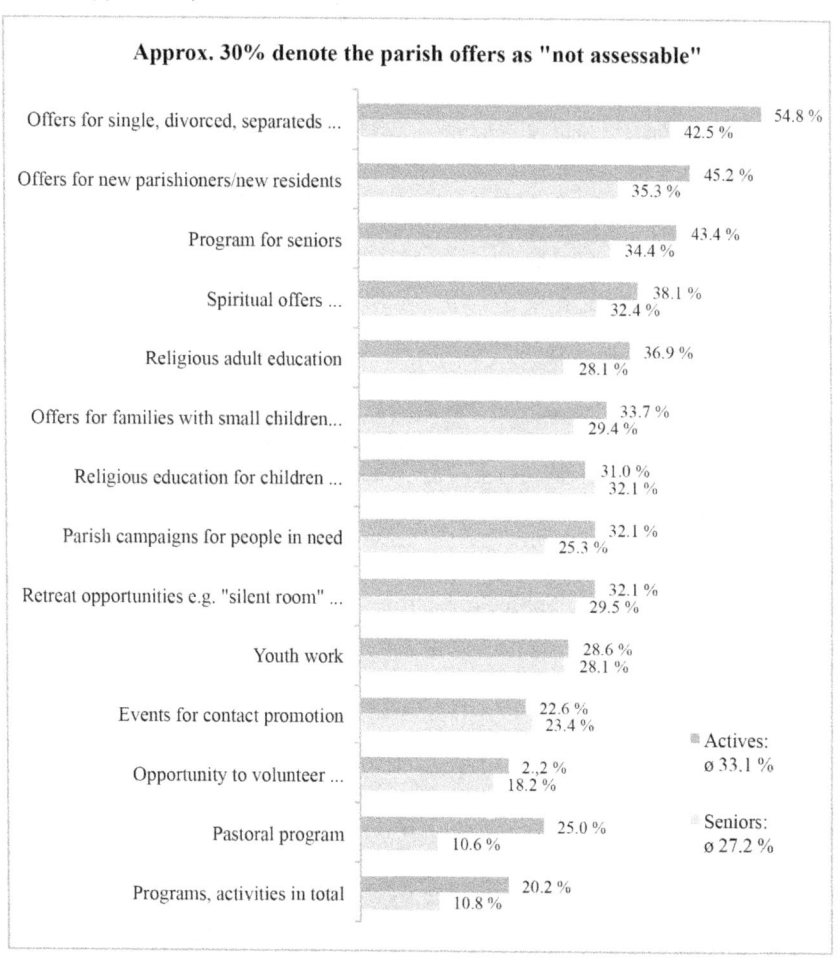

Approx. 30% denote the parish offers as "not assessable"

Offer	Actives	Seniors
Offers for single, divorced, separateds ...	54.8 %	42.5 %
Offers for new parishioners/new residents	45.2 %	35.3 %
Program for seniors	43.4 %	34.4 %
Spiritual offers ...	38.1 %	32.4 %
Religious adult education	36.9 %	28.1 %
Offers for families with small children...	33.7 %	29.4 %
Religious education for children ...	31.0 %	32.1 %
Parish campaigns for people in need	32.1 %	25.3 %
Retreat opportunities e.g. "silent room" ...	32.1 %	29.5 %
Youth work	28.6 %	28.1 %
Events for contact promotion	22.6 %	23.4 %
Opportunity to volunteer ...	2.2 %	18.2 %
Pastoral program	25.0 %	10.6 %
Programs, activities in total	20.2 %	10.8 %

Actives: ø 33.1 %

Seniors: ø 27.2 %

5.2.5.2   Characteristics of the Parish Life

Alongside the various charity and social offers presented by a parish to its members, neighbours and interested persons, there are also other attributes of relevance to the life of parishes such as the sense of community in the parish, leadership qualities of the parish priest, suitability of his assistants as well as the liturgical events during church services etc.[371].

Figure 5-22 on the next page provides the prevalently very good assessments of these characteristics by the respondents. These appreciate in particular physical proximity to the church (85.3%), quality of (Sunday) church services (75.3%), the liturgy on the whole (74.9%) as well as the musical (72.4%) and verbal (66.1%) aspects of the church services.

In contrast to the assessment of concrete activities, the "non assessable" indications in connection with the life of the parishes and their liturgical offers are more sporadic (Fig. 5-22). As for the sample of the surveyed CVers their above-average religiousness and affinity to church obviously was confirmed, the liturgical offers and the parish life can be deemed to be profiled in a more targeted way.

As "inadequate" and "less good", in particular 'presentation of a vision/perspective for the parish' (46.8%), 'presentation of a Catholic point of view on current topics' (42.3%) and 'information of parishioners and the parish media' (37.4%) were assessed, with the first of the points of criticism additionally also judged by almost a quarter (23.3%) of the surveyed CVers as "not assessable". Further about a third of the respondents judged as less good to inadequate the topics of 'proclamation, evangelisation' and 'community feeling, sense of belonging' (33.5% and 30.2%) respectively. The assessments also were fully confirmed in a targeted back query as to which aspects were most in need of improvement (see Fig. 5-23 on the page after next).

---

[371] See CARA – CENTER FOR APPLIED RESEARCH IN THE APOSTOLATE: CARA's seven elements of parish life. Ibidem.

Figure 5-22: "Please evaluate the following characteristics of your parish life" (Question 13)

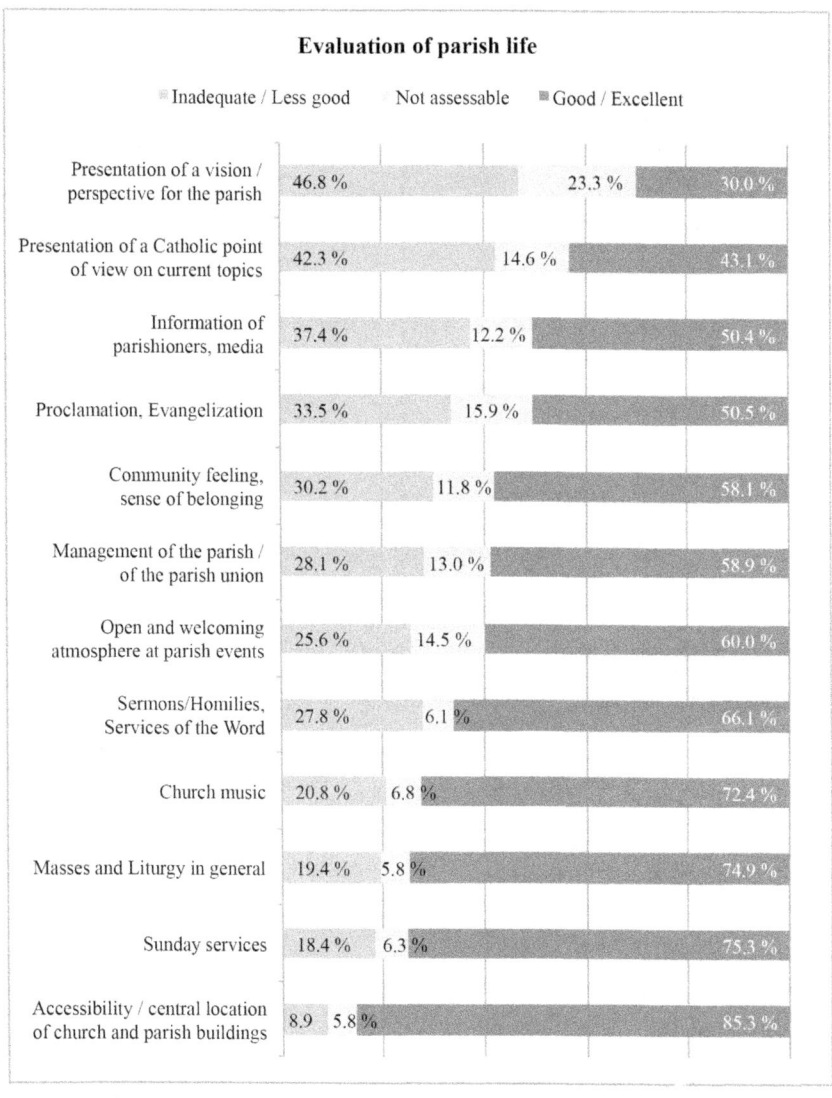

Evaluation of parish life

▪ Inadequate / Less good   Not assessable   ▪ Good / Excellent

	Inadequate / Less good	Not assessable	Good / Excellent
Presentation of a vision / perspective for the parish	46.8 %	23.3 %	30.0 %
Presentation of a Catholic point of view on current topics	42.3 %	14.6 %	43.1 %
Information of parishioners, media	37.4 %	12.2 %	50.4 %
Proclamation, Evangelization	33.5 %	15.9 %	50.5 %
Community feeling, sense of belonging	30.2 %	11.8 %	58.1 %
Management of the parish / of the parish union	28.1 %	13.0 %	58.9 %
Open and welcoming atmosphere at parish events	25.6 %	14.5 %	60.0 %
Sermons/Homilies, Services of the Word	27.8 %	6.1 %	66.1 %
Church music	20.8 %	6.8 %	72.4 %
Masses and Liturgy in general	19.4 %	5.8 %	74.9 %
Sunday services	18.4 %	6.3 %	75.3 %
Accessibility / central location of church and parish buildings	8.9	5.8 %	85.3 %

In times of great change, as currently experienced by parishes in Germany due to the ongoing demographic shift and progressive differentiation in society [372], guidance statements and clear answers to people's questions are a vital need. In this respect in particular the mainly criticised topics such as conveying a vision/perspective for the parish and presentation of a Catholic point of view on current topics imply a keen interest in these topics and/or a high pertinent need of communication of the surveyed CVers. This means that:

⇨ **HK8 can be deemed confirmed.**

Figure 5-23: "What is the most important topic for improvement?" (Question 14)

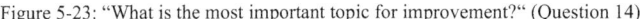

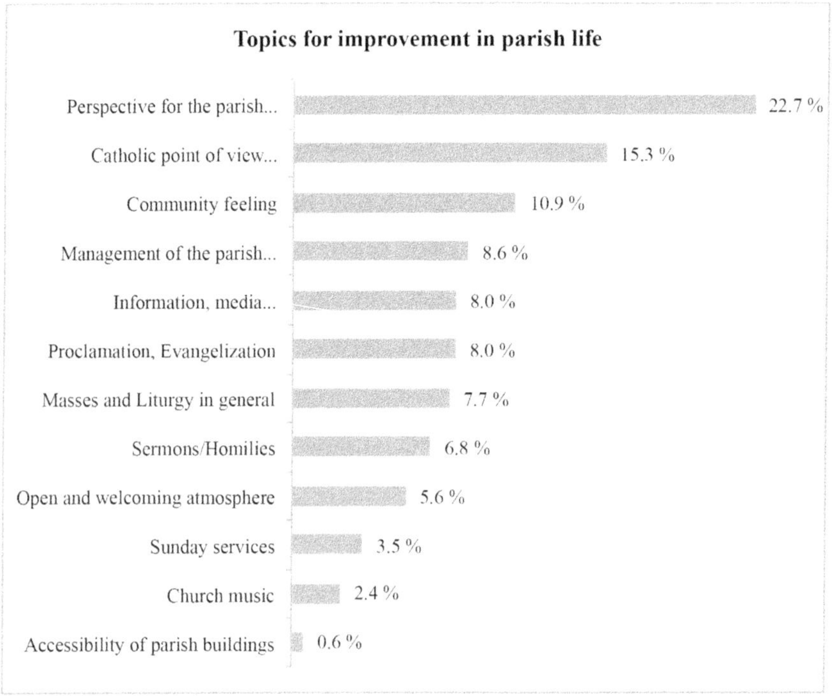

Topics for improvement in parish life

Topic	Percentage
Perspective for the parish...	22.7 %
Catholic point of view...	15.3 %
Community feeling	10.9 %
Management of the parish...	8.6 %
Information, media...	8.0 %
Proclamation, Evangelization	8.0 %
Masses and Liturgy in general	7.7 %
Sermons/Homilies	6.8 %
Open and welcoming atmosphere	5.6 %
Sunday services	3.5 %
Church music	2.4 %
Accessibility of parish buildings	0.6 %

---

[372] HILLEBRECHT, Steffen W. (2000): *Die Praxis des kirchlichen Marketings*. Ibidem, pp. 13-22.

5.2.6   Voluntary Engagement

5.2.6.1   The Type and Scope of Direct Engagement in Church

Of the 469 CVers surveyed, 356 (75.9%) indicated having been directly involved in ecclesiastical activities. This means that among the Catholic Corporates, the share of those involved in church is higher by about 20 percent than for the bulk of voluntarily engaged German academics [373] (55.2 %).

Figure 5-24: "Are you or have you been directly involved in ecclesiastical activities? (Question 16)

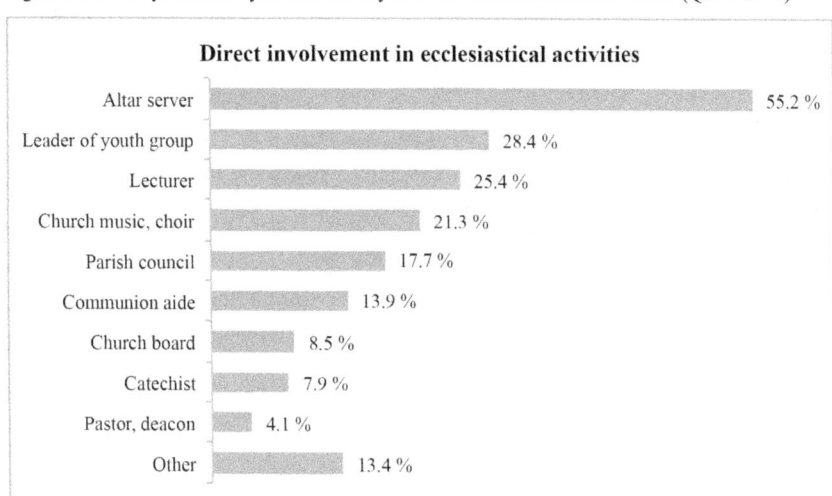

Direct involvement in ecclesiastical activities

Altar server	55.2 %
Leader of youth group	28.4 %
Lecturer	25.4 %
Church music, choir	21.3 %
Parish council	17.7 %
Communion aide	13.9 %
Church board	8.5 %
Catechist	7.9 %
Pastor, deacon	4.1 %
Other	13.4 %

On adding to the absolute number of all the indicated activities the optional entries under the heading "Other", there are a total of 918 ecclesiastical activities for the total of 356 respondents, which is on average well in excess of two ecclesiastical activities per person.

Particularly notable in the engagement in church is the high share of altar servers at 55.2 percent. 28.4 percent were or had been active as leaders of a youth group, a quarter (25.4%) was active as lecturers and one in five of the respondents (22.6%) was engaging in church musically. 17.7 percent were taking their share of responsibility for the parish council, and 8.5 percent for the church board.

---

[373]   TESCH-RÖMER, Clemens et al. (2016): *Der deutsche Freiwilligensurvey 2014*. Ibidem, table annex, Table 16-1, p. 222: Percentages of volunteers in 2014 by gender, age and education.

5.2.6.2   Engagement in Different Areas of Life

On exploring in general terms the areas of life in which the surveyed students and academics were currently active or had been active within the last 12 months, there was according to the findings a generally higher level of engagement compared to highly educated German male average[374] with activities beyond the standard level in the church, cultural, political and social contexts (Fig. 5-25) – apparently 'at the cost' of sports and other activities. In particular in church contexts, the CVers were engaged at 37.3 percent substantially more than the German academic average (11.0%). Consequently on accounting for the results from Part 5.2.6.1 (see Fig. 5-24):

⇨   **HF1 can be deemed confirmed.**

59.3 percent of the surveyed CVers further indicated having taken as part of their activities special responsibilities or volunteering appointments, which again points to a clear emphasis within the church contexts:

Figure 5-25: "Were you particularly engaged in one or more of the above areas, e.g. by taking over specific tasks or honorary offices?"
(Question 22 with specification based on predefined answer options from Question 21)

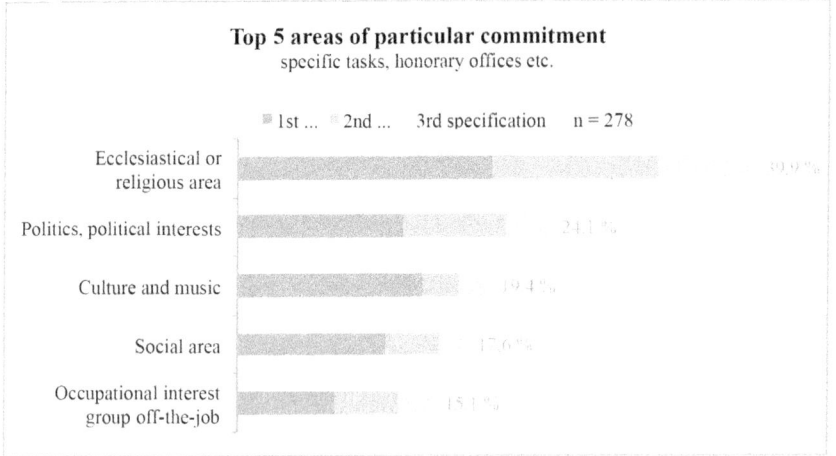

---

374   See TESCH-RÖMER, Clemens et al. (2016): *Der Deutscher Freiwilligensurvey* 2014. Ibidem, table annex, Table 3-15, pp. 26-28: Percentage of active persons in a time comparison by gender, area and education. Basis: All respondents, n = 28,689, selected data: Highly educated men.

Figure 5-26: "In which of the following areas of life are you or have you been active within the last 12 months?" (Question 21)

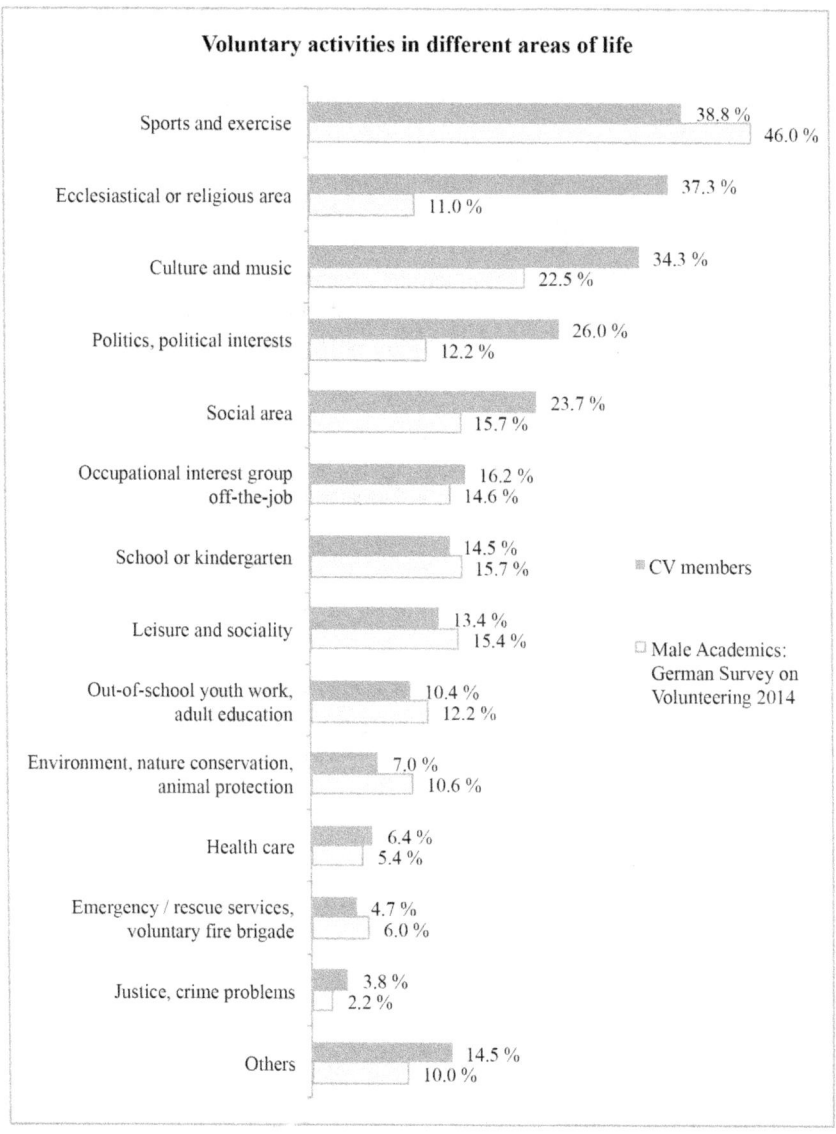

Voluntary activities in different areas of life

5.2.6.3   Fields of Activities and Motivation

Those CVers who had taken as part of their voluntary engagement a responsibility or a special honorary office (Fig. 5-25), were then asked about the scope of the tasks they assumed and the motives for their engagement (Fig. 5-27 as well as Fig. 5-28 on the next page).[375]

As answers to the question about the assumption of specific tasks or an honorary office (Fig. 7-24), almost a half of the Catholic Corporates (48.2 %) indicated 'organization/implementation of aid projects' followed by 'practical work that has to be done' (27.7%) and 'administrative activities'. These focus areas of activities are only partly confirmed by the results of the 2014 German Survey on Volunteering:[376] accordingly, those with higher education most often inserted themselves in 'organization of meetings or events', also followed by 'practical work that has to be done'.

Figure 5-27: "What tasks do you primarily undertake in your voluntary commitment?" (Question 23)

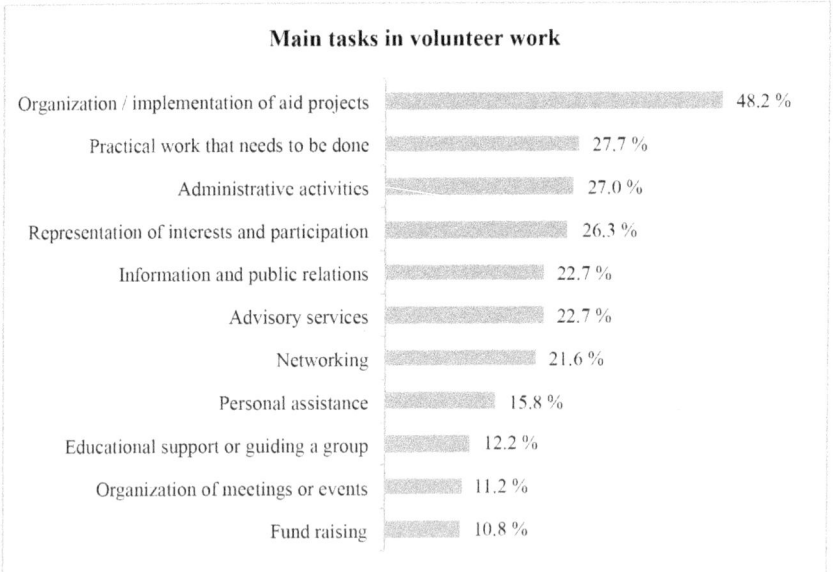

Main tasks in volunteer work

Organization / implementation of aid projects	48.2 %
Practical work that needs to be done	27.7 %
Administrative activities	27.0 %
Representation of interests and participation	26.3 %
Information and public relations	22.7 %
Advisory services	22.7 %
Networking	21.6 %
Personal assistance	15.8 %
Educational support or guiding a group	12.2 %
Organization of meetings or events	11.2 %
Fund raising	10.8 %

---

[375] Answering Questions 23 and 24 only was possible for those 278 participants who had filled in at least the first field in Question 22 - Areas of particular commitment.

[376] See TESCH-RÖMER, Clemens et al. (2016): *Der deutsche Freiwilligensurvey 2014*. Ibidem, pp. 304-307.

Thus from the focus points of the CVers in their engagement in church (Fig 5-25) and the pronounced emphasis in their activities on social and charitable matters (Fig. 5-27), the following conclusion can be drawn:

⇨ **HF3 can be deemed confirmed.**

On comparing the motivations of the CVers for their special engagement with the key motivations of male academics in Germany, alongside the social causes primarily their interest becomes evident in shaping society:

Figure 5-28: "Which motives were or are decisive for your particular commitment?" (Question 24)

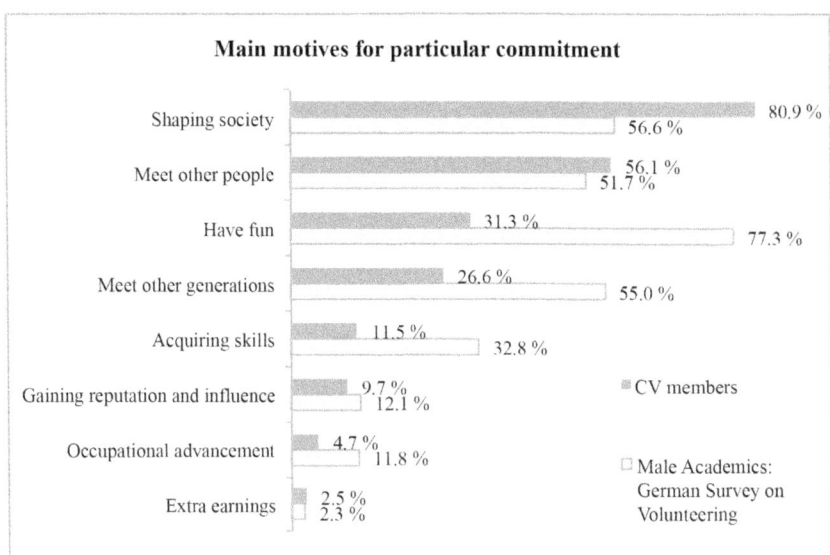

On connecting this strong motivation to shape society with the pronounced engagement of the CVers particularly in the church, cultural and political fields (Fig. 5-26), it follows that:

⇨ **HF4 can be deemed confirmed.**

5.2.6.4 *Engagement in Student Corporations*

Of the 469 CV members participating in the survey, about a fifth (20.9%) counted among the sc. Aktivitas (Actives), meaning they had not yet completed their studies, while the prevalent majority of the participants (78.9%) qualified with their status as 'Seniors'. One survey participant (0.2%) did not specify their status.

When asked about the intensity of contacts of their student association with the local parish, more than a half of the surveyed students and academics (62.3%) declared having been in such contact, irrespective of its actual form. More than a third of the respondents actively inserted themselves in the life of their parishes (35.2%), and a near quarter (23.3%) held joint events with their parish.

Figure 5-29: "To what extent do you agree with the following statements?" (Question 20)

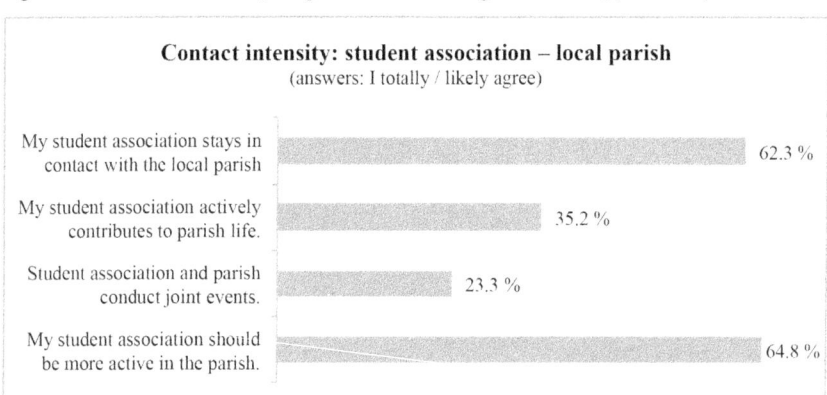

Despite this extent of contacts that can be deemed generally positive, more than a half of the surveyed CVers (64.8%) desired a stronger involvement of their association within the parish. This desire comes as no surprise as among the uniformly Catholic members of parishes, there are also young graduates from secondary schools and students as well as older academics who qualify as strong candidates for membership in respective student associations. Given this, the following conclusion can be drawn:

⇨ **HF2 can be deemed confirmed.**

5.2.7   Generalizability of the Sample (Representativeness)

The reference base of the study was a survey among students and academics organized in Catholic student associations. In the study, a total of n=694 Catholic persons were approached. Of these, n=468 were identified as members of a Catholic student association organized under the CV umbrella; n=370 (79.1%) had an academic education, and n=98 persons (20.9 %) had student status.

According to data of the German Federal Statistical Office, there are in Germany N=2164800 (81.2%) male Catholic persons with completed academic education and N=500200 (18.8%) male students of the Catholic faith. On comparing now the survey sample in statistical terms as regards distribution of male Catholic persons with completed academic education and those still studying, the survey sample corresponds to the distribution from the Statistical Yearbook (chi-square=0,78, df=1, Alpha=1%, not significant)[377]. The survey sample thus is (without further weighting) for the attributes "male Catholic academics" and "male Catholic students" representative in its distribution[378].

Figure 5-30: Structural Comparison of the Sample with the Statistical Population

		Academics	[%]	Students	[%]
Study	468	370	0.7906	98	0.2094
CV	29000	25000	0.8621	4000	0.1379
Germany	2665000	2164800	0.8123	500200	0.1877

The distribution of student and non-student members of the CV-affiliated associations differs slightly from the distribution according to the Statistical Yearbook. For example, there are in CV about 25,000 male Catholic members with

---

[377] See STATISTISCHES BUNDESAMT (2017): *Jahrbuch der Statistik 2017*, ibidem. As method, the unidimensional chi-square test was used that allows to verify whether a distribution within a sample matches a distribution within a population. As under this test, the "desired hypothesis" is the null hypothesis in that the sample matches the statistical population, a non-significant result is positive and welcomed.

[378] "Representative" means that a sample corresponds in its structure to the statistical population (either the German population or the entirety of CV members), with the structural attribute here relating to the ratio of Catholic persons with completed academic education and Catholic students. The advantage of the structural similarity found here is that the results for the sample are applicable (though still cautiously) to all male Catholic academics and male Catholic students in Germany, and to CV members.

an academic degree (86.2%) and approx. 4,000 male students (13.8%) (which is due to the fact that given demographic and societal changes, there is a steady decline in the percentage of students who become members in a student association). On comparing the survey sample also with the CV membership structure, although there are larger deviations (chi-square=4.86, df=1, Alpha=1%, not significant), there is still a general match. Thus the survey sample is generalizable also for members of the CV-affiliated student associations.

5.3 Summary and Recommendations

Due to the progressive loss of membership, church activities and offers are ever more difficult to implement relying on and with the aid of volunteers and voluntary helpers. Instead, such activities must be performed ever more often and at a substantial cost by full-time staff members and/or external service providers. Due to this in further parts of this thesis, firstly the relationship has been explored between engagement in volunteer organizations and the social capital in society, and the social economic determinants discussed of voluntary engagement and the positive correlations between education, income, religion and gender. In reference to the German Survey on Volunteering 2014, exceptionally high levels of voluntary engagement have been posited particularly for Catholic academics.[379]

5.3.1 Summary Assessment of the Hypotheses

In conclusion, the hypotheses posited and verified and/or falsified in this thesis can be evaluated as follows:

5.3.1.1 Religiousness and Affinity to the Church

On religiousness and affinity to the church of the surveyed students and academics, it can be concluded that the majority of them (85.5%) have a positive attitude towards the Church and their parishes. This clear-cut result further is sustained in practice both by regular presence at church services – more than a half of the CVers (52.7%) visit the Holy Mass at least once a week as compared to 10.2% of all Catholics – as well as a clearly distanced attitude to leaving the Church (80.2%).

All the three pertinent hypotheses have been confirmed based on the empirical study, so that the CVers can be testified an above average religiousness and affinity to the church overall.

---

[379] TESCH-RÖMER, Clemens et al. (2016): *Der Deutsche Freiwilligensurvey 2014*. Ibidem.

5.3.1.2   Church Communication and Parish Life

The eight core hypotheses can be comprised under the headings of "Communication Preferences", "Information Behaviour" and "Integration of Members" and attest to a generally positive perception of the Church offers and activities by the surveyed academics and students.

As before though, there is still a substantial need for the Catholic Church and its parishes to make efforts to keep up if it wants to be perceived and preferred in a highly technicized, ubiquitous and increasingly subjectively consumed world of communication as a competent guide towards oneself and in finding sense and meaning as well as a brand for top quality religious and social services. This is because although the Church has been tinkering with all types of media, it still lacks the precision and the sleight of hand including the ability to listen out to the very delicate tones (target group orientation) to get its messages right more than on an occasional basis. For example the high acceptance of and preference towards electronic information and communication channels as determined for the surveyed sample by now has been relatively underrepresented in the communication mix of parishes that still is skewed towards the traditional print media.

Proactive information behaviour such as researching in own effort and forwarding church-related information to one's personal and social networks by particularly communicative target groups such as the CVers still are not being used systematically by the Church and its parishes. Specifically this target group though that is communication-friendly and close to the Church generally views parish offers highly positively, however also with (age-specific) criticism and information deficiencies as regards offers of the catechetical and contact-inviting type. Although there is a prevalent satisfaction with liturgical events, what the respondents miss in particular is a clear communication of the points of view and development perspectives of the Catholic Church.

Seven of the hypotheses on information and communication of parishes have been confirmed in the study; the only one falsified is the hypothesis that Catholic Corporates are comprehensively informed on the activities and offers of their parishes.

5.3.1.3   Voluntary Engagement

The four hypotheses on voluntary engagement of Catholic Corporates have been all confirmed:

Out of the Christian desire to participate in shaping society, the CVers take on alongside cultural, political and social tasks in particular honorary functions in the Church and/or in various spheres of religious life. In doing so they focus on organizing aid projects, on practical and administrative tasks as well as on the wealth of activities in promoting and spreading the messages of the Church.

5.3.2 Recommendations

The communication attributes and interest focus points explored herein of corporate academics can be used by parishes and church establishments for a target-group specific communication with members, but also to present news and innovations/changes, and communicate emergencies.

Strategically, the insights gained may be used for designing and marketing concrete activities and offers, mainly however for targeted recruitment of volunteers and sponsors with academic background for example to organize church education and cultural events, for administrative support and for implementation of targeted aid and relief projects.

From the present thesis, the following practical recommendations concerning marketing and marketing communication of parishes can be derived in order to successfully approach (male) social circles with higher education:

(1) Knowledge

- Create a parish feedback system for regularly surveying the opinions, priorities, ideas, and potentials of the different parish members and their private environment.

- Identify milieu-specific influencers[380] ("advocates, ambassadors/evangelists, professionals, celebs") as direct contact persons for academic parish members.

(2) Parish Program

- Develop targeted offers for academic church members, such as.
  - Religious adult education,
  - Religious and spiritual lectures and discussions,
  - Church services in the Latin rite.

- Develop an academic-specific portfolio for voluntary engagement e.g. in the areas of

---

[380] WORD-OF-MOUTH MARKETING ASSOCIATION: *WOMMA Influencer Guidebook - 2013.* Ibidem, pp. 21-38.

- Parish administration, council/board, marketing/public relations,

- Religious education for children and adults, member support,

- Funding and organization of church events and aid projects, networking.

- Involve the church-related activities of Catholic student associations and organizations proactively in parish life.

(3) Contact Points

- Create opportunities to meet 'high potential' parish members.

- Organize milieu-specific events for contact promotion.

- Get in direct touch with Catholic academics, especially with CV members and their local organizations (student associations, senior associations and circles, educational and aid institutions).

(4) Communication

- Differentiate the communication of your parish according to media use, content preferences and information behaviour in specific social milieus:

  - Create milieu-specific content and boost content sharing (viral marketing).

  - Use CVers systematically as 'proactive communicators' for word of mouth both in their personal and online social networks (word-of-mouth marketing).

- Close the communication gap to academics:

  - Focus on informative websites and e-newsletters.

  - Ensure attractive presences on leading social media platforms and networks.

  - Align your classic (print) communication with academic awareness and perception.

  - Create apps related to faith, religion and parish activities.

- Communicate directly on detected information needs such as the perspective of the Church, Catholic point of view, academic-specific activities and projects.

- Use the advanced media competence of students and young parishioners with academic background to establish modern communication tools.

5.3.3   Further Research Questions

5.3.3.1   Interpersonal and Milieu-Specific Communication

A comprehensive examination into how far (digital) word of mouth within the framework of parish communication can be systematically activated and used strategically (seeding [381]) may yield valuable insights not just for marketing communication of church organizations and establishments but also for the basic church practice of proclamation and evangelization.

In the implementation of target group-specific direct marketing campaigns and in particular in directly approaching specific target groups with a view to their participation or voluntary engagement, care should be taken that the contact persons and media of parishes are compatible with the target group at hand in order to mitigate or minimize preferably in advance any milieu-specific acceptance problems.

In this respect, an examination into how far the milieu-specific background of the contact persons of a parish, or the milieu-specific homogeneity/diversity of a leadership or pastoral team is of any significance to the success of the church offers and/or the parish life could yield sustainable insights for training,[382] selection and the deployment of pastoral workers and other full-time staff members of the parish who come into "contact with the customer".

5.3.3.2   Applicability of the Results to Other Catholics

Both the German Survey on Volunteering 2014 as well as the best4planning database imply an applicability of the results of the present thesis to all the (male) Catholic academics in Germany.[383] However, in order to reach in this context verifiable conclusions, a detailed analysis of the data of at least the studies mentioned is necessary as well as a qualitative verification of the insights gained for example using academic focus groups.

5.3.3.3   Applicability of the Results to Other European Countries

Given the historical similarities and parallels in the formation and developments of Catholic corporations in German speaking areas, the results of this thesis may be

---

[381] HINZ, Oliver, SKIERA, Bernd, BARROT, Christian, BECKER, Jan U.: Seeding Strategies for Viral Marketing: An Empirical Comparison. In: *Journal of Marketing 75 (6)*, pp. 55-71 (American Marketing Association), 2011, pp. 55-71.

[382] In this respect see also: STELZER, Marius: *Wie lernen Seelsorger?* Ibidem.

[383] See Chapters 5.1.1.2 – 5.1.1.3.

principally applicable also to members of Catholic student associations in Austria and in Switzerland.

At the end of 2016, there were about 5.16 million Roman Catholics in Austria, with a strongly falling tendency.[384] This corresponds to a share in total population of 58.8 percent, which implies in comparison with Germany a substantially higher acceptance and weight of the Catholic Church in society. The Catholic student associations under the umbrella of the present-day Austrian Cartel Confederation (ÖCV) were up until 1933 a part of the German CV; since 1963, there is an official treaty between the two umbrella confederations.[385]

In Switzerland, there were a total of 2.57 million Roman Catholics in 2015,[386] which corresponds to a share in total population of 37.3 percent. In terms of the significance of the Catholic Church in society in Switzerland, generally similar conditions to Germany can be presumed, not least as there are also in Switzerland significant variations between the different cantons in mutual proportions of the Catholic and Protestant parts of the population respectively. The CV and ÖCV are associated with the Swiss Student Association (SchwStV) under a three-confederation treaty.[387]

These general framework conditions underscore the substantial similarities between corporate Catholic academics in Germany, Austria and Switzerland as such and also in their attitudes towards the Catholic Church.

Not just in Germany but also in Austria and Switzerland, there is additionally comprehensive information on voluntary engagement of the population;[388] there are also analyses of the respective Sinus Milieus based on which the specific attributes

---

[384] See MEDIENREFERAT DER ÖSTERREICHISCHEN BISCHOFSKONFERENZ: *Webportal "Katholisch.at"*. [retrieved on 2018-04-30] Available from: https://www.katholisch.at/statistik-60000

[385] cf. CARTELLVERBAND: *Der CV in Europa.* [retrieved on 2017-12-08] Available from: https://www.cartellverband.de/akademiker-netzwerk/der-cv-in-europa/ – as well as: ÖSTERREICH-ISCHER CARTELLVERBAND: *Die Entwicklung des CV in Österreich in der Zwischenkriegszeit.* [retrieved on 2018-04-30] Available from: https://www.oecv.at/Home/ Verband/21

[386] cf. SCHWEIZERISCHES BUNDESAMT FÜR STATISTIK: *Sprachen und Religionen.* [retrieved on 2018-04-30 Available from: https://www.bfs.admin.ch/bfs/de/home/statistiken/bevoelkerung/ sprachen-religionen.html – as well as SCHWEIZER BISCHOFSKONFERENZ: *Statistik der katholischen Kirche in der Schweiz.* [retrieved on 2018-04-30] Available from: http://www.bischoefe.ch/wir/schweiz/statistisches

[387] cf. SCHWEIZERISCHER STUDENTENVEREIN: *Webseite Schw.StV* [retrieved on 2018-04-30] Available from: http://www.schw-stv.ch/index.cfm?Sprache=DE

[388] See ZULEHNER, Paul: *87393 Kirchenaustritte – was nun? Information zum Forschungsbericht 2010 der Langzeitstudie "Religion im Leben der Menschen"* [retrieved on: 2018-04-30] Available from: http://zulehner.org/site/zeitworte/article/198.html | cf. STOLZ, Jörg, KÖNEMANN, Judith, SCHNEUWLY PURDIE, Mallory, ENGLBERGER, Thomas, KRÜGGELER, Michael: *Religiosität in der modernen Welt: Bedingungen, Konstruktionen und sozialer Wandel.* Lausanne: Université de Lausanne, Observatoire des religions en Suisse (ORS), 2011.

of Catholic academics in terms of the sociology of religion can be explored and mutually correlated.[389] For such intercultural comparisons, for example the Sinus institute of Heidelberg offers national milieu information currently for 18 European countries (including Austria and Switzerland) as well as transnational meta-milieus for identifying shared patterns in fundamental values, lifestyles and preferences of the people.[390] Additionally, multinational value studies such as the *European Values Study (EVS)* provide comprehensive and comparative information not least on religiousness, connectedness to church and religious socialization in a variety of European countries.[391] In order to ultimately reach scientifically verifiable conclusions on transferability of the present results to the Austrian and Swiss environments, an additional analysis is needed of both country-specific and transnational data and information collected using the means of the sociology of religion.

An examination of transferability of the insights from this study to other European countries is unlikely due to the lack of the cultures of Catholic student associations and confederations there to yield any usable results.

---

[389] cf. SINUS-INSTITUT: *Die Sinus-Milieus in Österreich.* [retrieved on 2018-04-30] Available from: https://www.sinus-institut.de/sinus-loesungen/sinus-milieus-oesterreich/ – as well as: SINUS-INSTITUT: *Die Sinus-Milieus in der Schweiz.* [retrieved on 2018-04-30] Available from: https://www.sinus-institut.de/sinus-loesungen/sinus-milieus-schweiz/

[390] cf. SINUS-INSTITUT: *Sinus-TGI-Mediadaten international.* [retrieved on 2018-04-30] Available from: https://www.sinus-institut.de/sinus-loesungen/mediendaten-international/

[391] cf. EUROPEAN VALUES SURVEY: *Atlas of European Values.* [retrieved on 2018-04-30] Available from: http://www.atlasofeuropeanvalues.eu/new/ – in reference to the World Values Survey and the Inglehart-Welzel cultural map of the world, cf. WORLD VALUES SURVEY: *Welcome to the World Values Survey site.* [retrieved on 2018-04-30] Available from: www.worldvaluessurvey.org

6   Conclusions

6.1   Conclusions

The research question of this thesis was: "How must church communication be ideally designed in order to successfully approach Catholic Corporates?" The present study provides concrete answers to this from the ideal typified perspective of student and graduate members of Catholic student associations organized under the umbrella of the Cartel Confederation (CV) that represents as the largest German and European association of academics the bulk of Catholic Corporates in Germany.

The key component of the church marketing mix is communication including marketing communication that is ascribed an equally interpersonal, faith conveying and community building function as well as media and marketing functions and the function of spreading the message of salvation and faith.[392] Particularly within the context of the stark decline in membership and the corresponding loss of importance and weight of the Catholic Church in an increasingly disparate society, it is becoming ever more difficult and demanding for parishes to successfully communicate in a target group- and milieu-specific manner the nature and benefits of their liturgical and social activities and offers on the one hand, and their need for personal and financial support on the other.

Given this, the present study has explored the current status of communication of Catholic parishes with their student and graduate members in terms of analyzing the specific perception of the offers of and the media used by parishes and correlating these with the communication preferences and information behaviour of the surveyed student and academic CV members. According to the findings made as for church media, these mostly include in general alongside the typical "above the line" communication channels that accompany church visits (publicanda, church announcement boards, flyers with schedules and event dates, parish news) the occasional parish letters/parish newsletters and parish websites.[393] For the surveyed CVers however, a comparatively strong preference was found for digital communication channels – e-mail newsletters, social media, apps.[394]

---

[392]   See EBERTZ, Michael N.: Religion, Kommunikation und Medien. In: FÜRST (2013): *Katholisches Medienhandbuch.* Ibidem, p. 40, as well as Chapter 3.6.3.2 herein (Interpersonal Communication).

[393]   See Chapter 3.6.3.1 – The Church Media Portfolio.

[394]   cf. Fig. 5-16 (The Communication Gap) in Chapter 5.2.4 herein.

The "below the line" components primarily used in communication with younger people such as social media, mobile marketing, viral marketing and search engine marketing still are being neglected or delivered in poor quality by many parishes due to the lack of support or lack of preference for and/or proficiency with such media of the competent persons. Here the concrete solutions appear to be identifiable with the affinity of CV-affiliated students and academics for digital communication channels and their respective support potential.

Specifically, as regards communication of church establishments and organizations with children and youth, there is a need for convincing concepts that account for the dwindling religious socialization and the increasing diversity of the coming generations away from the church and that are successful on a long-term basis with relevant content and with technically attractive means.[395]

In order to successfully approach academically educated CV-affiliated persons and to recruit them more consequently than before to support parish life, what is mainly needed is a specific address that clearly outlays the aims, perspectives, scope and needs of the parish life, accounting in the effort both for the wide acceptance typical of the milieus of print media as a means of communication, and for the pronounced preference towards up-to-date and mobile online communication channels.

In this respect, what may become particularly valuable for church communication is targeted content marketing: by generating target group specific and relevant, meaning appealing and valuable information for CVers for example on current topics of theological relevance, on current religious education events, on project-specific need for aid and support, or simply about surprising, extraordinary, intelligent, entertaining or useful matters – parishes as well may score effects that aid the spread of the communication message up to viral effects.[396]

Given their information behaviour of actively researching information and actively informing others as confirmed through the findings herein, the CV members can be termed "proactive communicators": The academics and students research in own active effort and with great interest church-related content and event dates and spread these proactively as a form of invitation within their personal social networks. The latter is done primarily through classical and digital word of mouth (personally, by phone, via SMS, e-mail, social media) – a communication discipline that has long

---

[395] See Fig. 3-14 (Topics of Interest to Catholics: An Overview) and Fig. 3-15 (Preferred Information Sources of German Catholics 2009) in Chapter 3.6.3.1 herein, as well as OETTING, Martin (2009): *Ripple Effect.* Ibidem.

[396] cf. Chapter 3.6.3.3 (Word of Mouth and Viral Marketing).

become established to great success in consumer goods marketing, however is not being systematically used by churches as of yet. On comprising the Catholic students and academics organized under the CV umbrella strategically as communicative "hubs" and "bridges"[397], that either wield large networks or function as bridges between different networks, then on a systematic activation of this communication-friendly target group for the classical and electronic word of mouth, the success of church communication campaigns could be significantly improved.

Within the context of the decline in membership, the shortage of priests, the lack of volunteers and the sweeping changes in communication landscapes, this thesis further posed a question about potential target groups with substantial resources the direct and indirect support by which can be secured primarily for the needs and purposes of the Church.

The Sinus institute of Heidelberg that has been used on a commissioning basis since many years by the Catholic Church found mainly in the conservative and economically established milieus an above average proportion of Catholics that are faithful to the Church. A targeted evaluation of the results of the German Survey on Volunteering 2014 as part of the effort herein supplied an additional proof that in particular male Catholic academics voluntarily engage on behalf of their church on a comprehensive basis.[398] Finally, a specific localization of male Catholic academics in the Sinus and SIGMA Milieus confirmed their concentration in the upper class, conservative, liberal-intellectual and social climber milieus.[399]

This finding applies also and in particular to members of confessionally defined student associations. These academics, also referred to as "Catholic Corporates", typically undergo during their studies an additional religious socialization phase that reinforces their religiousness and their commitment to church membership and predestines them over further course of their life to serve the needs of the Church.[400] In this respect, the sc. *Lebensbundprinzip*, or the principle of getting bound for life, of the student associations promotes not just support and cohesion across generations in the respective corporations themselves but also readiness of the Catholic

---

[397] Ibidem in reference to HINZ et al. (2011), who supplied a proof of up to 8-times higher success of such communication campaigns.

[398] cf. TESCH-RÖMER, Clemens et al. (2016): *Der Deutsche Freiwilligensurvey 2014*. Ibidem – as well as Chapter 5.1.1.2 herein (Social Capital and Voluntary Engagement of Catholic Academics).

[399] cf. Chapter 5.1.1.3 (Milieu-specific Classification of Catholic Academics).

[400] cf. Chapter 5.1.1.4 (Sociological Particularities of Catholics Organized in Confessional Student Associations and Academic Confederations).

academics to voluntarily engage in society, in politics and in particular in the Catholic Church.

On the example of members of Catholic student associations organized in CV, the largest European association of academics, a proof has been supplied in the empirical part of the present thesis that this group of persons with higher education levels is particularly suitable credit to its above average connectedness to the Church, its often comprehensive anchoring in society and its milieu-specific resources to support local parishes and church establishments in the performance of their core tasks in liturgy and in spreading the message of salvation and faith, but also in their service to others and to society in a more comprehensive and targeted manner than before. The sample examined by means of an online survey only represents a very small, but a positively highly engaged portion of the entirety of male Catholic academics that amounts in total to about 3.25 percent of the entire German population and to 9.5 percent of the Catholic population of Germany.[401]

The form and extent of this support though depend both on the quality of the particular address (marketing communication) as well as the target group match of the event offerings to be supported: "Where associations intend to recruit more workforce for voluntary and honorary activities, then they should firstly open themselves up more to new target groups. (...) These new target groups can be reached by making them matching offers that are both low-threshold and attractive." [402] Where the persons are approached personally, the adequate professional and social status of the parish representative initiating the contact is a key prerequisite for respective success and in order for the contact making effort to meet its purpose.

The interests of CVers are substantially focused on the field of religious education and theological lecture and discussion events. Though this area in particular as well as all the integrative and contact-promoting events of parishes are criticized as insufficient, there is on the whole a high level of appreciation of church activities and programs by CVers. Consequently, parishes should consider specifically adjusting or extending their education offers to include top quality theological and other scientific lecture and discussion events. In doing so, the obvious choice is to make CV-affiliated academics actively participate in planning and organizing such

---

[401] cf. B4P - BEST FOR PLANNING: *b4p 2016 III.* [retrieved on 2017-07-27] Available from: https://online.mds6.de/mdso6/b4p.php | Own research. Demographic parameters of the respondents: [Gender = male + Religious community = Catholic + General/vocational education = study] (1.84 million persons) as well as [Gender = male + Religious community = Catholic + Occupation = in training/student] (0.42 million persons).

[402] TESCH-RÖMER, Clemens et al. (2016): *Der Deutsche Freiwilligensurvey 2014.* Ibidem.

programs and/or implement these in collaboration with the student associations, local societies or regional corporations organized under the CV umbrella.

Last but not least alongside the financial resources and the comprehensive social anchoring of Catholic CV-affiliated academics, mainly their professional, technical, administrative, organizational and didactic skills and abilities can be meaningfully deployed and used by way of specific voluntary functions.

6.2 Closing Remarks

There are perhaps as many conceptual approaches and ideas for church marketing and communication as there are church parishes, groups and initiatives. Key in any considerations on market place-like solutions though is comprehensive and critical (including self-critical) perception of the respective church establishment or organization from the perspective of those the offers are aimed at. The relevant factors in this perception include the condition of the buildings and facilities as well as care in the selection, preparation and staging of events up to personal style and demeanour of the persons acting in the name or on behalf of the parish, or aiding and helping the parish.

In an era of excess offer, pluralism and freedom of choice, only those offers and activities will actually appeal to the many different target groups that are consequently designed to satisfy their needs, hence provide an obvious benefit, and that are communicated and marketed in the reality of living and the specific "language" of the respective target group.

Irrespective of what marketing activity or activities a parish ultimately opts for, from a certain point onwards any campaign, promotional action and every event gets reduced to the basics of all communication, which is the direct personal interaction between humans, the direct perception of the fellow human being and their individual response to one's own utterances via facial expressions and gestures – and through the thought, felt and said word.

Not least, the Gospel of John [403] as well opens with

ἐν ἀρχῇ ἦν ὁ Λόγος –

In the beginning was the Word.

---

[403] BISCHÖFE DEUTSCHLANDS, ÖSTERREICHS, DER SCHWEIZ et al.: *Die Bibel.*, ibid., Joh 1.1.

Acknowledgements

This dissertation would not have been a reality had it not been for the guidance of my supervisor Prof. Mgr. Peter Štarchoň, PhD. It is also imperative that I thank the other members of my committee for their advice and constructive commentary.

On a personal note, thanks are owed to those who stood by me while I found my way with this thesis; those who listened, those who questioned, and those who knew which varietal was appropriate.

Special thanks are also owed to my friend Elmar for his mentoring as well as to my wife Özlem Sophia who tolerated the many late evenings of research and who always motivated me once more.

I am also grateful to my parents, and to all those marketing collegues in the Catholic church environment who work with me on spreading the Gospel and inspiring people to the Christian faith and its diverse communities.

Tom Peters, December 2018

List of Literature

ABREU, Madalena: The brand positioning and image of a religious organisation: an empirical analysis. In: *International Journal of Nonprofit and Voluntary Sector Marketing 11 (2)*, 2016. DOI 10.1002/nvsm.49

ANGENENDT, Arnold, DAMBERG, Wilhelm: *Geschichte des Bistums Münster: Moderne und Milieu*. Münster: Dialogverlag, 1998. ISBN 3-933144-10-8 1

ANGHELUTA, Alin Valentin, STRAMBU-DIMA, Andreea, ZAHARIA, Razvan: Church Marketing. Concept and Utility. In: *Journal for the Study of Religions and Ideologies (JSRI), Vol. 8, No. 22*, p. 171-197. Bucharest: Acad Econ Studies, 2009. ISSN 1583-0039

APP, Reiner, BROCH, Thomas, MESSINGSCHLAGER, Martin: *Zukunftshorizont Kirche: Was Katholiken von ihrer Kirche erwarten. Eine repräsentative Studie*. Ostfildern: Grünewald, 2014. ISBN 9783786730125

ARN, Win, ARN Charles: *Master's Plan for Making Disciples*. Pasadena: Church Growth Press, 1984. ISBN 0-934408-05-X

BADELT, Christoph (ed.): *Handbuch der Nonprofit-Organisation: Strukturen und Management*. 5. revised edition. Stuttgart: Schäffer-Pöschel, 2013. ISBN 3791031910

BÄHR, Jürgen, JENTSCH, Christoph, KULS, Wolfgang: *Bevölkerungsgeographie*. Berlin, New York: de Gruiter, 1992. ISBN ISBN 3-11-008862-2

BECKER, Jochen: Marketing-Konzeption : *Grundlagen des ziel-strategischen und operativen Marketing-Managements*. 7., revised and amended edition. München: Vahlen, 2001. ISBN 9783800645275

BECKER, Patrick, DIEWALD, Ursula (ed.): *Die Zukunft von Religion und Kirche in Deutschland – Perspektiven und Prognosen*. Freiburg: Verlag Herder, 2014. ISBN 345133299X

BERGER, Jonathan: *Contagious. Why Things catch on*. New York: Simon & Schuster, 2013. ISBN 9781451686593

BERGER, Peter L.: *The Sacred Canopy: Elements of a Sociological Theory of Religion*. Garden City: Doubleday, 1967. ISBN 9781453215371

BIEBERSTEIN, Ingo: *Dienstleistungs-Marketing*. 4., revised and updated edition, Ludwigshafen: Kiehl, 2006. ISBN 3470471541

BIRKELBACH, Klaus: The decision to end church membership: Affiliation vs. church taxes. In: *Zeitschrift für Soziologie 28 (2)*, 1999. p.136-153. ISSN 0340-1804

BISCHÖFE DEUTSCHLANDS, ÖSTERREICHS, DER SCHWEIZ et al. (eds.): *Die Bibel. Altes und Neues Testament.* Einheitsübersetzung. Freiburg: Verlag Herder, 1980. ISBN 3451280000

BLÖMER, Michael: Die Kirchengemeinde als Unternehmen : Die Marketing- und Managementprinzipien der US-amerikanischen Gemeindewachstumsbewegung. Münster: LIT-Verlag, 1998. ISBN 3-8258-3915-X

BÖCKENFÖRDE, Ernst-Wolfgang: *Kirchlicher Auftrag und politisches Handeln : Analysen und Orientierungen.* Freiburg: Herder, 1989. ISBN 3-451-21593-4

BRUHN, Manfred, GRÖZINGER, Albrecht: *Kirche und Marktorientierung – Impulse aus der Ökumenischen Basler Kirchenstudie.* Freiburg (CH) Universitätsverlag, 2000. ISBN 3-7278-1240-0

BRUHN, Manfred: *Marketing. Grundlagen für Studium und Praxis.* 12., revised edition. Wiesbaden: Springer Gabler, 2014. ISBN 3658051124

BRUMMER, Arndt, NETHÖFEL, Wolfgang (ed.): *Vom Klingelbeutel zum Profitcenter? : Strategien und Modelle für das Unternehmen Kirche.* Hamburg: DS - Das Sonntagsblatt, Hanseatisches Druck- und Verlagshaus, 1997. ISBN 3-00-001475-6

BUGHIN, Jacques, DOOGAN, Jonathan, VETVIK, Ole Jørgen: A new way to measure word of mouth marketing. In: *McKinsey Quarterly*, April 2010

CALMBACH, Marc, EILERS, Ingrid, FLAIG, Berthold Bodo: *MDG-Milieuhandbuch 2013 : Religiöse und kirchliche Orientierung in den Sinusmilieus.* Heidelberg/München: SINUS Markt- und Sozialforschung GmbH, 2013

CALMBACH, Marc, BORGSTEDT, Silke, BORCHARD, Inga, THOMAS, Peter Martin: *Wie ticken Jugendliche 2016? : Lebenswelten von Jugendlichen im Alter von 14 bis 17 Jahren in Deutschland.* Wiesbaden: Springer Fachmedien, 2016. ISBN 9783658125325

CAREY, James W.: *Communication as Culture: Essays on media and society.* New York: Routledge, 2009. ISBN 978-0415989763

CARTELLVERBAND (CV) (ed.): *Charta '15 : Gesellschaftspolitische Grundsätze des CV.* Bad Honnef: Cartellverband, 2015

CASANOVA, José: *Europas Angst vor der Religion.* Berlin: University Press, 2009. ISBN 9783737413046

CASIDY, Riza: How great thy brand: the impact of church branding on perceived benefits. In: *International Journal of Nonprofit and Voluntary Sector Marketing 18 (3), pp.231-239*, 2013

CARA – CENTER FOR APPLIED RESEARCH IN THE APOSTOLATE: *Parish Life Survey Compilation of Questions, 2014*. Washington, D.C.: Center for Applied Research in the Apostolate (CARA), Georgetown University, 2014

DAEHN, Michael: Marketing the Church: *How to Communicate Your Church's Purpose and Passion in a Modern Context*. St. Louis: Lulu, 2006. ISBN 141167071X

DAVIS, Justin L, BELL, R. Greg, PAYNE, G. Tyge: Stale in the pulpit? Leader tenure and the relationship between market growth strategy and church performance. In: *International Journal of Nonprofit and Voluntary Sector Marketing 15 (4), pp. 352-368,* 2010

DENZLER, Georg, JANSCHE, R., KÜNG, Hans, ROSENDORFER, Herbert: *Der Ketzer Rupert Lay und das Versagen der Kirche. Sinnsuche in einer komplexen Welt*. Düsseldorf: ECON-Verlag, 1996

DIETLEIN, Georg: Kirche im Aufbruch: Ein Change Management-Ansatz für die katholische Kirche. Norderstedt: Books on Demand, 2015. ISBN 978-3734798429

DOPPLER, Klaus, LAUTERBURG, Christoph: *Change Management: Den Unternehmenswandel gestalten*. 12., updated und extended edition, Frankfurt am Main: Campus Verlag, 2008. ISBN 3593387077

EBERHARDT, Tim (ed.), MEFFERT, Heribert, KENNING, Peter: *Zufriedenheitsstudie „Katholiken des Bistums Münster"* (presentation for press conference, March 2, 2015). Münster: Münster Research Institute, 2015

EBERTZ, Michael N.: *Hinaus ins Weite. Gehversuche einer milieusensiblen Kirche*. Würzburg: Echter, 2008. ISBN 9783429029760

EBERTZ, Michael N. (ed.): *Milieupraxis: Vom Sehen zum Handeln in der pastoralen Arbeit*. Würzburg: Echter, 2009. ISBN 9783429031619

EGLI, Norman: *Virales Marketing: Ohne Geld und mit Mundpropaganda zum Erfolg*. Norderstedt: Books on Demand, 2009. ISBN 9783837083811

EICKEN, Joachim, SCHMITZ-VELTIN, Ansgar: Die Entwicklung der Kirchenmitglieder in Deutschland. Statistische Anmerkungen zu Umfang und Ursachen des Mitgliederrückgangs in beiden christlichen Volkskirchen. In: Statistisches Bundesamt: *Wirtschaft und Statistik 6/2010*. Wiesbaden: Statistisches Bundesamt, 2010

ETSCHEID-STAMS, Markus, LAUDAGE-KLEEBERG, Regina, RÜNKER, Thomas (ed.): *Kirchenaustritt – oder nicht? : Wie Kirche sich verändern muss.* Freiburg: Herder, 2018. ISBN 3451380714

EVERS, Adalbert, LAVILLE, Jean-Louis (ed.): *The Third Sector in Europe.* Cheltenham / Northampton: Edward Elgar, 2004. ISBN 1 84376 400 8

FACHSCHAFTSRAT DER PHILOSOPHISCHEN FAKULTÄT DER UNIVERSITÄT GÖTTINGEN: *Studentenverbindungen gestern und heute : Kritische Perspektiven auf Korporationen in Göttingen und Deutschland.* Göttingen: Aktiv Druck & Verlag, 2017. ISBN 978-3-00-055720-0

FAMOS, Cla Reto, KUNZ, Ralph (eds.): *Kirche und Marketing : Beiträge zu einer Verhältnisbestimmung.* Zürich: TVZ Theologischer Verlag, 2006. ISBN 3290173801

FISCHER, Ralph: *Kirche und Zivilgesellschaft : Probleme und Potentiale.* Stuttgart: Kohlhammer, 2008. ISBN 3170204327

FLÜGGE, Erik: Der Jargon der Betroffenheit. Wie die Kirche an ihrer Sprache verreckt. 2. Aufl., München: Kösel, 2016. ISBN 9783641188535

FÜRST, Gebhard (ed.), HOBER, David, HOLTKAMP, Jürgen: *Katholisches Medienhandbuch: Fakten - Praxis - Perspektiven.* Kevelaer: Butzon & Bercker, 2013. ISBN 9783766642097

GABRIEL, Karl, SPIESS, Christian, WINKLER, Katja: Modelle des religiösen Pluralismus: Historische, religionssoziologische und religionspolitische Perspektiven. Padernborn: Schöningh, 2012. ISBN 9783506774071

GEILING, Heiko (ed.): *Probleme sozialer Integration. agis-Forschungen zum gesellschaftlichen Strukturwandel.* Reihe ‚Soziale Milieus im gesellschaftlichen Strukturwandel' Band 1. Münster-Hamburg-London: LIT, 2003. ISBN 3-8258-6255-0

GERHARD, Joachim, MATTHIS, Karsten: *Öffentlichkeitsarbeit praktisch in Kirche und Gemeinden.* Göttingen: Vandenhoeke & Ruprecht, 2008. ISBN 9783525691014

GIESEN, Rut von: Ökonomie der Kirche? : Zum Verhältnis von theologischer und betriebswirtschaftlicher Rationalität in praktisch-theoretischer Perspektive. Stuttgart: Kohlhammer, 2009. ISBN 9783170208186

GRAY, Mark M., GAUTIER, Mary L.: *Catholic Media Use in the United States, 2011.* Washington, D.C.: Center for Applied Research in the Apostolate (CARA), Georgetown University, 2011

GRAY, Mark M., GAUTIER, Mary L.: *Catholic New Media Use in the United States, 2012.* Washington, D.C.: Center for Applied Research in the Apostolate (CARA), Georgetown University, 2012

HABERMAS, Jürgen: *Theorie des kommunikativen Handelns.* Frankfurt/Main: Suhrkamp, 1981. ISBN 9783518575833

HANIFAN, Lyda Judson: *The Community Center.* New York: Silver, Burnett & Company, 1920

HÄUSEL, Hans-Georg (ed.): *Neuromarketing: Erkenntnisse der Hirnforschung für Markenführung, Werbung und Verkauf.* 3. Auflage. Freiburg: Haufe Lexware, 2014. ISBN 9783648041017

HELD, Dirk, SCHEIER, Christian: *Wie Werbung wirkt: Erkenntnisse des Neuromarketing.* München: Haufe Lexware, 2008. ISBN 9783448072518

HELM, Sabrina: *Kundenempfehlungen als Marketinginstrument.* Wiesbaden: Springer-Verlag, 2013. ISBN 9783322904324

HEMPELMANN, Heinzpeter: *Gott im Milieu: Wie Sinusstudien der Kirche helfen können, Menschen zu erreichen.* 2. extended edition. Gießen: Brunnen, 2013. ISBN 9783765520174

HERMELINK, Jan: Praktische Theologie der Kirchenmitgliedschaft: Interdisziplinäre Untersuchungen zur Gestaltung kirchlicher Beteiligung. Göttingen: Vandenhoeck & Ruprecht, 2000. ISBN 9783525623626

HERMELINK, Jan (ed.), LATZEL, Thorsten: Kirche empirisch: Ein Werkbuch zur vierten EKD-Erhebung über Kirchenmitgliedschaft und zu anderen empirischen Studien. Gütersloh: Gütersloher Verlagshaus, 2008. ISBN 9783579055879

HILLEBRECHT, Steffen W.: *Kirche vermarken! : Öffentlichkeits-Arbeitsbuch für Gemeinden.* Hannover: LHV, 1999. ISBN 9783785907801

HILLEBRECHT, Steffen W.: Die Praxis des kirchlichen Marketings: Die Vermittlung religiöser Werte in der modernen Gesellschaft. Hamburg: E.B.-Verlag, 2000. ISBN 9783930826582

HINZ, Oliver, SKIERA, Bernd, BARROT, Christian, BECKER, Jan U.: Seeding Strategies for Viral Marketing: An Empirical Comparison. In: *Journal of Marketing 75 (6), pp. 55-71* (American Marketing Association), 2011

HIRSCHLE, Jochen: "Secularization of Consciousness" or Alternative Opportunities? The Impact of Economic Growth on Religious Belief and Practice in

13 European Countries. In: *Journal for the Scientific Study of Religion 52 (2), pp. 410-424,* 2013

HÖFELSCHWEIGER, Rainer: Mitglied, wer bist Du? : Eine kirchetheoretische Studie zur Differenzsensiblen Inklusion der religions-soziologischen pluralen Mitglieder evangelischer Kirchen. Leipzig: Evangelische Verlangsanstalt, 2011. ISBN 9783374028658

HOHM, Hans-Jürgen: *Soziale Systeme, Kommunikation, Mensch. Eine Einführung in soziologische Systemtheorie.* 2. überarb. Auflage, Weinheim/München: Juventa-Verlag, 2006. ISBN 9783779923503

HOLTKAMP, Jürgen: Fremde Welten entdecken. Marketing für, Pfarrgemeinden Verbände und Vereine. Münster: Dialog-Medien, 2010. ISBN 3941462237

HOOF, Matthias: Freiwilligenarbeit und Religiosität: Der Zusammenhang von religiösen Einstellungen und ehrenamtlichem Engagement. Berlin: LIT-Verlag Dr. W. Hopf, 2010. ISBN 9783643105523

HUSTINX, Lesley, VON ESSEN, Johan, HAERS, J. / MELS, S. (Hg.): *Religion and Volunteering. Complex, Contested and Ambiguous Relationships.* Cham: Springer International Publishing, 2015. ISBN 9783319045856

INSTITUT FÜR DEMOSKOPIE ALLENSBACH: Kirchenaustritte: Eine Untersuchung zur Entwicklung und zu den Motiven der Kirchenaustritte (IfD-Umfrage 5065). Allensbach, 1992

INSTITUT FÜR DEMOSKOPIE ALLENSBACH: Kommunikationsstile und -welten zwischen Männern und Frauen : Ergebnisse einer bevölkerungs-repräsentativen Befragung (Gesprächskultur in Deutschland). Allensbach, 2011

INSTITUT FÜR DEMOSKOPIE ALLENSBACH: *Chatroom Familie: Die Brücke zwischen den Generationen* (Jacobs Krönung-Studie). Allensbach, 2013

KAPLAN, Andreas M., HAENLEIN, Michael: Users of the world, unite! The challanges and opportunities of Social Media. In: *Business Horizonts* 53 (1), 2010. ISSN 0007-6813

KELLER, Ed, FAY, Brad: *The Face-to-Face Book.* KellerFay Group LLC, New York: InkWell Publishing, 2012. ISBN 1451640064

KLENK, CHRISTIAN: Zustand und Zukunft katholischer Medien. Prämissen : Probleme – Prognosen. Berlin: LIT Verlag, 2013. ISBN 9783643121820

KLÖCKER, Michael: Religionen und Katholizismus, Bildung und Geschichtsdidaktik, Arbeiterbewegung; ausgewählte Aufsätze. Frankfurt am Main: Verlag Peter Lang, 2011. ISBN 9783631617144

KLÖCKNER, Jennifer: Freiwillige Arbeit in gemeinnützigen Vereinen: Eine vergleichende Studie von Wohlfahrts- und Migrantenorganisationen. Wiesbaden: Springer Fachmedien, 2015. ISBN 9783658104221

KOTLER, Philip: *Marketing für Nonprofit-Organisationen.* Stuttgart: Poeschel, 1978. ISBN 3791001892

KOTLER, Philip, ROBERTO, Eduardo: *Social Marketing.* Düsseldorf: Econ-Verlag, 1991. ISBN 3430156467

KÜNKLER, Tobias, FAIX, Tobias, SANDMANN, Tim: Aufwachsen in einer christlichen Familie. Eine empirische Studie zur christlich-familiären Erziehung. Forschungsbericht. Kassel: empirica, 2017

KUNZ, Ralph, SCHLAG, Thomas (eds.): *Handbuch für Kirchen- und Gemeindeentwicklung.* Neukirchen-Vluyn: Neukirchener Verlag, 2014. ISBN 9783788728403

KURTH, Alexandra: *Männer – Bünde – Rituale: Studentenverbindungen seit 1800.* Frankfurt/Main: Campus Verlag, 2004. ISBN 9783593376233

KURYLO, Anastacia: *Inter/Cultural Communication: Representation and Construction of Culture.* Los Angeles: SAGE Publications, 2013. ISBN 9781452289496

LANGNER, Sascha: *Viral Marketing: Wie Sie Mundpropaganda gezielt auslösen und Gewinn bringend nutzen.* 3. extended edition, Wiesbaden: Gabler / GWV, 2009. ISBN 9783834914903

LEPSIUS, Mario Rainer: Demokratie in Deutschland: soziologisch-historische Konstellationsanalysen : ausgewählte Aufsätze. Göttingen: Vandenhoeck & Ruprecht, 1993. ISBN 9783525357637

LICHTSTEINER, Hans, PURTSCHERT, Robert: *Marketing für Verbände und weitere Nonprofit-Organisationen.* 3., updated edition. Bern: Haupt, 2014. ISBN 9783258078267

LICHTSTEINER, Hans, GMÜR, Markus, GIROUD, Charles, SCHAUER, Reinbert: *Das Freiburger Management-Modell für Nonprofit-Organisationen.* 8. edition, Bern: Haupt, 2015. ISBN 9783258079264

LINDSTRÖM, Martin: *Buy·ology: Warum wir kaufen, was wir kaufen.* Frankfurt am Main: Campus, 2009. ISBN 9783593389295

LISKOWSKY, Anne Elise, EVANGELISCHE KIRCHE IN DEUTSCHLAND: *Engagement und Indifferenz. Kirchenmitgliedschaft als soziale Praxis. Fünfte EKD-Erhebung über Kirchenmitgliedschaft.* Hannover: Evangelische Kirche in Deutschland (EKD), 2014. ISBN 9783878430292

MAGATH, Allan J.: When Marketing Services 4 Ps Are Not Enough. In: *Business Horizonts, Volume 29, Issue 3,* May-June 1986, Pages 44-50. ISSN 0007-6813

MAI, Paul (ed.) et al.: *CV-Handbuch.* 3. extended edition. Regensburg: Gesellschaft für Studentengeschichte und studentisches Brauchtum, 2000

McCARTHY, Edmund Jerome: *Basic Marketing: A managerial approach.* University of California: R.D. Irwin, 1960

McGAVRAN, Donald Anderson: *Effective Evangelism - A Theological Mandate.* Phillipsburg: Presbyterian and Reformed Publishing Company, 1988. ISBN 9780875522890

McGAVRAN, Donald Anderson: *The Bridges of God. A Study in the Strategy of Missions.* Eugene: World Dominion Press, 1995. ISBN 9781597522502

MEFFERT, Heribert, BURMANN, Christoph, KIRCHGEORG, Manfred: *Marketing : Grundlagen marktorientierter Unternehmensführung ; Konzepte, Instrumente, Praxisbeispiele.* 12. revised and updated edition, Wiesbaden: Springer Gabler, 2015. ISBN 3658023430

MERTES, Martin: *Controlling in der Kirche : Aufgaben, Instrumente und Organisation dargestellt am Beispiel des Bistums Münster.* 2. edition, Gütersloh: Gütersloher Verlagshaus, 2000. ISBN 3-579-02621-6

MEYNS, Christoph: *Kirchenreform und betriebswirtschaftliches Denken : Modelle, Erfahrungen, Alternativen.* Gütersloh/München: Gütersloher Verlagshaus / Verlagsgruppe Random House, 2013. ISBN 978-3-579-08166-3

MÖDINGER, Wilfried: *Kirchenmarketing: Strategisches Marketing für kirchliche Angebote.* Stuttgart: Lucius und Lucius, 2001. ISBN 9783828201774

MULYANEGARA, Riza Casidy, TSARENKO, Yelena, MAVONDO, Felix T.: An empirical investigation on the role of market orientation in church participation. In: *Int. Journal of Nonprofit and Voluntary Sector Marketing 15 (4), pp. 339-351,* 2010

OETTING, Martin: *Ripple Effect: How Empowered Involvement Drives Word of Mouth.* Wiesbaden: Gabler, 2009. ISBN 9783834920096

OTTE, Gunnar: Sozialstrukturanalyse mit Lebensstilen: Eine Studie zur theoretischen und methodischen Neuorientierung der Lebensstilforschung. Wiesbaden: VS Verlag für Sozialwissenschaften, 2009. ISBN 9783322993359

PELZ, Waldemar: Strategisches und Operatives Marketing. Ein Leitfaden zur Erstellung eines professionellen Maketingplans. Norderstedt: Books on Demand, 2004. ISBN 978-3833406348

PEPELS, Werner: Kommunikationsmanagement : Marketing-Kommunikation vom Briefing bis zur Realisation. Stuttgart: Schäfer-Poeschel, 1994. ISBN 3791008005

PEPELS, Werner: *Marketing-Kommunikation. Einführung in die Kommunikationspolitik.* 3., revised and amended edition. Berlin: Duncker & Humblot, 2015. ISBN 3428145135

PERL, Paul, OLSON, Daniel V.A.: Religious Market Share and Intensity of Church Involvement in Five Denominations. In: *Journal for the Scientific Study of Religion 39 No. 1, pp. 12-31,* 2000

PESTOFF, Victor, DEFOURNY, Jacques, HULGÅRD, Lars: *Social Enterprise and the Third Sector. Changing European landscapes in a comparative perspective.* New York: Routledge, 2014. ISBN 9781134619641

PETERS, Stephan: Elite sein. Wie und für welche Gesellschaft sozialisiert eine studentische Korporation? Marburg: Tectum Verlag, 2004. ISBN 9783828886353

PETERS, Tom, WATERMAN, Robert Jr.: *In Search of Excellence: Lessons from America's Best-Run Companies.* New York: HarperCollins, 1982. ISBN 9780060150426

PICKEL, Gert: *Religionsmonitor. Religiosität im internationalen Vergleich.* Gütersloh: Verlag Bertelsmann Stiftung, 2013

POLLACK, Detlef, MÜLLER, Olaf: *Religionsmonitor. Religiosität und Zusammenhalt in Deutschland.* Gütersloh: Verlag Bertelsmann Stiftung, 2013

PÖTZSCH, Olga, RÖSSGER, Felix: *Bevölkerung Deutschlands bis 2060. 13. Koordinierte Bevölkerungsabrechnung* (28. April 2015). Wiesbaden: Statistisches Bundesamt, 2015

PUTNAM, Robert D., LEONARDI, Robert, NANETTI, Raffaella: *Making Democracy Work: Civic traditions in Modern Italy.* Princeton: Princeton University Press, 1994. ISBN 0691037388

PUTNAM, Robert D.: Turning In, Turning Out: The strange Disappearance of Social Capital in America. In: *Political Science and Politics XXVIII/4,* 1995

PUTNAM, Robert D. (ed.): *Gesellschaft und Gemeinsinn*. Gütersloh: Verlag Bertelsmann Stiftung, 2001. ISBN 3892048401

REINHOLD, Kai, SELLMANN, Matthias (eds.): Katholische Kirche und Gemeindeleben in den USA und in Deutschland: Überraschende Ergebnisse einer ländervergleichenden Umfrage. Münster: Aschendorff, 2011. ISBN 9783402128886

REISING, Richard L.: *Church Marketing 101: Preparing your church for greater growth*. Michigan: Baker Books, 2006. ISBN 9781441200310

RODRIGUE, Christina S.: Marketing Church Services: Targeting Young Adults. In: *Services Marketing Quarterly 24 (1), 2002*

RUPP, William T., SMITH, Alan D.: A Study of the Interrelationships between the internet and religious Organizations : An Application of Diffusion Theory. In: *Services Marketing Quarterly 24 (2)*, 2002

SALAMON, Lester M., ANHEIER, Helmut K.: *Defining the nonprofit sector: A cross-national analysis*. Manchester: Manchester University Press, 1992. ISBN 9780719049026

SALAMON, Lester M., ANHEIER, Helmut K.: *The International Classification of Nonprofit Organizations: ICNPO-Revision 1, 1996*. Working Papers of the Johns Hopkins Comparative Nonprofit Sector Project, no. 19. Baltimore: The Johns Hopkins Institute for Policy Studies, 1996. ISBN 1-886333-23-8

SANTOS, Jessica, MATHEWS, Brian P.: Quality in religious services. in: *Int. Journal of Nonprofit and Voluntary Sector Marketing 6 (3)*, pp. 278-288, 2001

SARGEANT, Adrian: *Marketing Management for Nonprofit Organizations*. New York: Oxford University Press, 2009. ISBN 9780199236152

SCHMIDT, Jan-Hinrik (ed.) et al.: Heranwachsen mit dem Social Web: Zur Rolle von Web2.0-Angeboten im Alltag von Jugendlichen und jungen Erwachsenen. Landesanstalt für Medien Nordrhein-Westfalen, 2009. ISBN 9783891585092

SCHMIDT, Stephan: *Mundpropaganda als steuerbares Marketinginstrument*. Hamburg: Igel-Verlag, 2009. ISBN 9783868151787

SCHÜRMANN, Mathias: *Marketing. In vier Schritten zum eigenen Marketingkonzept*. Zurüch: vdf Hochschulverlag, 2011. ISBN 9783728134080

SCHULZ, Rüdiger, DE SOMBRE, Steffen, CALMBACH, Marc: *MDG-Trendmonitor : Religiöse Kommunikation 2010*, München: MDG Medien-Dienstleistung GmbH, 2010

SCHWARZ, Christian A.: *Praxis des Gemeindeaufbaus. Gemeindetraining für wache Christen.* Neukirchen-Vluyn: Schriftenmissionsverlag, 1987

SCHWARZ, Christian A.: *Das 1x1 der Gemeindeentwicklung.* Glashütten: C&P-Verlag, 1998. ISBN 3867700648

SCHWARZ, Christian A.: *Natürliche Gemeindeentwicklung in der katholischen Kirche.* Vallendar: Patris Verlag, 2003. ISBN 3932842405

SCHWARZ, Christian A.: Gemeindeentwicklung 3.0: Eine Einführung in die Natürliche Gemeindeentwicklung. Emmelsbüll: NCD Media, 2015. ISBN 3928093150

SEKRETARIAT DER DEUTSCHEN BISCHOFSKONFERENZ (ed.): *Katholische Kirche in Deutschland: Zahlen und Fakten 2010/2011.* Bonn: DBK, 2011 – annual editions untill and including: – *Katholische Kirche in Deutschland: Zahlen und Fakten 2016/2017.* Bonn: DBK, 2017

SELF, Donald R., WYMER, Jr., Walter W. HENLEY, Teri Kline (eds.): *Marketing Communications for Local Nonprofit Organisations: Targets and Tools.* New York: Haworth, 2001. ISBN 9781136403712

SELLMANN, Matthias et al.: *CrossingOver – Inspirationen aus den USA.* Lebendige Seelsorge 3/2011, pp. 153-231. Würzburg: Echter, 2011

SELLMANN, Matthias, WOLANSKI, Caroline (eds.): *Milieusensible Pastoral: Praxiserfahrungen aus kirchlichen Organisationen.* Würzburg: Echter, 2013. ISBN 9783429035181

SEPEHR, Philipp: Die Entwicklung der Marketingdisziplin: Wandel der marktorientierten Unternehmensführung in Wissenschaft und Praxis. Wiesbaden: Springer Fachmedien, 2013. ISBN 9783658038991

SHAWCHUCK, Norman, KOTLER, Philip, WRENN, Bruce, RATH, Gustave: *Marketing for Congregations: Choosing to serve People more effectively.* Nashville: Abingdon Press, 1992. ISBN 9780687235797

SHELL Deutschland Holding (ed.): *Jugend 2015* (17. Shell Jugendstudie). Frankfurt am Main: Fischer-Verlag, 2015. ISBN 9783596034017

SHIFMAN, Limor: *Meme: Kunst, Kultur und Politik im digitalen Zeitalter.* Berlin: edition suhrkamp (2681), 2014. ISBN 9783518738078

SOBETZKO, Florian, SELLMANN, Matthias: *Gründer*innen Handbuch für pastorale Start-ups und Innovationsprojekte.* Würzburg: Echter, 2017. ISBN 9783429043407

STELZER, Marius: Wie lernen Seelsorger? : Milieuspezifische Weiterbildung als strategisches Instrument kirchlicher Personalentwicklung. Würzburg: Echter-Verlag, 2014. ISBN 9783429037482

STEVENS, Robert, LOUDON, David, WRENN, Bruce, COLE, Henry: *Concise the Encyclopedia of Church and Religious Organization Marketing.* New York: Haworth Press, 2005. ISBN 9781135792596

STIELSTRA, Greg, HUTCHINS, Bob: *Faith-Based Marketing: The Guide to Reaching 140 Million Christian Consumers.* New Jersey: John Wiley & Sons, 2012. ISBN 9780470483060

STOLZ, Jörg, KÖNEMANN, Judith, SCHNEUWLY PURDIE, Mallory, ENGLBERGER, Thomas, KRÜGGELER, Michael: *Religiosität in der modernen Welt : Bedingungen, Konstruktionen und sozialer Wandel.* Lausanne: Université de Lausanne, Observatoire des religions en Suisse (ORS), 2011

TESCH-RÖMER, Clemens (ed.), SIMONSONS, Julia, VOGEL, Claudia: *Freiwilliges Engagement in Deutschland. Der Deutsche Freiwilligensurvey 2014. (German Survey on Volunteering 2014.)* Berlin: Deutsches Zentrum für Altersfragen (DZA) / Bundesministerium für Familie, Senioren, Frauen und Jugend (BMSFSJ), 2016

THOMÉ, Martin (ed.) et al: *Theorie Kirchenmanagement. Potentiale des Wandels.* Bonn: Lemmens, 1998. ISBN 3932306112

TKACZYNSKI, Aaron: Take me to church: What ministries are of perceived value for attendees from a nonprofit marketing perspective? in: *International Journal of Nonprofit and Voluntary Sector Marketing 22 (3), p. e1581,* 2017

TSCHEULIN, Dieter K., DIETRICH, Martin: Zur (Un-)Vereinbarkeit von Marketing und Kirche – Eine anbieterorientierte Analyse des kirchlichen Marketings. Freiburg: Albert-Ludwigs-Universität, 2003

TRAUNMÜLLER, Richard: Religiöse Vielfalt, Sozialkapital und gesellschaftlicher Zusammenhalt: Religionsmonitor - verstehen was verbindet. Gütersloh: Verlag Bertelsmann Stiftung, 2014. ISBN 9783867936392

USUNIER, Jean-Claude, STOLZ Jörg (eds.): Religions as Brands. New Perspectives on the Marketization of Religion and Spirituality. London: Routledge, 2014. ISBN 9781317067092

VAN DER LANS, Ralf et al.: A viral branching model for predicting the spread of electronic word-of-mouth. In: *Marketing Science 2010, 29 (2), pp. 348-365,* 2010

VOKURKA, Robert J., MCDANIEL, Stephen W., COOPER, Noelle: Church Marketing Communication Methods. The Effect of Location and Impact on Growth. In: *Services Marketing Quarterly 24 (1), 2002.* DOI 10.1300/J396v24n01_02

WAGNER, C. Peter: *Your Church can Grow.* Eugene: Wipf & Stock Publishers, 1981. ISBN 9781579105891

WALTER, Christian: Religionsverfassungsrecht in vergleichender und internationaler Perspektive. Tübingen: Mohr Siebeck, 2016. ISBN 9783161489907

WEISKORN, Richard (ed.): *Gesamtverzeichnis des CV 2015.* Bad Honnef: CV-Sekretariat, 2015

WESTLE, Bettina, GABRIEL, Oscar W. (ed.): *Sozialkapital. Eine Einführung.* Baden-Baden: Nomos, 2008. ISBN 9783832935290

WHITE, Darin W., SIMAS, Clovis F.: An empirical investigation of the link between market orientation and church performance. In: *International Journal of Nonprofit and Voluntary Sector Marketing 13 (2), 2008.* DOI 10.1002/nvsm.314

WHITE, Michael, CORCORAN, Tom: *Rebuilt : Awakening the Faithful, Reaching the Lost, and Making Church Matter.* Indiana: Ave Maria Press, 2013. ISBN 9781594713873

WIPPERMANN, Carsten, MAGALHAES, Isabel de: *MDG-Milieuhandbuch. Religiöse und kirchliche Orientierungen in den Sinus-Milieus® 2005.* Zielgruppen-Handbuch. München / Heidelberg: MDG / Sinus Sociovision, 2005

WIPPERMANN, Carsten, BDKJ / Misereor (ed.): *Wie ticken Jugendliche : Sinus-Milieustudie U27.* Düsseldorf: Verlag Haus Altenberg, 2008. ISBN 9783776102154

WULLHORST, Heinrich: *Leuchtturm oder Kerzenstummel? Die katholischen Verbände in Deutschland.* Paderborn: Bonifatius Verlag, 2017. ISBN 9783897107441

WUTHNOW Robert: *Acts of Compassion : Caring for Others and Helping Ourselves.* Princeton: Princeton University Press, 1991. ISBN 9781400820573

WYMER, Walter, WYMER, Walter W., KNOWLES, Patricia, GOMES, Roger: *Nonprofit marketing: Marketing management for charitable and nongovernmental organizations.* London: SAGE Publications, 2006. ISBN 9781412909235

ZULEHNER, Paul M.: Verbuntung. Kirchen im weltanschaulichen Pluralismus : Religion im Leben der Menschen 1970-2010. Ostfildern: Schwabenverlag, 2011. ISBN 9783796615382

Online Sources

AMERICAN MARKETING ASSOCIATION (AMA)   *Holder of Official Definitions of Marketing:* [retrieved on 2018-04-30] Available from: https://www.ama.org/AboutAMA/Pages/Definition-of-Marketing.aspx

APOSTLESHIP OF PRAYER INTERNATIONAL, EYM (Eucharistic Youth Movement): *Click to pray (clicktopray.org).* [retrieved on 2018-04-30] Available from: https://clicktopray.org/de/

BENTHAUS-APEL, Frederike: Lebensstilspezifische Muster der Kirchenmitgliedschaft. Ergebnisse aus der vierten Kirchenmitgliedschaftsstudie der Evangelischen Kirche Deutschlands (EKD). Frankfurt am Main: Campus, 2016 [retrieved on 2018-04-30] Available from: http://nbn-resolving.de/urn:nbn:de:0168-ssoar-143773

BISTUM ESSEN: *Kirchenaustritt hat viele verschiedene Gründe.* [retrieved on 2018-04-30] Available from: http://zukunftsbild.bistum-essen.de/die-bistums-projekte/die-bistumsprojekte/initiative-fuer-den-verbleib-in-der-kirche/kirchenstudie/ergebnisse-stimmungsbild-und-interviews/

BISTUM ESSEN: *Das Zukunftsbild-Projekt.* [retrieved on 2018-04-30] Available from: http://zukunftsbild.bistum-essen.de/die-bistums-projekte/die-bistumsprojekte/initiative-fuer-den-verbleib-in-der-kirche/kirchenstudie/das-zukunftsbild-projekt/

BISTUM ESSEN: *Zukunftsbild im Bistum Essen.* [retrieved on 2018-04-30] Available from: http://zukunftsbild.bistum-essen.de/

B4P – BEST FOR PLANNING: *Database b4p 2016-III – b4p 20176-I.* GIK Media, München.   [retrieved   on   2017-10-09]   Available   from: https://online.mds6.de/mdso6/b4p.php

BUCHER, Rainer: Was geht und was nicht geht. Zur Optimierung kirchlicher Kommunikation durch Zielgruppenmodelle. In: *sinnstiftermag 04, (2007) Erreicht/Unerreicht – Welche Zielgruppen spricht Kirche heute noch an?* [retrieved on   2018-04-30]   Available   from: http://www.sinnstiftermag.de/ ausgabe_04/titelstory.htm

BUNDESINSTITUT   FÜR   BEVÖLKERUNSFORSCHUNG: *Fakten: Bevölkerungsentwicklung.* [abgerufen am 2018-04-30] Verfügbar unter: https://www.bib.bund.de/DE/Fakten/Bevoelkerungsentwicklung/Bevoelkerungsent wicklung.html

CARA – CENTER FOR APPLIED RESEARCH IN THE APOSTOLATE: *The CARA Story.* [retrieved on 2018-04-30] Available from: http://cara.georgetown.edu/about-us/cara-story/

CARA – CENTER FOR APPLIED RESEARCH IN THE APOSTOLATE: *Seven Elements of Parish Life.* [retrieved on 2018-04-30] Available from: http://cara.georgetown.edu/wp-content/uploads/2015/01/Seven-Elements-of-Parish-Life.pdf

CARA – CENTER FOR APPLIED RESEARCH IN THE APOSTOLATE: *Why in-pew surveys work best.* [retrieved on 2018-04-30] Available from: http://cara.georgetown.edu/wp-content/uploads/2015/01/Why-In-Pew-Surveys-Work-Best.pdf

CARA – CENTER FOR APPLIED RESEARCH IN THE APOSTOLATE: *What to do after the CARA report is delivered.* [retrieved on 2018-04-30] Available from: http://cara.georgetown.edu/wp-content/uploads/2015/01/What-To-Do-After.pdf

CARTELLVERBAND: *Webportal "Cartellverband.de"* [retrieved on 2018-04-30] Available from: https://www.cartellverband.de/

CARTELLVERBAND: *Der CV in Europa.* [retrieved on 2018-04-30] Available from: https://www.cartellverband.de/akademiker-netzwerk/der-cv-in-europa/

CARTELLVERBAND: *Wer wir sind.* [retrieved on 2018-04-30] Available from: https://www.cartellverband.de/cartellverband/wer-wir-sind/

CARTELLVERBAND: *Wesen der CV-Verbindungen.* [retrieved on 2018-04-30] Available from: https://www.cartellverband.de/studentenverbindungen/wesen-der-cv-verbindungen/

CARTELLVERBAND: *Charta '15. Gesellschaftspolitische Grundsätze des CV.* [retrieved on 2018-04-30] Available from: https://www.cartellverband.de/cartellverband/wer-wir-sind/charta-2015/

CARTELLVERBAND: *Was ist eine Studentenverbindung?* [retrieved on 2018-04-30] Available from: https://www.cartellverband.de/studentenverbindungen/ was-ist-eine-studentenverbindung/

CENTER FOR CHURCH COMMUNICATION: *Church Marketing Report: A casual look at the marketing and communication practices of churches across the U.S..* Los Angeles, 2005 [retrieved on 2018-04-30] Available from: http://www.cfcclabs.org/ 2005/12/communications-report/

CV-AKADEMIE: *Die CV-Akademie* [retrieved on 2018-04-30] Available from: https://www.cv-akademie.de/die-cv-akademie

CV-VORORT: *Facebook-Fanpage.* retrieved on 2018-04-30] Available from: https://www.facebook.com/DerVorort/

DAMBERG, Wilhelm: *CrossingOver. Kirche der USA erfahren, Kirche hier neu denken.* [retrieved on 2018-04-30] Available from: http://www.crossingover.de/

DEUTSCHE BISHOFSKONFERENZ: *Aufbau der katholischen Kirche.* [abgerufen am 2018-04-30] Verfügbar unter: https://www.dbk.de/katholische-kirche/aufbau/

DEUTSCHE BISHOFSKONFERENZ: *Kirchensteuer.* [retrieved on 2018-04-30] Available from: https://www.dbk.de/themen/kirche-und-geld/kirchensteuer/

DEUTSCHE BISHOFSKONFERENZ: *Wissenschaft und Hochschule.* [retrieved on 2018-04-30] Available from: https://www.dbk.de/katholische-kirche/aufgaben/wissenschaft-und-hochschule/

DEUTSCHE BISCHOFSKONFERENZ, Arbeitsstelle für Jugendseelsorge: *WJT – Weltjugendtag.* [retrieved on 2018-04-30] Available from: http://www.wjt.de/

DEUTSCHER BUNDESTAG: *Basic Constitutional Law of the Federal Republic of Germany.* [retrieved on 2018-04-30] Available from: https://www.bundestag.de/bundestag/aufgaben/rechtsgrundlagen/grundgesetz/gg_11/245152

DEUTSCHER CARTITASVERBAND e.V.: *Caritas in Deutschland. Millionenfache Hilfe.* [retrieved on 2018-04-30] Available from: https://www.caritas.de/diecaritas/wofuerwirstehen/millionenfache-hilfe

DIÖZESE ROTTENBURG-STUTTGART: *Entwicklungsschritte im Geist Gottes planen und gehen.* [retrieved on 2018-04-30] Available from: https://www.kirche-am-ort.de/entwicklungsplan-und-abschlussbericht.html

ERZBISTUM KÖLN: *Pastoraler Zukunftsweg.* [retrieved on 2018-04-30] Available from: http://www.erzbistum-koeln.de/erzbistum/pastoraler_zukunftsweg/

ERZBISTUM KÖLN: *Neue Wege für Pastoral und Verwaltung.* [retrieved on 2018-04-30] Available from: http://www.erzbistum-koeln.de/kirche_vor_ort/neue-wege/

EUROPEAN VALUES STUDY (EVS): *Website of the European Values Study (EVS).* [retrieved on 2018-04-30] Available from: http://www.europeanvaluesstudy.eu/

EUROPEAN VALUES STUDY (EVS): *Atlas of European Values.* [retrieved on 2018-04-30] Available from: http://www.atlasofeuropeanvalues.eu/new/

FEDERAL INSTITUTE FOR POPULATION RESEARCH: *Fakten: Bevölkerungsentwicklung.* [retrieved on 2018-04-30] Available from:

https://www.bib.bund.de/DE/Fakten/Bevoelkerungsentwicklung/Bevoelkerungsent wicklung.html

FLAIG, Bodo: Was wollen die Schäfchen? In: *ZEIT ONLINE. Christ & Welt, Ausgabe 52/2011.* [retrieved on 2018-04-30] Available from: https://www.sinus-institut.de/veroeffentlichungen/downloads/download/was-wollen-die-schaefchen/download-file/174/download-a/download/download-c/Category/

FOCUS ONLINE: *Missbrauchsskandal in der katholischen Kirche. Die wichtigsten Fakten seit 2010.* [retrieved on 2018-04-30] Available from: http://www.focus.de/politik/deutschland/rueckblick-zahlen-und-fakten-zum-missbrauchsskandal-in-der-katholischen-kirche_id_6511683.html

GALLUP: *Website of the GALLUP organization.* [retrieved on 2018-04-30] Available from: http://www.gallup.com

GERMAN CARITAS ASSOCIATION: *Caritas in Germany – Tasks, organisation, and financing.* [retrieved on 2018-04-30] Available from: http://www.caritas-germany.org/cms/contents/caritas-germany.org/medien/dokumente/info-graphic-on-task/caritas-infografik-2016_en-version_170421.pdf?d=a&f=pdf

INTERNATIONAL CATHOLIC STEWARDSHIP COUNCIL (ICSC): *Website of the ICSC* [retrieved on 2018-04-30] Available from: http://catholicstewardship.com/

JOHN HOPKINS UNIVERSITY: *Comparative Nonprofit Sector Project (CNP) of the Center for Civil Society Studies.* [retrieved on 2018-04-30] Available from: http://ccss.jhu.edu/research-projects/comparative-nonprofit-sector-project/

JOHN PAUL II.: *Encyclical "Redemptor hominis"* (1979). [retrieved on 2018-04-30] Available from: http://w2.vatican.va/content/john-paul-ii/en/encyclicals/documents/hf_jp-ii_enc_04031979_redemptor-hominis.html

KAMP / Katholische Arbeitsstelle für missionarische Pastoral: *Pastorale Innovationen.* [retrieved on 2018-04-30] Available from: http://www.pastorale-innovationen.de/

KAMP / Katholische Arbeitsstelle für missionarische Pastoral: *Internetseelsorge.de.* [retrieved on 2018-04-30] Available from: https://www.internetseelsorge.de/

KATHOLISCH.DE / Internetportal of the Catholic Church in Germany: *Unser Glaube.* [retrieved on 2018-04-30] Available from: http://katholisch.de/glaube/unser-glaube

KATHOLISCHE AKADEMIKERARBEIT DEUTSCHLANDS (KAD): *Website of the Academic Confederation.* [retrieved on 2018-04-30] Available from: http://www.k-a-d.de/

LEITLEIN, Hannes: Die zehn größten Probleme der Gemeinden. In: *ZEIT ONLINE. Christ & Welt, Ausgabe 03/2017.* [retrieved on 2018-04-30] Available from: http://www.zeit.de/2017/03/kirche-gemeinde-probleme-ehrenamtliche-befragung

MEDIENREFERAT DER ÖSTERREICHISCHEN BISCHOFSKONFERENZ: W*ebportal "Katholisch.at".* [retrieved on 2018-04-30] Available from: https://www.katholisch.at/statistik-60000

MEINTZ, René: *Kirchenaustritt.de: Informationen zum Kirchenaustritt.* [retrieved on 2018-04-30] Available from: http://www.kirchenaustritt.de/

MEFFERT, Heribert: Kirche im Zeitalter der Marken. In: sinnstiftermag 03, (2008) *Bekannt/Unbekannt – Was kann Kirche von moderner Markenführung lernen?* [retrieved on 2018-04-30] Available from: http://www.sinnstiftermag.de/ ausgabe_03/interview.htm

ÖSTERREICHISCHER CARTELLVERBAND: *Die Entwicklung des CV in Österreich in der Zwischenkriegszeit.* [retrieved on 2018-04-30] Available from: https://www.oecv.at/Home/Verband/21

RINKLAKE, Thomas: *Befragung "Pfarrbriefservice.de". Ergebnisse.* Nürnberg: xit GmbH, 2014. [retrieved on 2018-04-30] Available from: http://www.pfarrbriefservice.de/file/ergebnisse-der-pfarrbriefbefragung-2014#download

ROMAN CURIA: *Codes Iuris Canonici / Code of Canon Law.* Part II, Cann. 330-572. Vatican: Libreria Editrice Vaticana, 1983. [retrieved on 2018-04-30] Available from: http://www.vatican.va/archive/ENG1104/_INDEX.HTM

ROMAN CURIA / International Theological Commission (2004): *Communion And Stewardship. Human Persons Created in the Image of God (2004).* [retrieved on 2018-04-30] Available from: http://www.vatican.va/roman_curia/ congregations/cfaith/cti_documents/rc_con_cfaith_doc_20040723_communion-stewardship_en.html – http://catholicstewardship.com/

SCHWEIZERISCHES BUNDESAMT FÜR STATISTIK: *Sprachen und Religionen.* [retrieved on 2018-04-30] Available from: https://www.bfs. admin.ch/bfs/de/home/statistiken/bevoelkerung/sprachen-religionen.html

SCHWEIZER BISCHOFSKONFERENZ: *Statistik der katholischen Kirche in der Schweiz.* [retrieved on 2018-04-30] Available from: http://www.bischoefe.ch/ wir/schweiz/statistisches

SCHWEIZERISCHER STUDENTENVEREIN: *Webseite Schw.StV.* [retrieved on 2018-04-30] Available from: http://www.schw-stv.ch/index.cfm?Sprache=DE

SIGMA: *Über SIGMA.* [2018-04-30] Available from: http://www.sigma-online.com/de/About_SIGMA/

SIGMA: *SIGMA-Milieus für Deutschland.* [retrieved on 2018-04-30] Available from: http://www.sigma-online.com/de/SIGMA_Milieus/SIGMA_Milieus_in_Germany/

SINUS-INSTITUT: *Sinus-Milieus®* [retrieved on 2018-04-30] Available from: https://www.sinus-institut.de/en/sinus-solutions/sinus-milieus/

INUS-INSTITUT: *Sinus-Geo-Milieus®* [retrieved on 2018-04-30] Available from: https://www.sinus-institut.de/sinus-loesungen/sinus-geo-milieus/

SINUS-INSTITUT: *Die Sinus-Milieus® in Österreich.* [retrieved on 2018-04-30] Available from: https://www.sinus-institut.de/sinus-loesungen/sinus-milieus-oesterreich/

SINUS-INSTITUT: *Die Sinus-Milieus® in der Schweiz.* [retrieved on 2018-04-30] Available from: https://www.sinus-institut.de/sinus-loesungen/sinus-milieus-schweiz

SINUS-INSTITUT: *Sinus-TGI-Mediadaten international.* [retrieved on 2018-04-30] Available from: https://www.sinus-institut.de/sinus-loesungen/mediendaten-international/

STATISTISCHES BUNDESAMT: *Statistisches Jahrbuch 2017* (and elder editions) [retrieved on 2018-04-30] Available from: https://www.destatis.de/DE/ Publikationen/StatistischesJahrbuch/StatistischesJahrbuchAktuell.html

STATISTISCHES BUNDESAMT: *13th Coordinated Population Projection for Germany* [retrieved on 2018-04-30] Available from: https://service.destatis.de/ bevoelkerungspyramide/index.html#l=en

STELZER, Marius, HEYSE, Marko: *Typologie der Lebensführung.* [retrieved on 2018-04-30] Available from: https://lebensfuehrungstypologie.wordpress.com/ubersicht

TRINITY VINEYARD CHURCH: *What we do / Our mission.* [retrieved on 2018-04-30] Available from: http://www.trinityvineyardchurch.com/about-us/our-purpose/what-we-do/

UNITED NATIONS / DESA: *World Population Prospects 2017.* [retrieved on 2018-04-30] Available from: https://esa.un.org/unpd/wpp/

VEREIN UMWIDMUNG VON KIRCHENSTEUERN: *Kirchensteueraufkommen beider Kirchen 1967-2016.* [retrieved on 2018-04-30] Available from: http://www.kirchensteuern.de/

VETTER, Martin: Ein halbes Jahrhundert KMU. In: *Praktische Theologie, Vol. 51 (3), pp. 133-140,* 2016 ISSN 0946-3518

WIKIPEDIA: Liste der korporierten Bundestagsabgeordneten. [retrieved on 2018-04-30] Available from: https://de.wikipedia.org/wiki/Liste_der_korporierten_ Bundestagsabgeordneten

WILLOW CREEK COMMUNITY CHURCH: *Willow Creek History.* [retrieved on 2018-04-30] Available from: https://www.willowcreek.org/en/about/history

WORD-OF-MOUTH MARKETING ASSOCIATION: *WOMMA Influencer Guidebook – 2013.* Chicago, 2013. [retrieved on 2018-04-30] Available from: http://womma.org/free-womm-resources/

WORLD VALUES SURVEY: *Welcome to the World Values Survey site.* [retrieved on 2018-04-30] Available from: www.worldvaluessurvey.org

WORLD VALUES SURVEY: *Inglehart-Welzel Culture Map 2017* [retrieved on 2018-04-30] Available from: http://www.worldvaluessurvey.org/images/ Culture_Map_2017_conclusive.png

ZENTRALKOMITEE DER DEUTSCHEN KATHOLIKEN: *Deutscher Katholikentag.* [retrieved on 2018-04-30] Available from: http://www.katholikentag.de

ZULEHNER, Paul: 87393 Kirchenaustritte – was nun? Information zum Forschungsbericht 2010 der Langzeitstudie "Religion im Leben der Menschen" [retrieved on 2018-04-30] Available from: http://zulehner.org/site/zeitworte/ article/198.html

CPSIA information can be obtained
at www.ICGtesting.com
Printed in the USA
BVHW041052050419
544725BV00017B/533/P